谨以此书献给每一位为打造现代化可持续都市倾注心血的朋友。本书旨在通过讲述上海历史，重现大中里项目建设细节，向为兴业太古汇作出宝贵贡献的建设者们致以崇高敬意。

This book is dedicated to everyone who has ever thought about making a modern city sustainable. In addition to documenting the history of Shanghai and HKRI Taikoo Hui, it recognises the invaluable contribution of people who have made the Dazhongli project a success.

查懋成

Victor Cha

为了让读者更好地感受大中里的活力重生，编纂团队在筹备
阶段进行了详尽的调研，力求全面展现这片土地的历史风云。
唯年代变迁，部分史料的质量未臻完美，望能见谅。让我们
透过仅余的记录，一同来窥探逐渐远去的磅礴时代。

The editorial team conducted exhaustive research to
showcase Dazhongli's exciting past and put its vibrant
present into the proper perspective. Due to its historic
nature, the quality of some of the most important material
has suffered. We hope you will forgive us in such cases,
and look past the surface to enjoy these rare glimpses into a
bygone era.

# 传承未艾·成就方兴

查懋成

香港兴业国际集团
副主席兼董事总经理

"善待每一块土地，尊重历史人文的延续"是由我的父亲、香港兴业国际集团创始人查济民博士提出的企业立身之根本，多年来一直指引着香港兴业国际的前进方向。在集团40余年的发展历程中，我们秉承着"尊人重土"、"止于至善"的理念，精心铸就每一个项目。

查氏家族与上海的缘分始于20世纪40年代初。抗战期间，父亲曾在上海经营民族纺织工业，并在胜利后被上海工商界推荐为上海纱布染织业的"接管大员"之一，这座城市的魅力感染了他。

离开上海，父亲落户香港，他一直心系国家，努力将民族工业发扬光大，走向世界。在60年代，父亲被誉为亚洲以及非洲纺织大王。

70年代末，香港大屿山东北部的"愉景湾"面临落入外国政府银行手中的危险，出于拳拳爱国之心，父亲倾囊购入，才保住了这幅香港最大面积的私人开发土地留在国人手中。一位织染工业家也因此毅然走上地产开发之路。

彼时的大屿山仍是一片荒芜之地，水陆不通，这是一个即使有经验的大型开发商都不愿意碰的项目。面对被戏谑为"现代版愚公移山"，父亲依然没有动摇决心。兄长查懋声受命领军愉景湾项目，凭借他的革新思维，我们创造了亚洲首个可持续发展的环保小镇，包含多项"首创"的概念及"唯一"的纪录，这个传奇故事一直为人所津津乐道。

80年代末，响应改革开放的号召，查氏家族重回故土，先在故乡浙江海宁投资设厂，后又耗资以亿元计收购濒临破产的国营纺织企业，以实际行动报效祖国。

90年代，祖国科技发展滞后，查氏家族出资成立"求是科技基金会"和"桑麻基金会"，前者广纳诺贝尔奖华裔科学家，培育国内科研人才，鼓励科技兴国；后者则注重扶持传统纺织及印染工业迈向现代化。

世纪交接的时代节点，我们重回上海，再度被这座城市的强大活力所震撼，希望能参与到波澜壮阔的城市建设之中，为申城发展添砖加瓦。

21世纪初，国家重回国际舞台，先后取得奥运会和世博会的主办权，并顺利跻身世贸组织（WTO）行列，国际地位显著提升。上海的大型基础建设、轨道交通工程、机场扩建纷纷展开，城市更新更是重中之重。随着社会变迁，位于城市核心区域的老城厢急需注入新活力，紧密跟上城市发展的步伐。2002年，我代表集团洽谈大中里地块的重建项目。经过层层筛选，通过重重评定，我们有幸得到静安区政府的信任，拿下这片上海最大的石库门建筑群的开发权。我也终于回到父亲曾经奋斗过的城市，成为万千城市建设者的一分子。

查氏家族早有愉景湾的开发经验，深谙大型项目建设除了一腔热忱和赤诚之心，更需要迎难而上的勇气和毅力。如果说我的父兄是现代版的"愚公"，相信我也堪称新时代的"愚公2.0"。如果说是我成就了兴业太古汇，我更觉得是大中里成就了我。从大中里到兴业太古汇，15年的建设历程并非一段易走的路，但我对项目的热诚和信心没有一天动摇。细品回甘，这堪称一段非凡之旅。

每当回首，我都感慨万千。我们遇到了非典病毒、金融海啸等巨大挑战，一路上难题无处不在。在最困难的时候，我只好自我调侃："天将降大任于斯人也，必先苦其心志，劳其筋骨。"期间，最让我纠结的是城市发展与历史保育的博弈。大中里的宝贵之处不仅在于位处城市心脏位置，更重要的是其在上海市民心中的深厚感情。然而，我多次与区政府和保育专家深度走进项目，眼前的残破乱状不但潜藏安全隐患，也无法与上海这个大都会的发展势头接轨，重建才是负责任的行为。

深谙大中里对上海的重大意义，我更要秉承父亲教诲的"尊人重土"之道，将其建设成为能引领未来的商业综合体，方能不辜负土地厚重的历史价值。

完成了艰巨的居民动迁安置后，接踵而来的还有基坑建设、地铁施工、区域联动、交叉作业、绿色施工等种种技术难题。我们将不同工序的技术报告记录下来，以便后来者借鉴，薪火相传。这些过程组成了城市更新的营造史，我们希望借此鼓励年轻人不怕艰辛，发扬迎难而上的奋斗精神。

在多方协调后，我们坚持保留民立中学4号楼，延聘专家进行上海市少有的由企业出资进行的历史建筑移位工程，并展开细致的修缮工作，使其修旧如旧，重获新生，并赋以"查公馆"之名，以纪念父亲的爱国情怀，记录我们查氏家族与上海这座城市代代相传的情谊。为了一颗百年广玉兰古树，我们多番修改设计蓝图，即使牺牲容积率，也在所不惜。

关关难过关关过，事事难成事事成，这背后实在有赖各级领导和各方友好伙伴们的支持和帮助。这里包括了静安区政府对我们的信任、合资方太古地产的通力合作、顾问团队的专业和热情投入、施工单位的携手拼搏、原大中里居民的配合、周边居民的理解等等。每个参与者的努力，每个建设者的拼搏，每个兴业人的付出，还有上海市民对城市更新的期盼，都是我们的强大后盾。

时代的步伐是不会停下来的，在大中里项目准备以兴业太古汇的新颜面世时，整个零售行业早已发生了巨变。消费升级，品牌老化，新零售及电商网购模式不断涌现，这些都冲击着实体商店的生存空间。兴业太古汇零售部分的面积多达10万平方米，面对市场激烈的竞争，我们深入调研新生一代的消费模式，决定打破常规，为购物中心开创新定位，另辟新业态，面向消费者对个性化，定制化的需求，综合娱乐、社交、文化等功能，将商业区打造为充满生命力的社区。

2017年秋天，一个收获的季节，在万众瞩目之下，兴业太古汇终于呈现在大家面前。

结合古、今、中、西的元素，精雕细琢而成的兴业太古汇无疑是一座建筑艺术品，但我们更希望为这座大型商业综合体注入个性和活力，使其发挥犹如博物馆般兼收并蓄和变化万千的功能，在重塑海派建筑特色以及石库门里弄的社区情怀的同时，让"大中里"继续以新的形态滋润和丰富上海市民的生活。

开业三年来，我们深耕细作，不断优化业态，引进新概念，活用沉浸式、体验式、场景化营销，为消费者带来全新的购物、娱乐、社交新体验，创造品味生活。此外，我更订立目标，在金玉其外之余，亦要亮丽其中。我们马不停蹄提高后勤运营标准，加强绿色可持续应用，将后勤基地作为日后贵宾参观的重点之一，坚持以匠心打造"看不到的美好"。

如今，兴业太古汇作为上海潮流地标的代表之一，获得了市场和社会的广泛认可。作为一家将"传承"刻入企业文化血脉的公司，香港兴业国际不愿止步于此。我们知道，这片土地虽然有了新的名字，但背后书写着大中里厚重跌宕的历史，它不应就此湮没于时间长河之中。

为此，我特邀第一财经传媒执笔，采访十余位业内专家和项目参与者，共同写就了这本《未艾·方兴——从大中里到兴业太古汇》，通过小故事，诉说大时代，讴歌大情怀，记录大中里地块百年的风云变迁，传扬文化保育的初心，揭示城市更新的魅力与前景。最重要的是，再一次彰显"尊人重土"的精神。

字少声多难过去，助以余音始绕梁。

愿此书为读者打开一扇了解上海历史文化的窗户，让更多人了解，重建与保育并不是零和博弈，破旧的载体或许不能保留，但蕴藏在地块深处和心灵深处的历史文脉是永存不灭的，"立新不破旧"才是未来城市发展之道。兴业太古汇将继续用实际行动，为"上海文化"品牌建设贡献一份力量。

过去，我们是大中里历史的观察者。

现在，我们是兴业太古汇的建设者。

未来，期待能与更多有识之士一同，成为推动城市发展的助力者。

未艾方兴，一切，才刚刚开始。

写于 2020 年初秋

# On the RISE

**VICTOR CHA**

*Deputy Chairman and Managing Director,*
*HKR International Limited*

My father, Dr. Cha Chi-ming, the founder of HKR International, built his business on the core values of showing respect to people, and to the cultural heritage and history of each plot of land. These ideals have guided our group's development for over 40 years. Along with a constant drive for perfection, they have been the basis of each and every one of our projects.

My family's connections with Shanghai began in the early 1940s. During the Sino-Japanese war, my father operated a textile company in Shanghai. After victory, the Shanghai industrial and business sectors nominated him as one of the major "textile trade representatives". The city had charmed him.

Although he eventually left Shanghai and lived in Hong Kong, my father's heart always remained completely in the motherland. His dream was to build a strong national textile industry at home, and expand it across the world. And, he was largely successful. By the 1960s, he was well known in Asia and Africa as the "King of Textiles".

In the late 1970s, Discovery Bay on Lantau Island almost fell into the hands of a foreign government-controlled bank. My father didn't hesitate. He immediately invested a huge proportion of his personal wealth to keep the city's largest piece of private land for development in the hands of its citizens. Thus, the textile industrialist resolutely entered the world of real estate development.

At the time, Lantau Island was a remote place, which was accessible only by sea. This made Discovery Bay a project that no experienced large-scale developer would touch. Faced with the prospect of being ridiculed as a modern-day "Foolish Man Removing Mountains", my father's resolve remained unshaken. He beautifully demonstrated the spirit behind the idiom – where there's a will, there's a way. Payson Cha, my elder brother, was entrusted with the development project. With his innovative thinking and forward-looking mindset, Discovery Bay was built into the first eco-friendly and sustainable community in Asia. He introduced multiple cutting-edge concepts and set numerous unique records. Discovery Bay's legendary story never fails to fascinate.

The Cha family returned to our homeland towards the end of the 1980s, following calls for the reform and opening up of the Chinese economy. We started by setting up factories in our old hometown of Haining in Zhejiang, and spent hundreds of millions of RMB on procuring state-owned textile enterprises that were close to bankruptcy. It allowed us to give something tangible back to the country.

In the 1990s, when the pace of technological development in the country faltered, the Cha family took action and founded the Qiu Shi Science & Technologies Foundation and the Sang Ma Trust Fund. The former, which included several Chinese Nobel laureates, was established to cultivate scientific research, and encourage national development through science and technology. The latter focused on supporting the modernisation of the traditional textile and dyeing industry.

As the new century unfolded, we returned to Shanghai and were once again astonished by the vibrancy of the city. We hoped to take part in urban construction and contribute to the development of Shanghai.

In the 21st century, China returned to the world stage and obtained the rights to host the Olympics and the World Expo. It quickly joined the World Trade Organization (WTO), and its international standing has since improved significantly. Large-scale infrastructure construction in Shanghai, including rail transportation and airport expansions were implemented. Urban renewal became one of the most important projects. As society developed, the old parts of downtown Shanghai desperately needed renewal to keep up with the pace of the city's development. On behalf of the group, I negotiated the urban renewal project for Dazhongli in 2002. After careful selection, and passing rounds of evaluation, we were honoured to have gained the trust of the Jing'an District Government, and took over the development

rights for one of the largest clusters of Shikumen buildings in Shanghai. I had finally returned to the place where my father had worked so hard, and become one of the million of people building the new city.

The Cha family gained substantial development experience in the Discovery Bay project, and we learned that large-scale construction takes more than just passion and zeal. It also calls for courage and perseverance to overcome challenges. If my father and brother were called the modern "Foolish Men", then I would probably be the "Foolish Man 2.0" of this era. Instead of believing that I made HKRI Taikoo Hui, I believe that Dazhongli has made me the man I am today. The 15-year transformation from Dazhongli to HKRI Taikoo Hui was not easy. Nevertheless, my passion and confidence in the project never wavered for a single day. Looking back, it was quite a journey and a memorable experience.

We faced immense challenges and difficulties along the way – from SARS to the financial crisis. In times of hardship, I often remind myself of the saying: "Whenever God means to make a man great, he first breaks him into pieces." And then I try to do what the "Foolish Man" would do, and look on the bright side! What challenged me most during that period was the struggle between urban development and historical conservation. The most precious thing in Dazhongli is not simply its location in the heart of the city. It is the role it plays in the hearts and minds of the citizens of Shanghai. However, during my numerous visits to the project site, I was struck by the decay and hidden safety concerns. It was clear that these issues would prevent the site from integrating with the new Shanghai metropolis, and I resolved that reconstruction was the responsible thing to do.

I was deeply aware of the significance of Dazhongli to Shanghai, and I wanted to uphold my father's motto of "respecting the people and cherishing the land." I also wanted to transform the site into a commercial complex that could take the lead in the future, while remaining faithful to the land's heritage.

After completing the arduous process of relocating thousands of residents, we were faced with technical difficulties involving the construction of the foundations, accommodating the construction of the new metro line nearby, simultaneous operations, and introducing green construction techniques. We compiled the technical reports for different procedures as a reference for future engineers. This process became part of the history of urban renewal, and we hope to use the lessons gained from it to encourage young people to embrace challenges and demonstrate their resolve in overcoming difficulties.

Through multilateral negotiations, we maintained our goal of preserving Building No. 4 of Minli School. After appointing experts to conduct one of the few corporate-funded historical building relocation projects in Shanghai, the next step was a careful refurbishment programme to restore the building to its former glory. It was renamed Cha House in honour of my father's love for the nation, and to commemorate the Cha family's lasting connections to the city from one generation to the next. We modified the design blueprints multiple times to accommodate a single, century-old magnolia grandiflora tree, even if it meant sacrificing floor area.

We were able to overcome difficulties and surmount obstacles with the support and assistance provided by officials on all levels, and partners from various sectors. We benefitted from the trust the Jing'an District Government placed in us, and the full cooperation of our joint-venture partner Swire Properties. That was complemented by passionate dedication from the advisory team, the hard work of construction companies, cooperation from the original Dazhongli residents, and the understanding of people in nearby neighbourhoods. The hard work of each participant, the efforts of all the construction workers, the dedication of every employee, and the hope of successful urban renewal in the hearts of Shanghai's citizens became our greatest support.

Time never stops. As the Dazhongli Project prepared to face the world in the form of HKRI Taikoo Hui, the entire retail industry had already undergone significant changes. Evolving consumer behaviour, the aging of traditional brands, and the continuous rise of new online shopping models had taken over many of the roles previously played by physical stores. HKRI Taikoo Hui's retail space exceeded 100,000 square metres. Faced with intense market competition, we conducted in-depth studies of the new generation's consumption models, then decided to break free from tradition and reposition the shopping mall. We created new business patterns to satisfy emerging consumer demands for personalisation and customisation, while combining entertainment, social networking, and cultural offerings to transform a commercial complex into a vibrant community.

The fall of 2017 was the moment-of-truth, and the highly-anticipated HKRI Taikoo Hui finally opened to the world.

By integrating traditional, modern, Chinese, and Western elements, the meticulously constructed HKRI Taikoo Hui is undoubtedly an architectural work of art. However, we also hope to instil character and vitality into the large commercial complex, so that it can play the role of a museum and host all manner of events. After recreating

Shanghai-style architectural features and incorporating ideas from Shikumen communities, we hope to enable the new "Dazhongli" to continue to inspire and enrich the lives of the citizens of Shanghai in its new form.

In the three years since the opening of HKRI Taikoo Hui, we have continued to work hard, constantly optimising business models and introducing new ideas. For example, we have incorporated the flexible use of immersive, experience-oriented, scenario marketing. This provides consumers with brand new shopping, entertainment, and social networking choices for a more tasteful lifestyle. In addition, I also set targets to maintain the quality of the commercial complex's back-of-house. We are constantly improving logistical and operational standards and enhancing green and sustainable applications, to establish the logistics base as one of the key points for guest visits in the future. We remain resolved to creating "unseen wonders" through our craftsmanship.

HKRI Taikoo Hui has now become one of Shanghai's iconic landmarks and received wide acclaim from both society and the market. As a company with "heritage" thoroughly embedded in its corporate culture, HKR International has no plans to stop here. We know that although the land has a new name, it was built upon the immense history of Dazhongli, which should not be buried beneath the sands of time.

For this reason, I invited Yicai Media Group to write this book – "On the RISE – From Dazhongli to HKRI Taikoo Hui." Including interviews from dozens of project participants and industry experts, the book captures the history and emotions of an era through unique stories, and it records the changes Dazhongli has seen during the last century. It upholds our value of conserving cultural heritage, and demonstrates the charm and potential of urban renewal. More importantly, it once again exemplifies the spirit of "respecting the people and cherishing the land."

As the old Chinese saying goes, few words can travel over loud noises, so they must be accompanied by echoes to be passed down.

I hope this book can open a window for readers to learn about the history and culture of Shanghai, and help people understand that reconstruction and conservation are not zero-sum games. Broken vessels may not always be kept, but the heritage buried deep beneath the land and in our hearts lasts forever. "Building the new without breaking the old" is the only way forward for future urban development. HKRI Taikoo Hui will continue to contribute to the government's "Shanghai Culture" branding initiative, with the aim of making culture a compelling element in shaping Shanghai's future.

In the past, we were observers of the history of Dazhongli.

Now, we are the creators of HKRI Taikoo Hui.

In the future, we hope to work with Shanghai people who share our values, and become promoters of urban development.

This is just the beginning of a new chapter in our story, and everything is on the rise.

Written in the autumn of 2020

# 兴业太古汇
## ——静安区涅槃重生的新地标

孙建平

原静安区委书记

2013 年，我就任上海市静安区区委书记。静安区是上海繁荣而紧凑的市中心，在这不足 8 平方公里的土地上，老式上海弄堂、不同年代的私家花园、摩登高楼大厦等各式建筑汇聚，彰显着海派文化的新旧冲突与交融，拥有独特、优雅的城市韵味。

就职后，我最为关注的项目之一，就是静安区内的一片"明珠之地"——大中里地块，现今的兴业太古汇商业综合体。

大中里地块原为上海市中心规模最大的石库门建筑群之一，但在 21 世纪初的上海市中心，旧区旧里的土地利用率低，加上石库门建筑群的安全、民生要求都已跟不上时代发展，改造势在必行。

作为当时静安区内发展亮点，大中里项目的落成将会对上海的城市商业发展起到很大推动作用，一直受到区委、区政府的高度关注。因此，我曾数次到访正如火如荼建设中的项目工地，并与香港兴业国际诸位高层就建设过程中的安全、质量、进度、环境等问题进行多次会谈，要求严格排查安全隐患，消除事故苗子，采取切实措施，防患于未然，在保障安全的情况下精益求精地发展，成为优质工程、安全工程典范，并成为少瑕疵、好设计、有特色、与整个城市品位和要求相适应的里程碑式工程。

从个人角度来说，这亦代表着我对该项目的诸多期盼。从 2006 年规划变更，去除住宅业态、转为长期持有的商业综合体开始，兴业太古汇的发展也是对大中里地块经济利益最大化的最优选。我亦期望它能够作为南京西路商圈内的标杆性项目，在十里南京路上熠熠生辉。

但对项目的关注，不仅出于"老城改造"的需求，更因为其是"城市更新"的一部分。对于优质存量资源也需要发掘其新生功用——从建筑立面上看到城市的年轮、从文化上看到历史文脉，并赋予现代城市功能。而大中里项目中，有一座历经百年的老建筑，如何对这座原民立中学校舍进行优质保护，也是项目建设中需要高度关注的地方。

所幸项目方香港兴业国际主导了对这座百年老宅的移位和保护性修复工作，让地块的历史风貌文脉得以延续。2018 年 5 月 18 日，命名为查公馆的老宅经过八年的细致修缮后终于再次对外开放。我也受邀参加了查公馆揭幕展的开幕仪式，看见它在"修旧如旧"的基础上，被注入更多新功能后焕发出的新生，亦十分感慨与激动。

在国务院发布的《国务院关于上海市城市总体规划（2017-2035 年）的批复》中指出，要努力把上海建设成为创新之城、人文之城、生态之城，卓越的全球城市和社会主义现代化国际大都市。

兴业太古汇这个"十五年磨一剑"的项目，如今成为上海潮流地标之一，也为南京西路商圈的繁荣注入了新的活力。

但这还不够。在更多人的努力、创新之下，希望兴业太古汇能够持续发展，提升消费者体验度、感受度和满意度，打响"购物品牌"，为静安区核心商圈能级提升带来更多动力。

写于 2019 年末

# HKRI Taikoo Hui – A Rich and Iconic Landmark in Jing'an District

**SUN JIANPING**
*Former District Party Secretary of Jing'an District*

In 2013, I served as the District Party Secretary of the Jing'an District in Shanghai. It is a prosperous and close-knit community in the heart of Shanghai. Old Shanghainese houses, garden mansions from different eras, and modern high-rise buildings all congregate within eight square kilometres – exemplifying Shanghai's integration of old and new styles, which has created a unique and elegant urban flavour.

The project that kept me occupied after I took office was the "pearl" of Jing'an District – Dazhongli – which is now the HKRI Taikoo Hui commercial complex.

Dazhongli was once home to one of the largest clusters of Shikumen buildings in Central Shanghai. However, land usage rates in the old districts were low in the early twenty-first century. And, as Shikumen building clusters could no longer keep up with the safety and living standards of the era, a transformation project was inevitable.

As a highlight of development back then in Jing'an District, the completion of the Dazhongli project would greatly promote Shanghai's urban commercial development. Its progress had always been closely followed by the District Party Committee and the District Government. I visited the busy construction site numerous times and discussed the safety, quality, progress, and environmental issues with many of HKRI's senior executives to request strict safety inspections, eliminate potential accidents, and adopt rigorous measures to prevent incidents. I wanted to ensure safety while pursuing sophistication and development excellence, and make it a model for high quality construction. Dazhongli would also be a milestone project, with minimum defects, excellent design and unique features, while also satisfying aesthetic and functional requirements.

From a personal perspective, it also represented my high hopes for the district. After plans for changes were implemented in 2006, to remove residences and convert the area into a long-term commercial investment complex, the development of HKRI Taikoo Hui was the best choice for maximising the economic interests of Dazhongli. I also hoped it would become a benchmark project for the West Nanjing Road commercial district.

The project became more than a response to demands for the refurbishment of an old city, and turned into a part of Shanghai's urban renewal. We also needed to create many new functions that high-quality projects demand, while maintaining the history of the city in the external appearance of the buildings. This would enable people to observe the unity and coherence of history from a cultural perspective, without compromising the ability to provide modern urban functionality. The Dazhongli land plot included a century-old building – the former Minli School – which became a focus of the construction project, as high-quality protective measures had to be implemented.

Fortunately, HKR International led the relocation and restoration of the structure and preserved its historical and cultural value. On 18 May 2018, the old building, renamed Cha House, finally reopened to the public after eight years of meticulous work. I was invited to its opening ceremony and was touched and excited by its rebirth, which was based on a complete restoration, with additional new functionality.

The "State Council's Approval on the Overall Urban Plans for Shanghai City (2017-2035)" outlined goals for making Shanghai a city of innovation, culture and ecology, as well as a distinguished global city and a socialist metropolis.

HKRI Taikoo Hui was the result of years of hard work. It has now become one of Shanghai's iconic landmarks and injected new life and prosperity into the West Nanjing Road shopping district.

However, that alone is simply not enough. With the hard work and innovation of many more people, I hope that the development of HKRI Taikoo Hui can continue to improve consumer experience, bonding, and satisfaction, and create a true "Shopping Brand" that powers the further improvement and upgrading of Jing'an District.

Written in December 2019

# 建筑不语·下自成蹊

杨宇东

第一财经总编辑

上海这座伟大的城市，因商业而生，在她的成长过程中，商业也是最根本的动力源泉。那么，在她未来的发展中，又需要怎样的商业规划、商业建筑和商业内涵？这个问题这些天一直萦绕在我的思绪之中。

收到出版方的邀请为此书作序，刚开始时我是有犹疑的，毕竟平日里我更多关注的是偏宏观的财经领域，包括政策、市场和产业等话题，像城市更新和某个商业中心建设这样的具体项目，确实是没有什么积淀，写出来的东西怕是要贻笑大方。不过可能是缘分的关系，兴业太古汇恰好就在第一财经总部的隔壁，我几乎每天都要路过，也时常会进去消费，有不少的好感；再加上我又是个土生土长的上海人，眼看着几十年来这座城市的巨大变迁，有令人欣喜的新生，也有让人痛心的消逝，从老上海人人尽皆知的"大中里"、"斜桥"衍化重生的兴业太古汇究竟会给上海带来什么？这个话题也确实引发了我不小的兴趣。

上述两方面的缘由使得我答应了写序的邀请，尤其是看完初稿之后，才明了这个项目经历了多么漫长而艰辛的规划和建设，内里又蕴涵了多少关于商业，关于建筑，关于城市，关于文化传承的理念、原则和价值观！所以，把兴业太古汇的诞生从多个角度结集成册，供商业开发者和运营者，供城市规划者和建设者，供文化研究者和消费者来认真了解和品味，有很强的现实意义；也因为涉及"大中里"这座"魔都"中心地块的涅槃重生，故事的斑斓多彩会给读者带来愉悦的阅读体验。

城市离不开商业，更何况像上海这样一座完全因为商业而兴盛，直至成为中国最大商业中心的城市。上海具备先天的地理优势，地处长江入海口，背靠江南富庶之地，辐射广袤内陆地区，隔海近距离眺望日韩东亚诸国，在1843年开埠之后，海内外商人纷至沓来，文化思想包容并蓄，商业类型多元纷呈，迅速崛起为远东第一大都市。

从书中我们也可以看到，随着城市的快速繁荣，上海的商业中心区域也在不断扩大，尤其从19世纪末期开始，涌现出越来越多的商业建筑，无论从外观还是功能，都领一时风气之先，包括地处"大中里"附近的上海第一个乡村俱乐部"斜桥总会"和"张氏味莼园"（部分建筑保存至今，简称"张园"），建筑风格新潮，吃喝玩乐俱全，开业之后迅速成为当时的"网红打卡地"，游人如织，甚至经常阻塞交通。

回首上海100多年的商业发展史，我们会发现，随着商业的迅速繁荣，一大批优秀的商业建筑也迅速涌现，只有发达的商业才会催生优秀的商业建筑，我想这是一条颠扑不破的规律。从外滩沿线向西一路延伸，从黄浦到静安、卢湾，再到徐汇、长宁，数不胜数的优秀商业建筑坐落在各大商圈内，成为优秀的地标。包括住宅在内，上海近现代建筑数量之多，保存之完好，也是冠盖全国。

当你在街头端详这些地标建筑，再去翻看它们的史料之后，你都会发现一个共同规律：无论这座建筑当初是怎样的建造目的，是要做银行，还是要做商场抑或做酒店，建造者们都非常用心，从选址到设计再到施工，都是极其认真仔细，绝不急功近利，像是在做一件兼具高度实用价值的艺术品，也正因为如此，这些建筑才可能不仅在建成时红极一时，更能在日后流芳百年。

但殊为可惜的是，历史和文化总有潮起潮落，兴亡勃忽，总有时代视割断为创新，视拆毁为革命，在一些历史的断层中，城市的文脉商脉也难逃式微的命运。即便是当代，在商业重新复苏的近四十年，在大部分城市，急功近利的水泥森林已成不可阻挡之势，导致百城一面，千城一面，为了城市化的急速推进，为了地方长官的GDP业绩，最高效的手段就是大拆大建，推倒重来。这不是城市更新，而是水泥森林革命。无论是道路还是商场，人们行走在其间毫无愉悦感，商业中心只为刺激人们的购物欲而设计，最后造就了一批外观呆板，内观乏味的商场楼宇，尤其是在电商兴起之后，这批严重缺乏购物休闲体验感的商场迅速没落，要么人流量陡降，要么沦为早教和餐饮的混杂地。

上海有优秀的传统，无论是商业还是建筑，上海不缺商业中心，但是缺好的商业中心，雨后春笋般林立的大型商场已经数不胜数，能够体现城市个性和品位，能够传承历史和文脉的商业中心却屈指可数。当然，我们必须尊重商业的本质，满足消费者的需求依然是所有商业设施最根本的目的，但是深刻的变化依然发生：物质匮乏的时代早已经过去，在发达城市，高端购物场所已经过剩，人们去商业综合体，目的已经是多元化，购物或休闲体验，甚至是无目的的放松，消费精神产品和欣赏人文景观。好的商业中心必须能够满足这些多元化的需求，更高超的做法是，其自身就是城市肌理和个性的一部分，就是城市记忆的重要载体！

其实回想自己对于上海这座城市的早期记忆，除了生活在徐家汇附近而日日所见的天主教堂那些高大建筑之外，就是在徐家汇26路起点站坐上电车，一路向东，途径淮海路繁华的街衢，近西藏路时就可以听到远处江上轮船的汽笛，再到四川中路那些欧式建筑街区里，立即可以感受到潮湿清新的江风扑面而来，等到了外滩终点站，抬头就是那些伟岸的建筑了，如果恰逢整点，还可以听到海关大楼大钟洪亮的报时。所以，建筑就像声音和气味一样，构成了我们对一座城市全部的记忆，而建筑又是其中最持久的一部分。

但是所谓的"传承"，所谓的"记忆"并不是这么容易就可以实现的，它需要城市管理者、开发商、建筑师和市民们的一致选择才有可能达成。好在兴业太古汇的开发者们是非典型的商业地产开发商，"大中里"地块是香港兴业国际集团在上海拿的第一块地，从早期的坚定拿地，到随后决定"不赚快钱"取消住宅规划全部转为商业地产，全部长期持有，再到金融风暴和城市规划的影响带来的漫长等待，前后整整15年，历经波折！幸好查氏家族最看重的不是短期的投资回报，就像他们在香港开发著名的"愉景湾"项目一样，他们最看重的是好的建筑和社区"作品"，背后是"尊人重土"的核心价值观。

在大上海最心脏地带的"大中里"地块，他们带着对上海商业文明发自内心的敬畏和珍惜，从规划开始，就用购物中心、写字楼、酒店、公寓式酒店等近十栋高低建筑错落有致地形成社区生态，宁愿降低容积率也要沿袭旧时大中里和吴江路疏朗的空间格局。购物中心沿街部分被切分成多栋二三层楼、低密度的小型建筑，核心是贯穿南北的半月形大型中轴商场。写字楼和酒店在购物中心之上，各个建筑之间通过连廊相通，这样的逐级升高使得周边道路的视野顿时开阔，综合体被自然地融入街道之间，而且多个公共入口或开放或隐秘，人流可以随意在不同的建筑和街区中穿行，漫步，犹如我们儿时出入的四通八达的石库门弄堂，喧嚣可以瞬间遁入静谧。

除了通过模仿传统格局的新建筑向旧上海的记忆致敬之外，修旧如旧的查公馆也是兴业太古汇的点睛之笔。

我一直以为，城市更新的核心不在于"更新"，而在于如何"守旧"，或者说是在守旧基础上的更新。推倒一切不是更新，在旧的躯壳里创造出新的生机和灵魂，又能与传统一脉相承，这才是最高境界。

位于综合体南端的民立中学校舍（中华人民共和国成立前是著名的"邱氏大宅"）是一栋精美的历史保护建筑，既是重要的历史印记，也是宝贵的文化遗产，可惜失修多年，图纸也只留下一部分，修复面临的挑战极大，但是开发者和建筑师事务所耗费了极大的心血和成本，除了向南安全平移57.3米，更是以修旧如旧的方式对所有的外立面和内部装饰进行了复原，还增加了地下室和复古电梯，重新以"查公馆"命名。更有意义的是，通过修缮，赋予了这座百年建筑新的功能，让来到兴业太古汇的消费者能够在这座老宅里看展览，听讲座，举办各种文化活动。

在我看来，这种新旧共存像一座天平的两端，新与旧，动与静，历史与未来，时尚与传统，轻盈与稳重，都通过时空交错，寻到了平衡，也寻到了商业文明向未来延展的脉络。

当然，作为一个商业综合体，消费者的体验是一切评价的基础，从我的个人经验来看，兴业太古汇店铺的最大亮点是走独具品味的轻奢和潮牌风格，"不做大店做小店"，10万平方米的空间容纳整合了超过250个品牌，给白领消费者带来了极为新鲜、有趣和丰富的组合，其中一间单衣单价在千元以内的男装品牌让我迅速成为粉丝。而素凯泰和镛舍两个极度低调，极简风格，但又是极其讲究入住者"回家"体验的顶级现代酒店，又用最为感性的方式诠释了上海这座城市经典与现代完美结合的卓越品质。

作为一座伟大的商业城市，上海经历了开埠后令人炫目的高速发展，也经历过长期的战乱和商业化的停滞，再到改革开放四十年来的高歌猛进，一跃而成为世界级的中心城市，其商业文明、商业文化的传承虽然遭遇过无数的波折，但是依然保有顽强的生命力。这种顽强生命力的背后是她极其善于传承，包容，特别是在传承包容基础上的不懈创新。而所有创新的目的一定都是以人为核心，我认为这也是兴业太古汇项目取得巨大成功的根本所在，"尊人重土，以人为本，珍惜传统，传承创新"，这本书给我最大的收获是这十六个字，我也希望更多的上海城市建设者和参与者能够从中有所感悟。

写于 2020 年夏至

# The Allure of Architecture

**YANG YUDONG**

*Editor in Chief, Yicai Media Group*

Born through commerce, a great city like Shanghai, will continue to be powered by it as she grows. But what kind of commercial plans, architecture, and activities will she need to drive her future development? I've thought about this question for the past few days.

I was hesitant when I received an invitation from the publisher to write the preface for this book. After all, I pay more attention to macro financial and economic studies on topics such as policies, markets, and industries. I don't have much to say about specific projects, such as urban renewal or a particular commercial complex, and I was afraid that what I wrote might be ridiculed. However, fate may have played a part in this case, as HKRI Taikoo Hui happens to be located right next to the headquarters of Yicai Media Group. I walk past it almost every day, and I shop there often, since I really like the place. As I was born and raised in Shanghai, the immense changes in this city during the past few decades have given me a great sense of rebirth, along with a profound sadness for the things we left behind. What will HKRI Taikoo Hui bring to Shanghai after its transformation from the well-known Dazhongli and "Xieqiao"? This topic has inspired me profoundly.

The reasons above compelled me to accept the invitation. I gained a deeper understanding of the project's arduous planning and construction phases after reading the first draft. And I learned even more about the ideals, principles and values embedded in the project, with respect to commerce, architecture, the city and its cultural heritage. This book has compiled stories on the birth of HKRI Taikoo Hui from multiple perspectives, into a volume for commercial developers, operators, urban planners and builders, cultural researchers, and consumers to take time to learn from and understand. It has strong practical significance. Involving the rebirth of "Dazhongli" – a plot of land in the centre of the "Fascinating City". These spectacular stories will offer readers a joyful experience.

A city is nothing without commerce. This is particularly true for a big city like Shanghai, which has relied on commerce to prosper and become one of the largest business centres in China. Shanghai is endowed with geographical advantages. Positioned at the mouth of the Yangtze River and beside the prosperous south-eastern provinces, it reaches far inland and looks out over the horizon to Japan, Korea and the countries of East Asia. Chinese and foreign businessmen flocked to the city after its port opened in 1843. Inclusive in terms of culture and values, its businesses diversified and flourished, and Shanghai quickly became the largest city in the Far East.

The book also presents to us the continuous expansion of Shanghai's central commercial zone, and the rapid development of the city. More and more commercial buildings have risen, particularly since the end of the 19<sup>th</sup> century. They were the first of their kind, both in appearance and function. The buildings included the first Country Club and Zhang Garden located near Xieqiao. The trendy architectural style and abundant supply of food, drink and entertainment, quickly made them contemporary "check-in spots". So many tourists flocked in that traffic often became congested.

Looking back at more than 100 years of history in Shanghai, we discover that the rapid development of commerce has given rise to large areas of exceptional commercial buildings. In fact, I believe it is an unbroken rule that only advanced commercial activities can give birth to such structures. Buildings extended westward from the Bund along the Huangpu River to the Jing'an and Luwan districts, and further to the Xuhui and Changning districts. More rose in the major commercial districts and became landmarks in their own right. Shanghai ranks first in China in the sheer quantity of early modern structures (including residential buildings) and the state of their preservation.

When you observe these landmarks and read their histories, you will discover that they have something in common. Regardless of the purpose of the building when it was built – be it a bank, a commercial outlet, or a hotel – the builders were very thorough in everything from site selection to design and construction. They were careful and took no shortcuts. It was as though they were making a highly functional work of art. As such, these buildings became immensely popular when they were built, and their reputation continues to live on.

It is regrettable that history and culture have their ebbs and flows. There are always eras in which severing ties with the past is considered as innovation, and demolition is regarded as

a revolution. At critical times in history, even the cultural and commercial heritage of cities cannot escape their fate. And in modern times, nearly forty years after the start of the opening-up policy, the shortcuts taken to build mazes of concrete had become unstoppable in most cities. The result was that every city looked the same. For local officials, the most effective way to expedite urbanisation and achieve GDP targets was to remove everything and start over. It was not urban renewal, but a revolution of concrete forests. People walk on roads and in malls with no sense of joy. Commercial centres exist for the sole purpose of stimulating the desire to shop. And this has culminated in large swathes of commercial buildings that are dull on the outside and tedious on the inside. This is particularly true after the rise of e-commerce. Malls with severe deficiencies in shopping and leisure experiences saw a drastic decline in visitors, or became a blend of preschool education institutions and catering facilities.

Shanghai has exceptional traditions, commercial activities, and architecture. And, while there is no shortage of commercial centres, what Shanghai lacks are good ones. Mega malls have risen rapidly and become too numerous to count. We must of course respect the essence of business, as the satisfaction of consumer demands remains the most basic purpose of all commercial facilities. There aren't many commercial centres that exemplify the characteristics and tastes of their cities – centres that can pass on history and heritage. However, profound changes have begun: The era of material deprivation has passed and there is now an oversupply of high-end shopping venues in developed cities. People now visit commercial complexes for a variety of reasons, including shopping, leisure or simply to relax. And they consume products with humanistic spirit and appreciate culture. A good commercial centre must satisfy these diverse demands. The best way to do this is to be part of the urban character and landscape, and become an important medium for the memories of a city.

As I look back on my early memories of Shanghai, the most lasting ones are of the tall buildings that stood outside the Catholic Church near my home in Xujiahui, and the busy streets stretching from the No. 26 tram station in Xujiahui all the way east along Huaihai Road. You could hear the steam whistle from the Huangpu River ferry in the distance as you approached Xizang Road, and feel the fresh breeze from the river when you passed the European-style buildings on Sichuan Road. Upon arriving at the terminal on the Bund, you could simply look up and see the buildings that lined the shore. If you happened to get there at the top of the hour, you could hear the bell on the Customs House telling the time. Architecture is just like sound or smell – it constitutes an important, and perhaps the longest-lasting part of our memory of a city.

However, preserving "heritage" and "memory" is not so easily accomplished. It takes a consensus among the city's administrators, developers, architects, and residents to achieve such goals. Fortunately, the developers of HKRI Taikoo Hui were not typical commercial real estate developers. "Dazhongli" was the first land lot obtained by HKR International in Shanghai. It took 15 years and a lot of hardship, from the resolute desire to acquire the land, to the subsequent decision not to pursue fast cash when it cancelled residential plans and converted the property to commercial real estate for long-term ownership. This is not to forget the delay caused by the financial crisis and the impact on urban planning. Fortunately, the Cha family does not prioritise short-term investment returns. The HKRI Taikoo Hui project is similar to their renowned Discovery Bay development in Hong Kong, where they placed a high value on the work of creating good buildings and communities, and upheld their core values of "respecting the people and cherishing the land."

In "Dazhongli", the group upheld their respect for Shanghai's commercial development. From the planning stage, they began to form an ecosystem of communities, amidst nearly ten buildings of varying heights that would soon become shopping malls, office buildings, hotels, and serviced apartments. They chose to sacrifice floor area to maintain the open spaces of Dazhongli and Wujiang Road. The portion of the shopping mall that ran along the street was divided into multiple small, low-density, two-to-three-storey buildings surrounding a core area that included a large crescent-shaped mall stretching from north to south. The office towers and hotels are situated above the shopping mall, with each connected through footbridges. The gradual increase in elevation opens up the view of surrounding roads, and the complex blends effortlessly into the neighbourhood. With multiple public entrances that can be opened or discreetly hidden, people can pass through different buildings in a way that is reminiscent of those Shikumen building clusters from our childhood. They can leave the noise behind them and enter a place of tranquillity in mere moments.

In addition to using new buildings that mimic traditional floorplans and layouts in a tribute to the memories of old Shanghai, the HKRI Taikoo Hui project also included the complete restoration of Cha House as its keystone.

I've always believed that the core value of urban renewal does not lie in renewal, but in the means of heritage preservation. Renewal does not mean the removal of everything. The highest level of achievement is to create new life and soul in an old shell while preserving heritage.

The Minli School building (the famous "Qiu Mansions" before the founding of the People's Republic of China) located at the south of the complex, was a beautiful preserved building that acted as an important historical site and a treasured piece of cultural heritage. Unfortunately, it had fallen into disrepair and only a portion of the original schematics remained. There were immense challenges in the restoration, but the developers and the architecture firm still spent a large amount of energy and resources to faithfully refurbish the structure. In addition to safely relocating the building 57.3 metres southward, they fully restored the structure and all the external facades and internal decorations to their original state. They also added a basement and a retro-look elevator, renaming the building Cha House. Importantly, the restoration has given it new functionality, and enabled the century-old building to hold exhibitions, seminars, and various cultural events.

For me, harmony and coexistence between new and old are like two sides of a scale. The new and the old, the moving and the static, history and future, fashion and tradition. They all find balance through the intersection of space and time, and this balance gives way to the future expansion of commercial civilisation.

For a commercial complex, consumer experience is naturally the basis for all appraisals. From my personal experience, the biggest highlight of HKRI Taikoo Hui is its unique blend of tasteful luxury and trendy styles, presented in small boutiques instead of large stores. The 100,000 square metre space contains more than 250 brands that provide white-collar consumers with fresh, interesting and abundant combinations. I quickly became a fan of a menswear brand. The Sukhothai Shanghai and the Middle House are two first-rate, minimalist, modern hotels that make guests feel like they have come home. They portray Shanghai's classicism and modernity in a sensitive and thoughtful manner.

As a great city, Shanghai has experienced dazzling development since its port opened. It has also undergone war and stagnation, prior to the last forty years of rapid expansion fueled by China's opening-up policies. It has become a world-class city – one that has retained its resilience and vitality despite countless difficulties – thanks to its ability to preserve its heritage and the endless pursuit of innovation. All innovation must be human-oriented, and I believe that is the source of HKRI Taikoo Hui's tremendous success. The greatest things I learned from this book were the values of respecting the people and cherishing the land, preserving heritage, and passing on the spirit of innovation. I hope it will also inspire more developers and participants in Shanghai's urban development.

Written in mid-2020

# 城市建设的匠心

**贾坚**

同济大学建筑设计研究院（集团）
有限公司副总裁，兼轨道交通与
地下工程设计院院长

大中里项目地处上海静安区核心地段，被称为"南京西路上的最后一块商业拼图"，是上海近十年来超大型商办综合体建设的典型代表作之一。大中里项目不仅开发体量大，而且周边环境条件极为复杂，其地下工程的设计及实施极具挑战性。

　　十二年前我和我的同事有幸成为大中里项目地下工程的设计顾问，欣喜之余也倍感压力。当时地块西侧有在建的地铁13号线南京西路站，地铁建设期间须将石门路的交通和管线全部翻排到大中里的场地内，如何统筹协调二者建设的场地安排和施工进度，并保证相邻开挖的稳定和结构安全等等都是摆在项目团队面前的难题。而在地块内部，还有一座近百年的历史保护建筑——民立中学，在百年建筑下方如何安全地开挖四层地下室，让老建筑在延续历史文脉的同时适应城市更新的发展，这也是我们面临的另一个考验。此外，运营中的地铁2号线盾构隧道在地块北部穿过，以往将上海的地铁隧道建造形容为"在豆腐里打洞"，而大中里项目在地铁隧道上方加盖建筑，则相当于"在有洞的豆腐上盖楼"，其难度之大可想而知。大中里项目占地面积超过6万平方米，总地下空间开发面积超过18万平方米，基坑挖深达20米，属于深大地下工程，还涉及深层承压水降压及控制等问题，我们必须兼顾周边环境的保护。诸如此类的工程难题非常多，可以说大中里项目几乎遇到了上海地下空间开发中面临的各类难题，这既是挑战，也驱动我们去创新。

　　在中国地下工程建设理念和建造技术方面，上海一直走在最前沿。我们按照"大楼要造、地铁要保"的原则，对大中里项目和地铁工程进行了科学合理的总体设计筹划，并在项目实施中成功地运用了多项创新技术，包括"轨道交通与地块的统筹同步合建技术"、"骑跨运营地铁盾构隧道上方的开挖技术"、"历史保护建筑的平移盖挖技术"、"软土深基坑分区卸荷控制环境变形技术"、"承压水抽灌一体化控制大地沉降技术"、"超高层建筑基础沉降耦合控制技术"等等，此外我们还创新开发了"基坑支撑下挂临时管廊技术"，从而便捷实现了交通翻交与管线翻排的分离，大大降低了场地多次周转和交通迁改的难度及成本。可以说大中里项目是近年来上海地下工程建设创新系列技术的集中体现。

　　大中里地块从曾经的里弄石库门街区转变为当今的兴业太古汇商业地标，它既承载了上海人旧时的记忆，又凝结了工程建造者的辛勤付出，还承担了上海全新商业景象的期望。大中里项目建设体现的"历史传承"、"新老交融"、"统筹互利"、"绿色环保"和"创新发展"理念，同样也将在中国方兴未艾的城市建设中得到进一步推广和发展。

写于2020年7月

# Craftsmanship in
# Urban Development

**JIA JIAN**

*Deputy CEO, Tongji Architectural Design
and Research Institute (Group) Co., Ltd.,
Dean of the Rail Transportation and
Underground Engineering Institute*

The Dazhongli Project is located in the core of Shanghai's Jing'an District, and is known as the "last piece in the commercial jigsaw of West Nanjing Road." As a classic example of a commercial complex development in Shanghai, the project was not only large in scale, but also involved dealing with extremely tough conditions in the surrounding environment. The design and implementation of its underground construction was particularly challenging.

Twelve years ago, when my colleagues and I had the good fortune to be made design consultants for the Dazhongli Project's underground construction, our joy was tempered by the sense of pressure we felt. At that time, the West Nanjing Road station of Metro Line 13 was under construction on the west side of the lot, and it was necessary to re-route traffic and pipelines along Shimen Road to the Dazhongli Project site. Coordinating site arrangements and the construction of the two projects, while ensuring the stability and structural safety of all areas and structures around the excavation work, were among the difficulties that the project team had to face. In addition, a nearly century-old historic structure – the Minli School building – was also located within the lot. How to safely excavate the project's four basement floors under this old building, and meet the needs of urban renewal while preserving the building in its historic context, was yet another challenge that we had to confront. Furthermore, the shield tunnel for the in-operation Metro Line 2 passed beneath the northern portion of the lot. Shanghai's metro tunnels have been described as "holes made in tofu". That made the construction of buildings above them in the Dazhongli Project tantamount to "constructing buildings on top of tofu with holes in it." The Dazhongli Project site covers a floor area of over 60,000 square metres, and the total developed underground space exceeds 180,000 square metres. The foundation pit was 20 metres in depth, which constitutes deep underground work. The project also faced other problems, such as the reduction and control of confined water, while ensuring that the surrounding environment was protected. The difficulties in a project like this were numerous and extreme, and the Dazhongli Project in particular included nearly all of the problems faced by any underground construction work in Shanghai. In short, the circumstances were very challenging. Those problems brought challenges, but also drove us to innovate.

Shanghai has consistently been at the forefront of underground construction technology and methodology in China. In accordance with the principle of "metros must be protected when high-rise buildings are built," the overall design planning for the Dazhongli Project and metro work was conducted scientifically. In the course of the project, we successfully deployed numerous innovative techniques, including coordinated rail transit and lot co-construction, and excavation above the operating subway shield tunnels. We also performed excavation under a historic building, sectional excavation to control environmental deformation in soft soil, dewatering while recharging confined water, coupled with controlling super high-rise building foundation subsidence. In addition, we developed an innovative way to temporarily hang pipe racks beneath foundation pit supports, which enabled us to conveniently separate the process of re-routing traffic and pipelines, while greatly reducing the difficulty and cost of multiple site changes.

The Dazhongli Project lot has been transformed from a neighbourhood block featuring Shikumen architecture, into a contemporary landmark known as HKRI Taikoo Hui. It bears the memories of Shanghai residents, while also embodying the intense dedication and commitment of the project builders, and meeting the expectations of Shanghai's all-new commercial cityscape. The Project showcases the concepts of historical preservation, the blending of new and old, planning for mutual benefit, green environmental protection, and innovative development. It is also an example of excellence amidst China's unfolding urban development landscape.

Written in July 2020

# 1990 - 2019 大事年表

## Milestones
### 1990 ~ 2019

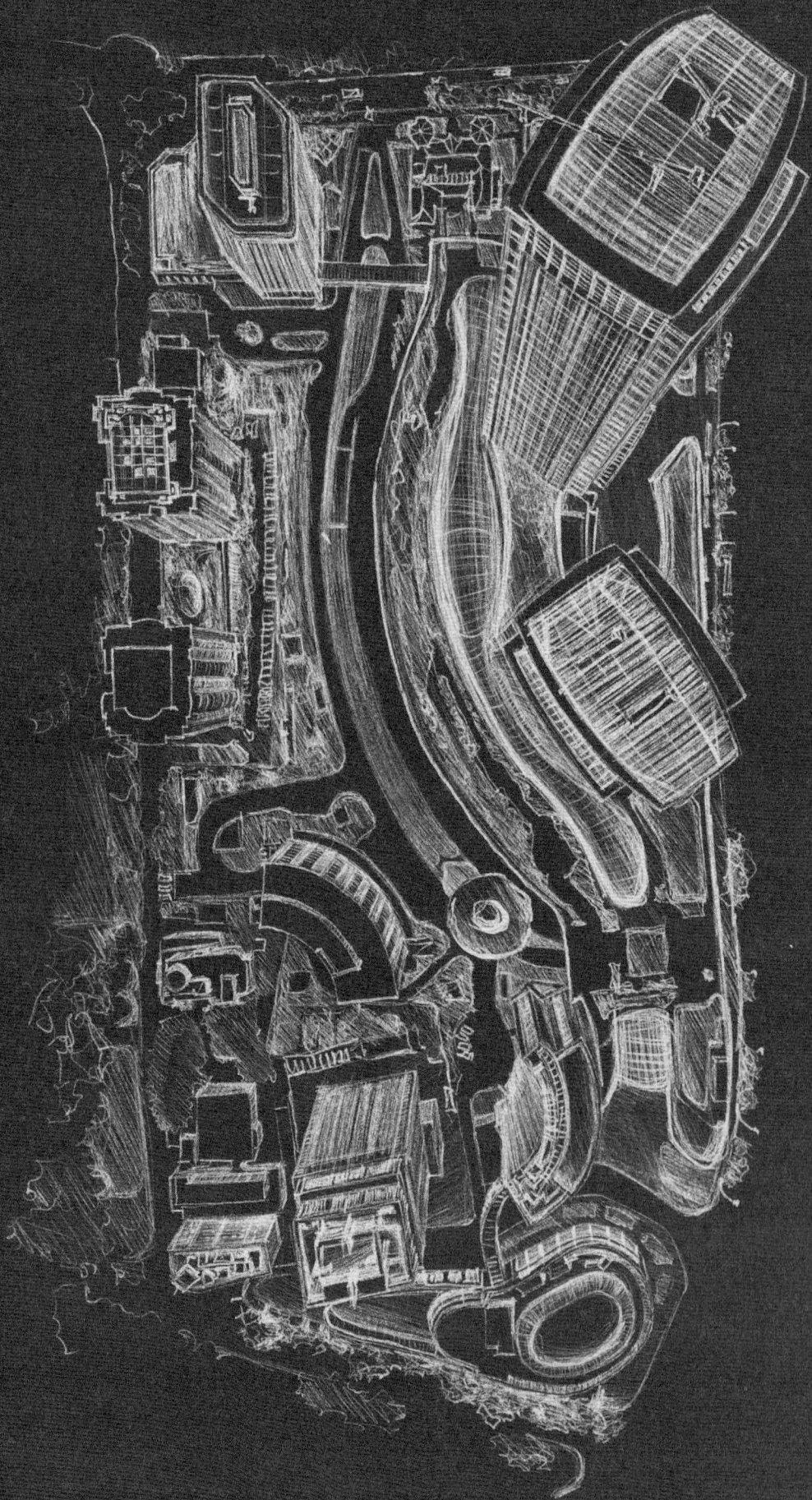

# Chapter I

# UNIQUE ARCHITECTURE SHAPES SHANGHAI

第 一 章

走进

海派厅堂

兼容并蓄的海派文化
Shanghai-style — An Inclusive Culture

西为中用的社区设计
West-meets-East Community Design

百年树人的文化沿革
The History of a Cultural Icon

上海近代的海派文化，是以明清江南文化为底蕴，并吸收了西方的风格元素所形成。新旧市民的习惯、经历、思想在日常生活中碰撞交融，又使其逐渐发展为一种务实奋进、灵活多变的城市精神。

Modern Shanghai's unique style is rooted in the Southern Yangtze River culture, which evolved from the Ming and Qing dynasties. One of its key features is the incorporation of western aesthetic elements. Over time, many of the ideas and experiences of its long established and newer residents gradually merged, until they developed into the pragmatic, progressive and agile urban spirit we know today.

上海的历史，也是一部租界史和新移民史。自开埠以来，中外"冒险家"在这座新城中步步为营，不断寻找发展机遇。"远东第一都市"的蓝图在基础建设的推进下得以快速实现——当年依水系而成的郊野土地，也逐渐被开发为上海城市肌理中最为鲜活的居住社区。

The history of modern Shanghai is really a story of new immigrants and foreign settlements. Since its founding, countless Chinese and foreign "adventurers" have looked to the city as a source of exciting new opportunities. Things changed quickly when the Chinese government began to create the urban infrastructure, from which the blueprint of the "Greatest City in the Far East" took shape. The rural landscape along the great Yangtze River and its tributaries also developed into vibrant residential communities, becoming an intimate part of the metropolis we know as Shanghai.

1 – 1
1930 年代的上海外滩
The Bund in the 1930s

作为中西融合的典型代表，石库门一度是百万"新上海人"对城市梦想的写照。中国人最为重视的宗族桑梓、文化传承，通过建筑与家园的故事，展现出生生不息的强大韧劲。

For Chinese people, their ethnic clans and cultural heritage are both powerful and sacrosanct. These ideas are reflected in the architectural style of their homes – such as the unique Shikumen style formed by a classic fusion of Chinese and Western culture – which represented the realisation of the dreams of millions of newcomers to Shanghai.

在上海市中心，恰有这样一段独特的故事流传至今——从占据城市心脏位置的"斜桥"地区发展史，到以中华民族命名的"大中里"社区营造史，到为民而立的"民立中学"百年校史，再到如今破土重建的"兴业太古汇"商业进化史——都可感受到这种深植于土地和民族精神中的特质。

Located in the heart of the city, HKRI Taikoo Hui has a unique story. It is part of Shanghai's original Xieqiao district, which produced the cherished Dazhongli residential area, and was itself named in honour of the Chinese people. The site was also the long-time home of Shanghai Minli School, which educated many influential scholars during a tumultuous century. However, throughout its various transformations, the area has retained much of its original spirit.

# 兼容并蓄的海派文化

## *Shanghai-style*
## *– An Inclusive Culture*

　　水系资源是所有大城市格外珍视的地域天赋和文明底色。上海，不管是其气势宏伟、将城市与世界连通的大江大海，还是潺潺流淌、持续滋润一方土地的浦塘泾浜，都能以其灵动与柔和，为城市的发展增加独特韵味。

　　在高度现代化的上海市中心，数百年前的风貌早已深埋地下。年轻一代多只识得被保留至今的重要航路，如黄浦江、苏州河与吴淞口，却对"徐家汇"、"陆家嘴"、"肇嘉浜"等繁华地区的地名由来知之甚少。

　　历史上，上海实际是一个河流纵横、湖泊密布的典型水乡城邑。区域地名中"江"、"浦"、"塘"、"浜"、"泾"、"港"等用来形容水系规模及特点的词被如此广泛地应用，就是一个证据。这些水系所切分出的大小片区，形成了上海最早的城市肌底，之后又随着租界时代的快速城市化，以另一种特殊的形式被保留下来。

Water is a vital resource for any major city, and plays a defining role in shaping its destiny. In the case of Shanghai, both the Yangtze River and the East China Sea helped to form the city's essential character, while the smaller rivers and streams have added to its unique charm.

Although ultra-modern skyscrapers have sprung up across the city's central district, the roots of Shanghai's character reach deep into its past. While many younger residents are familiar with the city's longstanding maritime connections – like the Huangpu River, Suzhou Creek and the Wusong Estuary – most are completely unaware how bustling areas, such as Xujiahui, Lujiazui and Zhaojiabang got their names.

Shanghai is a typical water-oriented city. Coming in all shapes and sizes – from small streams to winding rivers and estuaries leading to the sea – water has formed Shanghai's fundamental character. You can see this clearly in the wide use of descriptive place names like 塘 (Táng), which means pond, and 港 (Gǎng), which means port. These were largely retained, albeit in unique ways, during the rapid urbanisation which took place during the concession era.

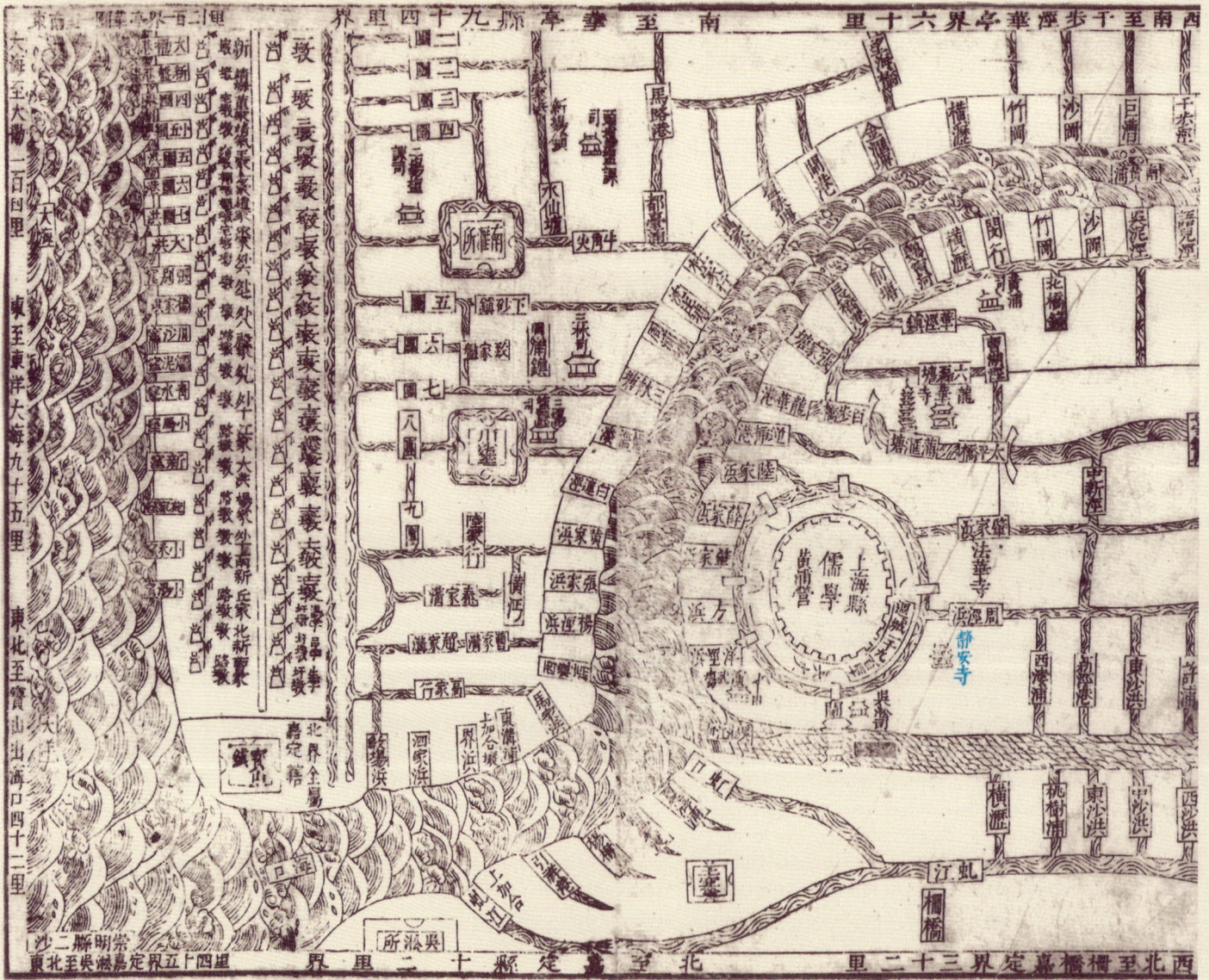

康熙年间的《上海县志》·1683
From the "Shanghai County Compendium" during
the regime of Qing Emperor Kang Xi (1683)

静安寺涌泉

　　以目前上海市中心的"静安寺"地区为例：在这座香火旺盛的古刹内，曾有一口特别的古井"涌泉"。清秦荣光《上海县竹枝词》中记载："涌泉，在静安寺前，昼夜沸腾，俗称海眼。"附近又有一条小河，因这口古井而得名"涌井浜"，其位置处于"大马路"（即如今的南京东路）和跑马场（即如今的人民广场）向西的延长线上，也就是如今上海繁华的商业街"南京西路"所在地。

　　1860 年后，上海的租界区域获批扩展，英商朝着静安寺方向填埋河道、修筑马路，将势力范围向上海内陆渗透。"涌井浜"在这一过程中逐渐消失，变成了当时的"静安寺路"，仅在其英文名"Bubbling Well Road"中有所体现。

　　伴随着"静安寺路"的逐步延伸，临近跑马场的周边位置最早获得进一步开发。根据当时的报纸记载：每当西人在跑马厅赛马时，许多住在附近的华人拿着板凳，隔河观赛。因人多拥挤，经常有人被挤入河中。

## The Yongquan Well at the Jing'an Temple

*Take the Jing'an Temple area in the centre of Shanghai for example. The ancient structure, which attracted visitors and devout followers for centuries, had a well which people called Yongquan (bubbling spring). Qin Rongguang, a noted scholar during the Qing Dynasty, published a series of books on Shanghai county. He wrote, "Yongquan, with its water that gushes day and night, is located in front of Jing'an Temple. It is colloquially known as the Eye of the Sea." The name of a nearby stream called Yongjingbang, was also inspired by the well. It was located to the west of the old Grand Avenue (today's East Nanjing Road) and the Racecourse (now People's Square), where today's bustling West Nanjing Road is located.*

*After 1860, Shanghai's Foreign Settlements grew rapidly. British merchants began filling in streams near the Jing'an Temple and building roads, as they tried to expand their influence. It was around this time that the name Yongjingbang lost its significance. Over time it was replaced by Jing'an Temple Road. All that was left of its former existence was the English name, Bubbling Well Road.*

*The nearby Racecourse was one of the first areas to benefit from the extension of Jing'an Temple Road. According to newspaper reports at the time, whenever westerners were at the Racecourse, many Chinese people living nearby would take their wooden benches and watch the horse races from across the river. When there were simply too many onlookers, some unfortunate souls would get shoved into the water.*

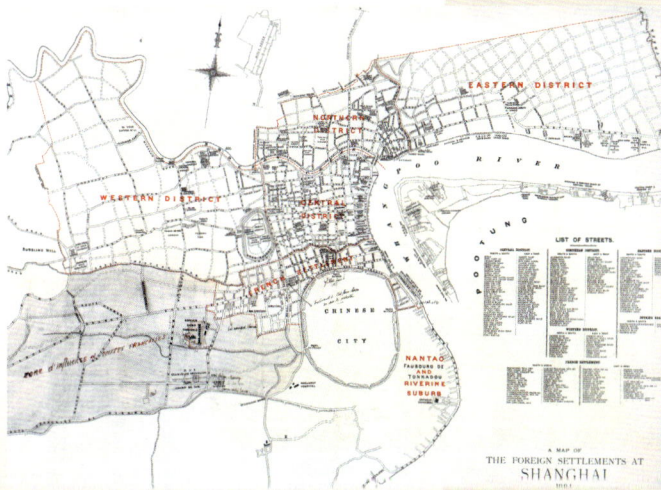

1 - 3
静安寺涌泉
The Yongquan Well
in the Jing'an Temple area

1 - 4
上海外国租界地图・1904
A map of the Foreign
Settlements in Shanghai

报道中所提及的"河",即是一条弯弯曲曲的吴淞江支流"东芦浦"。由于有碍交通,租界当局顺应水势,特意在河道上筑了一座呈东北往西南走向的"斜桥",整个区域也因此得名"斜桥"。根据上海市文化历史建筑研究专家娄承浩的考证,"斜桥"是清末民初上海城市建设中最具话题性,各类文化碰撞杂糅最强的区域之一。

The river mentioned in such reports was the East Lupu – a winding tributary of the Wusong River. Limited urban development meant that a bridge built at the time crossed the river at an angle, linking a road on the northeast bank to another on the southwest bank. Hence the name Xieqiao literally means "slanted bridge". According to Mr. Lou Chenghao, an expert on Shanghai's cultural and historical buildings, Xieqiao district was one of the places in Shanghai during the late Qing Dynasty and early Republic period which yielded the most interesting conversations and saw the greatest clash of cultures.

1-5
上海地图 · 1907
A map of Shanghai in 1907 showing where Xieqiao was located

**娄承浩**　上海市建筑学会历史建筑保护委员会顾问
上海老房子俱乐部理事长

　　"斜桥"可以说是上海市中心范围内最重要的历史地标之一。这里占据了地理位置要冲，又有很好的交通基础，使得当时已经式微的清政府系统、逐渐兴盛的民间资本和野心勃勃的西方力量，乃至更后期处于萌芽阶段的中国共产党政权，都试图在这里确立自己的基础。这也是当时上海城内"五方杂处"的一个典型案例。

## LOU CHENGHAO

Advisor of Historical Architecture Conservation Committee,
Architectural Society of Shanghai China
Governor-General of the Shanghai Old Homes Club

*Xieqiao district was one of the most important historical landmarks in Shanghai's city centre. It occupied a prime geographical location and possessed such excellent transport infrastructure that the waning Qing government, local businesses and ambitious western firms, and even the Chinese Communist Party which came much later, attempted to establish themselves there. It is also an example of the diverse mix of residents in Shanghai at the time.*

　　一方面，由于受到太平军的冲击影响，清末上海的政府势力已经不再固守于如今城隍庙所在的旧城，开始向外扩散。名门望族、官员士绅多选择比邻而居，互通婚姻，在清末民初成了显赫一时的"朋友圈"。时任上海道台的邵友濂府邸、"上海第一豪门"的盛宣怀家宅以及李鸿章五弟李凤章的住所，都位于斜桥区域。以当年的盛府为例，其占地足有105亩之多，极为豪华阔绰，以至于寄信不用强调地址，注明"斜桥盛公馆"五个字，即可送达。

The advance of Taiping Rebellion forces caused the imperial government in Shanghai to move beyond the old city where the Chenghuang Temple lies, which it occupied towards the end of the Qing Dynasty period. During this time, many famous people and government officials moved in. Wealthy families concentrated in the area, and formed a formidable social circle through frequent intermarriage. The official residence of the Chief Governor of Shanghai, Shao Youlian, as well as the family home of Sheng Xuanhuai, and that of Li Fengzhang, the fifth brother of Li Hongzhang, were all located in the Xieqiao district. Sitting on seven hectares of land, the Residence of Sheng Xuanhuai was said to be the "richest household" in Shanghai. It was so famous that any mail sent there didn't require a full address. Letters could simply be marked the Residence of Sheng, Xieqiao.

1-6
斜桥盛公馆
The Residence of Sheng in Xieqiao

另一方面，以张叔和为代表的沪上富商，已有足够的资本积累可以彰显其实力。在"斜桥"以东，张叔和自 1882 年购得一块私家园林后，即对其多次改建、扩建，最终于 1885 年建成一座占地 61.52 亩的"张氏味莼园"，开放予市民参观。到 1893 年，"张氏味莼园"内又建起当时上海市内最高的建筑物"安垲第"（Arcadia Hall），并设立魔术表演、游乐宫、中西式餐馆等，游人如织，一时甚至阻塞道路。

Then, there were the wealthy Shanghai merchants. One of the most flamboyant was Zhang Shuhe, who loved showing off his wealth. In 1882, he bought a piece of land to the west of Xieqiao to construct a private estate that would become known as Zhang Garden. After several rounds of expansion that saw the estate sprawl across four hectares, it was opened to the public. In 1893, Arcadia Hall – said to be the tallest building in Shanghai at the time – was added. With magic shows and other attractions, such as a games hall and Chinese and Western restaurants, Zhang Garden became so popular that the road leading to it regularly suffered from traffic congestion.

1 - 8
张氏味莼园内最高建筑 —— 安垲第
Old Shanghai's tallest building –
Arcadia Hall in Zhang Garden

1 - 7
昔日的张园盛况
Bustling Zhang Garden at the height of its popularity and prosperity

1 - 9
现今的张园
Zhang Garden today

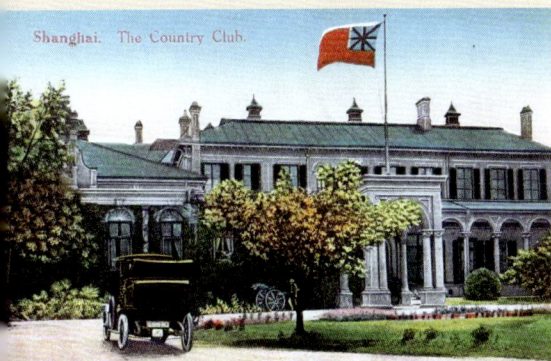
Shanghai. The Country Club.

1-10
斜桥总会明信片
A postcard of The
Country Club

1-11
斜桥盛公馆
The Residence of
Sheng in Xieqiao

以"填浜筑路"推动区域发展的租界势力，也延续了将这一区域用于休闲、娱乐的规划。1879 年，三位旅沪的英国人在"斜桥"以西建设了上海第一个乡村俱乐部"斜桥总会"（如今上海电视台所在地），内设网球场、高尔夫球场、桌球房、歌舞厅、酒吧、棋牌室、浴室等多种休闲活动设施，经扩建后总面积达到 65 亩，在旅沪英侨中影响极大。

依靠这些项目，斜桥区域在上海市中心的区位潜力已经获得了初步肯定，但整体仍处于开发早期。一个可以佐证的小案例是：斜桥总会的三位建设者之所以认定可以建设乡村俱乐部，是因为他们在已经建成的静安寺路附近散步时，"时时可见野鸡起落在草丛树间。"

直到民国早期，上海快速进入国际化发展的建设阶段，斜桥的魅力才真正被大量涌入的人口和机遇所点燃。

The powerful settlement forces, which drove development by filling up streams to build roads, were also responsible for creating the region's leisure and entertainment amenities. In 1879, three British men founded The Country Club, the first of its kind in Shanghai. It was located to the west of Xieqiao, where the Shanghai Television building sits today. The club boasted numerous attractions, including a golf driving range, tennis courts, a billiards room, a dance hall and a bridge room, as well as a bar and baths. Following several rounds of expansion, The Country Club eventually covered more than four hectares, and was an important fixture in the social life of British nationals living in Shanghai at the time.

Although such projects demonstrated Xieqiao's potential as part of Shanghai's city centre, it remained relatively undeveloped. The co-founders of The Country Club certainly valued the area's rural character, and when they strolled near the newly-completed Jing'an Temple Road, they "could spot pheasants among the bushes every now and then."

It was not until the early Republican Period when Shanghai began to rapidly internationalise, that the potential of Xieqiao district became fully apparent. This was not least because of the large number of immigrants arriving in the area and the business opportunities on offer.

# 西为中用的社区设计

## West-meets-East
## Community Design

　　如果说古老的河道水系，是数百年前上海的血管网络，那么成片兴建的里弄制式，则组成了近百年上海的肌理和总体样貌。

　　进入民国时期后，名噪一时的"斜桥三公馆"、"张氏味莼园"和"斜桥总会"这类大体量的园林府宅，都在政局动荡中逐渐从舞台中央退下。伴随着租界范围的大规模拓展以及各类基础设施的不断完善，斜桥区域逐渐被推至上海这座国际化大都市的核心地带，各类有工作和居住需求的移民人口快速涌入。

　　清末太平天国起义后，租界内就开始为当时的华人难民及新移民建设社区住宅，初期是以十分简陋的连排木板房为主。依靠保护政策以及这样的居住条件，上海租界就在清末吸引了超过 20 万新居民。

If the rivers can be called Shanghai's circulatory system, then the numerous small housing estates that sprang up during the last century were the muscles that made the city move.

When China entered the Republican Period, the resulting political upheaval spelled the end for some of the larger residences, along with Zhang Garden and The Country Club. As the Foreign Settlements expanded and new infrastructure was built, Xieqiao district gradually became the heart of Shanghai, attracting innumerable immigrants looking for work and somewhere to live.

Following the Taiping Rebellion towards the end of Qing rule, community estates were built inside the Foreign Settlements to house Chinese refugees and new migrants. Although they were initially fairly rudimentary wooden houses built in rows, the protection policy and relatively good living conditions attracted more than 200,000 immigrants during the late Qing period.

1-12

**上海老城厢航拍**
Aerial view of old Shanghai

当时迁入租界的，不完全是身无长物的难民，也包括许多避祸的江南富商。战局稳定后，他们开始期待更好的居住条件，于是有了各类规格更高的住宅建设需求。

上海的本土住宅以"石库门"样式闻名于世。这一样式糅合中国传统合院形式与西方建筑和装饰风格。住宅在中国传统的"立帖式"木结构上，加了砖墙承重。相比于传统的中式民居，石库门的优势在于省地、省工、省料，多用砖石的特点相较于纯木质结构更为安全。

It wasn't just penniless peasants or war refugees who moved into the Foreign Settlements. There were also many wealthy merchants from surrounding cities and regions. As the conflicts receded, these businesspeople began to yearn for better living conditions, and they demanded residences with nicer facilities and more stylish architecture.

Shanghai is known worldwide for its Shikumen-style houses, which combine the fundamentals of traditional Chinese courtyard homes with western architecture and decorative styles. Brick walls added to the traditional Chinese brick-nogging and timber structures, increased the floor-loading that these houses could bear, making them safer than pure timber structures. Shikumen homes also occupied less land than traditional Chinese houses, and saved on labour and materials.

1-13
石库门建筑
Shikumen buildings

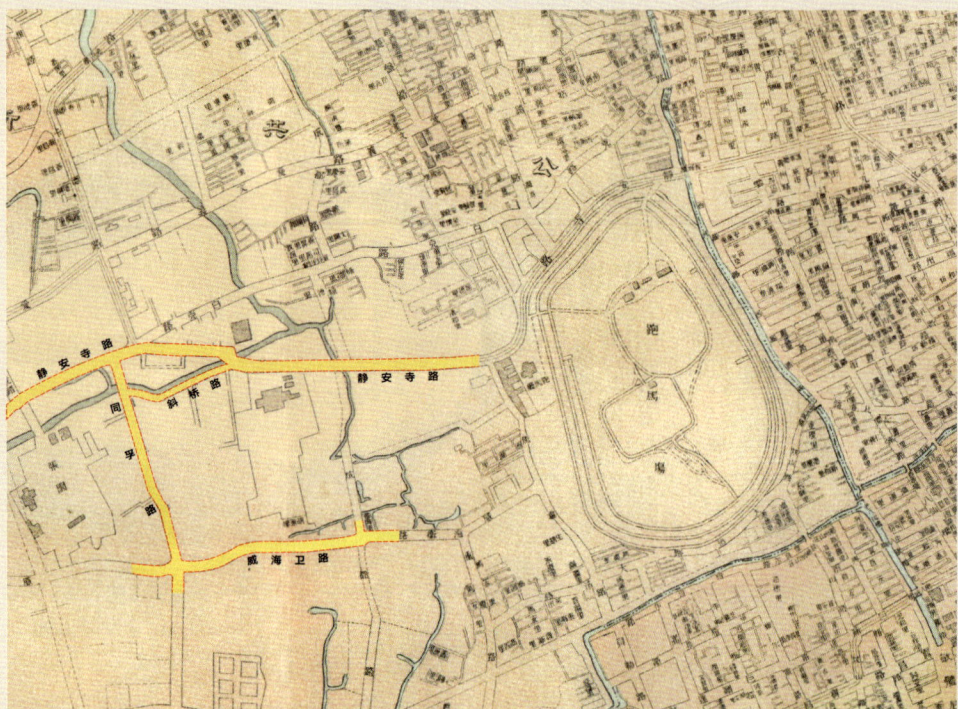

1-14

实测上海城厢租界图·1910

Map of Shanghai in 1910

根据住宅的规模、结构、配套设施，以及多栋住宅间的组织方阵、社区体量，石库门也演变出了"旧式"、"新式"里弄和社区之分。其中，旧式里弄单个院落的体量较大，更接近传统的江浙民居；新式里弄的石库门多是联排建设，整体规模缩小，并增设当时先进的卫生设施。

在民国早期的斜桥区域内，可供开发的地域主要位于"斜桥总会"与"张氏味莼园"之间。这里以农田为主，间或还有杂草丛生的墓地。1900年，斜桥所跨的"东芦浦"被租界工部局填埋筑路，与静安寺路打通，并逐渐向南延伸。这条基本保留了河流走向的道路建成后，以美国驻沪副领事晏摩氏之名，被命名为"同孚路"（Yates Road，也称"宴芝路"），也就是如今的石门一路。当年跨河通行用的"斜桥"，也被扩建成"斜桥弄"。

Shikumen houses were generally built in large estates, which increased their appeal among the immigrants flooding in from the nearby Jiangsu and Zhejiang provinces. The houses came in two varieties, with the original, or "old" Shikumen design, featuring traditional courtyards. The "new" Shikumen residences were more like townhouses, usually constructed in rows, and featuring indoor sanitation facilities, which were considered a tremendous advancement at the time.

During the early Republican Period, land for development within Xieqiao district could be found between The Country Club and Zhang Garden. It was mostly farmland, with a few plots used as graveyards. In 1900, the Wusong River's East Lupu tributary, which ran through Xieqiao, was filled in by the Construction Bureau of the Foreign Settlements to make way for a new road. The road connected the region with Jing'an Temple Road, and ultimately extended southwards, following the contours of the old river. It was eventually named Yates Road, in honour of the then U.S. Deputy Consul-General in Shanghai. Today it is called Shimen Road Number One. The Xieqiao bridge over the river was eventually rebuilt to become "Xieqiao Lane".

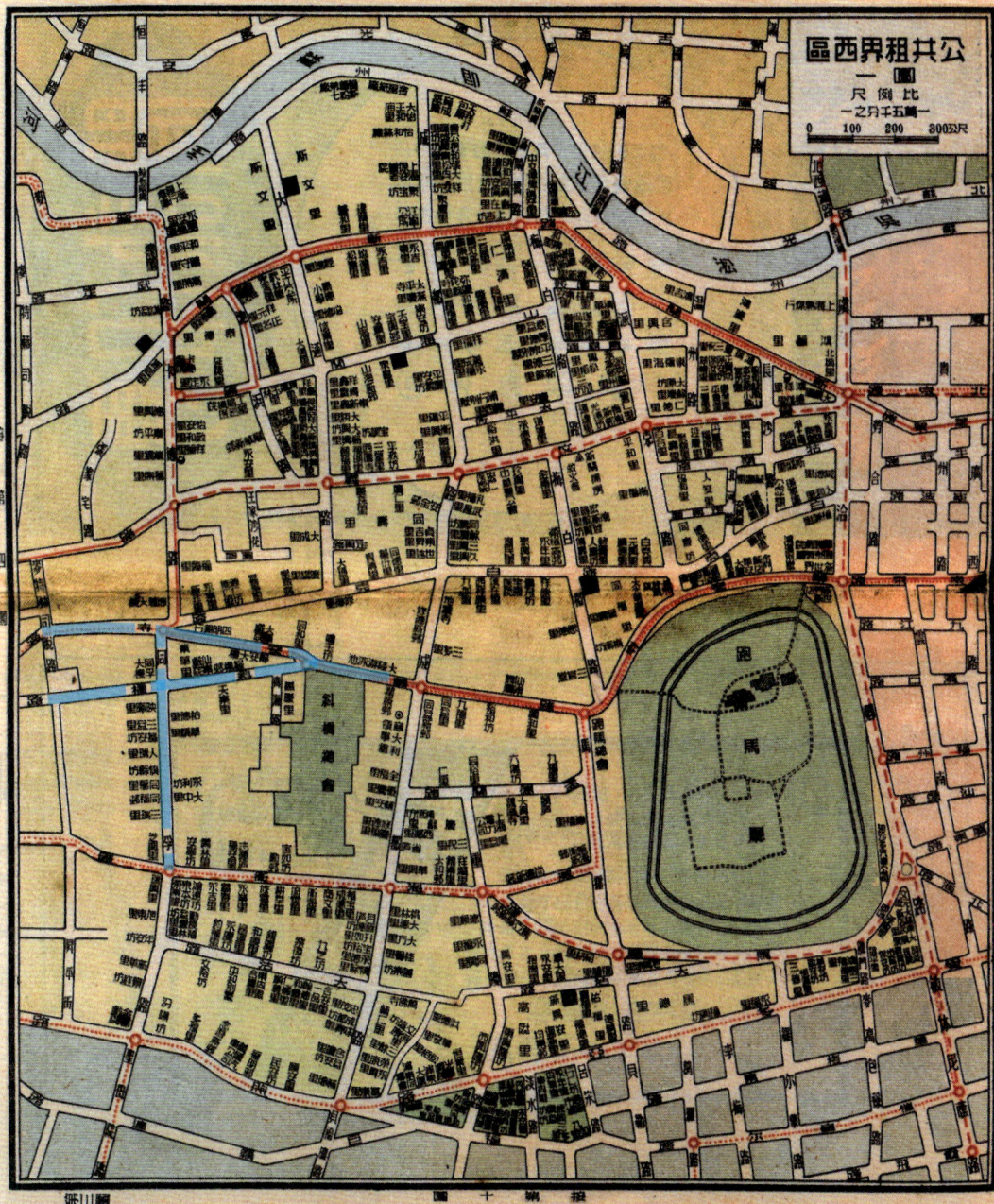

区域内其后的建设计划，多沿着这两条道路扩展，最终形成了多条（片）规模较大的里弄社区，包括天乐坊、大中里、华顺里、北映辉里、南映辉里、柏德里、武陵坊、福绥里等。其中，更靠近静安寺路的天乐坊、大中里、柏德里连成了一片。在之后的很长时间里，这里都以规模最大的大中里作为统称。

1 - 15
上海里弄地图·1942
Map of Shikumen houses
in Shanghai in 1942

Subsequent development in the area mainly involved expansion along these two roads, ultimately forming numerous large housing estates. They included Huashunli, North Yinghuili, South Yinghuili, Wulingfang, and Fusuili. Three other estates – Tianlefang, Dazhongli, and Bodeli – which were closer to Jing'an Temple Road, formed a larger community. For a long time after their development, they were collectively known as Dazhongli.

1 - 16
大中里 Dazhongli

1 - 17
昔日的柏德里 Old Bodeli

1 - 18
从前的天乐坊 Old Tianlefang

1 - 19
大中里鸟瞰图
A bird's-eye view of Dazhongli

　　始建于 1925 年的"大中里",实际上是区域内相对"年轻"的社区,它来自颜料商奚鹤年在当时房地产热潮中的一个投资决定。他将妻子刘莲仙在这里的陪嫁土地利用起来,兴建居住社区。由于其华商背景,在起名时,奚鹤年特意挑选了代表"大中华"的"大中"二字,在当时上海租界被"大英帝国"占据的状况中创造出不一样的声势。

Built in 1925, Dazhongli was actually a relatively "young" community. It was the result of an investment decision by a dye merchant named Xi Henian, which was taken amidst a real estate frenzy. Xi used the plot of land – which was actually his wife Liu Lianxian's dowry – to build a residential community. As a proud Chinese businessman, Xi purposely chose the words 大 (Dà) and 中 (Zhōng), which were derived from the term "Greater China", to distinguish his community from those of the British Empire in the Foreign Settlements.

围绕一条总弄和数条支弄，大中里由 111 幢砖木结构的二层石库门建筑所组成，总建筑面积达到 14,699 平方米。每栋住宅的前后客堂、前后厢房、亭子间、天井和晒台一应俱全，又在建筑式样上增添了些许西式风格的雕花门楣。当然，房价也不低——民国时期迁入"大中里"的人士，大都是上海洋行里的高级职工，房租用金条付，出入开小汽车，娶妻生子都在这里。

从民国时期到 21 世纪初，大中里区域一直是上海市中心各类商业、服务、文化配套最好的地方之一。

以买衣服为例：在 1920 年代至 1930 年代，同孚路沿街已有不少工艺考究、式样新颖的成衣铺、童装店和裁缝铺；到 1940 年代，整条路 70% 都是服装店，在侨民群体里都颇具口碑。中华人民共和国成立后这条路由"中正一路"改称为"石门一路"，虽商业网点性质向综合性发展，但仍以服饰、皮具、饰品等闻名，立于民居外立面的"开开百货公司"招牌，一度是整条街上最大的广告位。

Covering a total of 14,699 square metres, Dazhongli comprised 111 two-storey brick-and-wood Shikumen houses, built around a major lane and several sub-lanes. Each house included a living room in front and bedrooms in the back, a courtyard and a balcony. The builders also added some western-style carved door headers. Needless to say, the houses were not priced for the poor. Those who could afford to move into Dazhongli during this time were mostly senior employees of big trading houses in Shanghai. Rent was paid in the form of gold bars, and most residents also owned motor vehicles. They lived lavish lifestyles, getting married and having children in the community.

The region surrounding Dazhongli remained one of the best areas in Shanghai's city centre for businesses, services and cultural amenities, from the Republican era through to the 2000s.

Take fashion apparel for example. During the 1920s and 1930s, there were already a number of shops along Yates Road that offered stylish, high-quality apparel and childrenswear, as well as tailoring services. By the 1940s, some 70% of the shops on the road sold apparel, and were highly regarded by the Chinese population. After the founding of the People's Republic of China, the road was renamed Shimen Road No. 1. Although some other businesses crept in over time, shops selling apparel, leather goods and accessories continued to dominate the road's retail trade. At one time, the Kai Kai Department Store's sign, which occupied the facade of a number of residential buildings, was the largest advertising space on the entire street.

　　在大中里之外，面积不大的柏德里，以及片区内主入口位于斜桥弄上的天乐坊，也各有故事。

　　兴建于 1927 年的"柏德里"，社区名称来自德籍医生柏德。他在沪创办了宝隆医院（上海长征医院前身），也出资修建了这片里弄。社区建成后不久，正以上海为核心发展的中共中央政治局就选中了这里的一栋石库门住宅，作为日常联络点：一正一厢，坐北朝南，楼下是客堂，楼上是办公室，看似毫不起眼，实际极为重要，周恩来、邓小平都曾在此工作。

Bodeli, a small housing estate outside Dazhongli, and Tianlefang, with its main entrance at Xieqiao Lane, also boasts a rich history.

Built in 1927, Bodeli's name was inspired by a German doctor called Eduard Birt, who founded the Baolong Hospital (the predecessor of the Shanghai Changzheng Hospital). He also paid for the construction of the estate. Not long after the community was built, the Political Bureau of the CPC Central Committee, which at the time was developing aggressively in Shanghai, chose a Shikumen residence there as its secret office. The two-storey house had only two rooms – a reception hall downstairs, and an office upstairs. But, it is historically important because major Communist Party leaders, such as Zhou Enlai and Deng Xiaoping, worked there.

1 - 22
开开百货公司招牌
The Kai Kai Department Store's sign

[1] 参考资料: 节选自电视纪录片《邓小平与上海》。中共中央文献研究室、中共上海市委宣传部、上海文广新闻传媒集团联合摄制。2014年8月东方卫视、上海电视台纪实频道播出。

[1] Reference: A quote from the TV Documentary "Deng Xiaoping in Shanghai" jointly produced by the Party Documents Research Office of the CPC Central Committee, the Publicity Department of CPC Shanghai Municipal Committee and Shanghai Media Group.

1927年秋至1928年间，正值大革命失败到土地革命兴起的历史转折时期，中共中央要在上海领导全国各地进行武装起义，整顿、重建党的各级组织和恢复白区秘密工作，及红军初创时期农村革命根据地工作。对于每天来柏德里处理工作的干部，均要求"职业化打扮"，当时邓小平整天头戴礼帽，身穿长袍出入其中[1]。

The failure of the CPC's attempt to overthrow the Nationalist Kuomintang (KMT) Government was a turning point in China's history. From the autumn of 1927 to 1928 the Chinese Communist Party's Central Committee decided to instigate an armed nationwide uprising, revamp its organisation at various levels, resume work in KMT-controlled areas, and engage in revolutionary work during the early stages of the formation of the Red Army. This was done from the Party's base in Shanghai. CPC cadres who worked at Bodeli were required to "appear professional." As a result, Deng Xiaoping wore a top hat and long coat on a daily basis [1].

**舒浩仑**　上海大学上海电影学院讲师
纪录片《乡愁》导演

大中里周边21世纪初的商业布局，从现在的眼光看起来也是很齐全的。

当我还是小孩子时，印象里不远处是人民公园、瑞金电影院；往北走到南京西路，有当时上海唯一的一家少年儿童书店，对面是六一儿童商店；再走几步，就是静安区少年宫，现在已经变成818广场了；我还在更远一点的少年武校练过武术，就是现在的中信泰富。对大人来说，出弄堂走几步路就有菜场、粮店、酱店、油店、服装店，有钱的话也可以去南京西路，买东西很方便。

对我来说，大中里有意思的地方在于：整个社区建于1925年，最后一栋房子消失在我印象中是在2008年。它基本上是和整个上海同步发展的，相当于是历史的一个缩影。

**SHU HAOLUN**
Lecturer at the Shanghai Film Academy
Director of the documentary "Nostalgia"

*The mix of trade around Dazhongli during the 2000s was comprehensive, even by today's standards.*

*When I was a child, the People's Park and the Ruijin Cinema were nearby. If you walked north towards West Nanjing Road, you would see Shanghai's only bookshop for children and young people. The June 1st Children's Store was just opposite. A few steps further would be the Jing'an District Children's Palace – today it is the 818 Mall. I even learned martial arts at the Youth Martial Arts School a little further away. It was where CITIC Square is today. For the adults, wet markets and shops that sold grain, sauces, oil and apparel were just a few steps outside of their lanes. The wealthy ones could also visit West Nanjing Road.*

*For me, the memorable thing about Dazhongli was this: The community was built in 1925. In my recollection, the last house vanished in 2008. Its development was basically in tandem with that of Shanghai – it is a snapshot of Shanghai's developmental history.*

历史上的邱氏大宅（东楼）
The original east block of the Qiu Mansions

在大中里片区的联排石库门周围，民国时期还兴建过不少规格更高、更繁复的独栋建筑。例如如今青海路 44 号的岳阳医院青海路门诊部，即是旧上海地产大王周湘云的旧居。这些建筑中最受瞩目的，则是被称为"邱氏大宅"的两栋"欧式城堡"。

大中里源于颜料商奚鹤年，但在民国时期，上海滩上有着远比奚鹤年出名的四个"颜料大王"：贝润生、周宗良、吴同文、邱氏兄弟。这几位多是借着大型洋行开拓中国市场时参与买办工作，协助进口颜料到上海，又趁着两次世界大战的动荡时期掌握了实权和财富。

关于山东籍的邱氏兄弟邱信山、邱渭卿两人的发迹过程，说法不一。流传较广的说法是：两人聪明伶俐，在德商背景的谦信洋行从打工仔一路做到买办，之后自建"德和"颜料行，依靠货源渠道的优势发了横财。

谦信洋行此前在大中里以南曾兴建两栋高级职员宿舍，由德商倍高洋行建筑师卡尔·倍克设计，建筑面积约 3,600 平方米。但在民国政府宣布加入第一次世界大战、对德宣战之后，谦信洋行就将手中的颜料存货和这两栋欧式建筑低价抛售给邱氏兄弟，建筑也因此变成了"邱氏大宅"——哥哥邱信山住东楼，弟弟邱渭卿住西楼。

During the Republican Era, lavishly-furnished detached buildings dotted the area surrounding the townhouse district in Dazhongli. One example is the outpatient department of the Yueyang Hospital at No. 44, Qinghai Road, which was the former residence of the renowned property tycoon, Zhou Xiangyun. However, the most prominent of these buildings were two European-style developments called the Qiu Mansions.

Dazhongli was the achievement of the successful dye merchant, Xi Henian. However, during the Republican Era, there were many other wealthy men in Shanghai, like the so-called "Dye Kings". They included Bei Runsheng, Zhou Zongliang, Wu Tongwen and the Qiu brothers. Most of these prominent businessmen took advantage of their relationships with big foreign trading houses that were keen on developing the China market for imported dyes. They obtained power and untold wealth between the two world wars.

There are many different stories about the Qiu brothers – Qiu Xinshan and Qiu Weiqing – who came to Shanghai from Shandong province. One popular version describes them as a street-smart pair who began their careers at the German-owned China Export, Import & Bank Company, A.G. After working their way up from lowly positions to become compradors, they eventually founded their own dyestuff trading house and became incredibly wealthy.

The China Export, Import & Bank Company, A. G. built two residential blocks in Dazhongli to house its senior employees. Designed by Karl Baedeker of Becker & Baedeker, the buildings covered 3,600 square metres. After China declared war on Germany during World War I, the firm sold the buildings and its dye inventory to the Qiu brothers at modest prices. The brothers immediately renamed the buildings as the Qiu Mansions, with the elder Qiu Xinshan living in the east block, and the younger Qiu Weiqing living in the west block.

从设计风格上，"邱氏大宅"中现存的东宅融合了巴洛克风格与德国新古典主义风格，十分独特：砖石混合结构，主立面朝南、轴线对称。建筑中部的底层为大内廊开间，二层的内廊由六个圆形拱券支撑，三层退层建了阳台；建筑两侧向外凸出，切面为半六边形，高度都为四层，配以铜制花式尖顶，形似欧洲城堡。

东宅的整栋建筑墙面都为红砖，配以白色石材框架，色彩庄重而不失豪华、立面变化但不显混乱。西宅与东宅的设计思路相仿，只是将两侧建筑部分都削减为三层、尖顶由铜制改为敷瓦，装饰风格也明显更为朴素。

相比于好静的邱信山，喜欢动物的邱渭卿的西楼要热闹得多：花园中有虎、有蛇；水池里养了鳄鱼，水池外养了穿山甲。此外，每天清晨从花园内的鸽棚里还会飞出约两千只鸽子，在大中里片区一度是很有名的景观。

抗日战争爆发后，邱氏的生意不复往常，家族也有各立门户的想法，大宅失去了往日的热闹。直到 1940 年代，这两栋住宅又在一所著名学府"民立中学"的辗转过程中，获得了新的生机。

In terms of design, the Qiu Mansions – of which only the east block remains today – combined Baroque and German Neo-classical architectural styles. With symmetrical, south-facing facades, the buildings were a mix of brick and stone. They featured a large hall on the ground floor. On the second floor, the internal gallery was supported by six round columns, while the third floor had balconies. The left and right-hand corners of the buildings were highlighted with hexagonal, tower-like extensions, topped off with fancy bronze spires, giving them the look of European castles.

The facade of the east block was constructed using red brick. White stone was used for the window frames, giving the building a lavish and stately look. The west block had a similar design, but its side extensions were three storeys instead of four. The spires were tiled rather than covered with bronze, and the building's decorative style was more understated.

In contrast to his introverted elder brother, the extrovert Qiu Weiqing loved animals. His garden was home to tigers and snakes; crocodiles could be seen in the pond, and there were even pangolins. Every morning, about two thousand pigeons would be released from the loft in the garden, creating an impressive sight around Dazhongli.

The Qiu brothers' business was devastated by the Sino-Japanese War. Fractures began to appear in their families and the Mansions lost their former lustre. In the 1940s the buildings received a new lease of life when Shanghai Minli School – a famous institution of the time – moved in.

1 - 24
邱氏大宅东楼和西楼
The east and west blocks of the Qiu Mansions

香公馆

## 〔三〕　百年树人的文化沿革

### The History of a Cultural Icon

　　围绕"城隍庙"建立起来的清末上海市中心，集中了大量政治、经济、文化和教育资源，开埠早期不少知名学校也诞生于此，民立中学就是其中之一。

　　1904 年，上海的工商业巨子、沪上名门苏氏家族大家长苏本炎顺应母亲的遗嘱，为了让宗族中的成员都获得读书的权利，决定在其宅院旁的民房里兴建一座"民立上海中学堂"。师资力量和日常管理，则由他两位刚从圣·约翰大学毕业的弟弟苏本铫、苏本浩负责组织。

　　苏本炎从小被祖父送入上海的洋学堂研习商业知识，之后又在圣·约翰大学修读法律，一毕业就是上海商业法的专家。他学以致用，大量参与实业投资，将家族带上了发展之路。因此，"民立上海中学堂"在课程设置上，也格外重视外文、法律、商业，逐渐发展为上海清末最有名的中学。

Shanghai was built around the Chenghuang Temple, which was dedicated to the city's deity. However, since the earliest days, the heart of the city has always been the concentration of political, economic, cultural and educational institutions. Minli Shanghai Middle School – which later changed its name to Shanghai Minli School – was destined to become one of them.

In 1904, Su Benyan, one of Shanghai's industrial and business tycoons and a member of a distinguished clan, decided to build the Minli Shanghai Middle School on a plot adjacent to his residence. It was the fulfilment of his mother's dying wish, to secure access to education for members of their clan. Responsibility for the teaching staff and daily management tasks was placed in the hands of his brothers, Su Benyao and Su Benhao, both of whom had recently graduated from Shanghai's prestigious St. John's University.

His grandfather sent the young Su Benyan to western schools in Shanghai to study business, and he went on to study law at St. John's University. As an expert in Shanghai's business and legal landscape, he used his knowledge to invest in industrial projects and took his family to new heights of success. As a result of his experience, the curriculum of Minli Shanghai Middle School was dominated by foreign languages, the law and business studies. The school ultimately became an educational icon during the late Qing period.

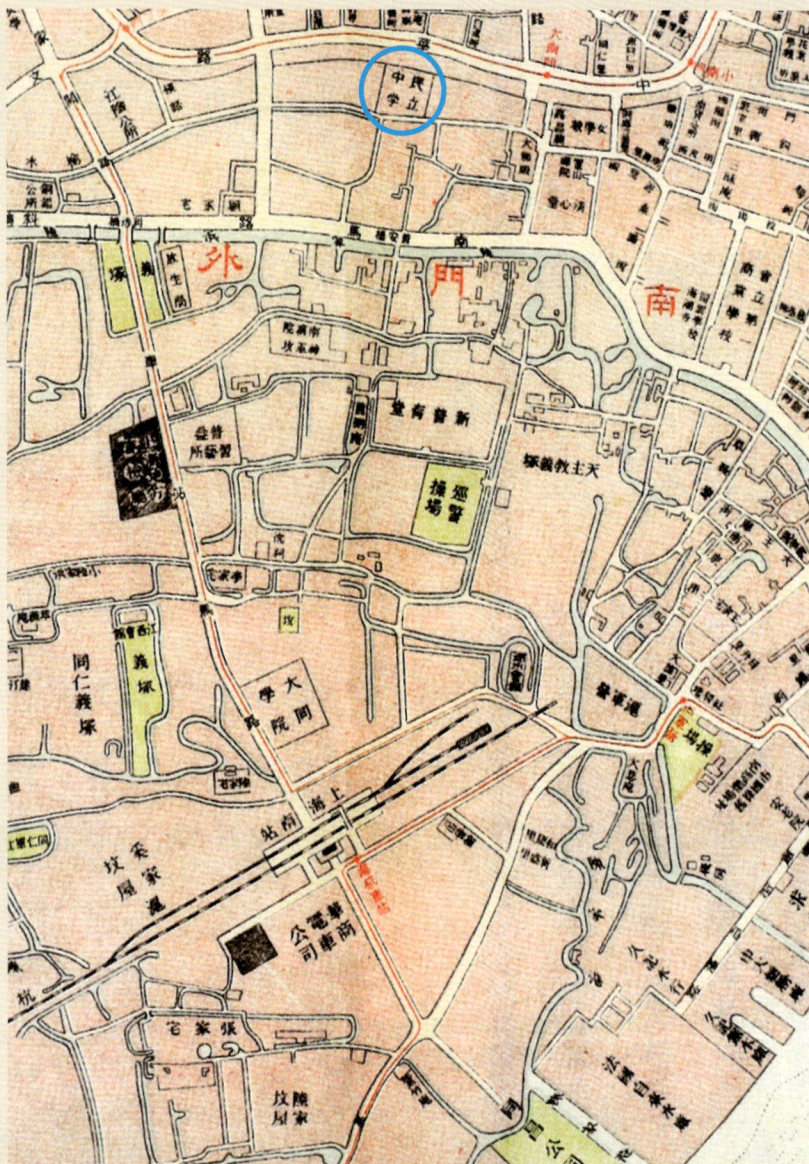

1-25
实测上海城市租界分图·1918
A survey map of Shanghai's Foreign Settlements in 1918

**薛理勇** 上海市历史博物馆研究员

　　苏氏兄弟均是圣·约翰大学的毕业生，苏本炎还是上海商界巨子，这就使民立中学从创办日始就注意学生的独立思考和适应社会能力。因而，大多数学生毕业后就可以在上海的商事机构中谋得一份好的职业。1905年商业事务大臣来上海时视察了学校，对民立上海中学的教育方法给以高度评价，并"奏奉传旨嘉奖"，上海学政唐景崇也特赠"教术修明"的匾额。

——摘自作者著作《上海老城厢掌故》

## XUE LIYONG
Research Fellow of Shanghai Municipal History Museum

*The Su brothers were graduates of St. John's University, and Su Benyan himself was a successful business leader in Shanghai. Thus, since its founding, Minli School emphasised independent thinking and social adaptability in its pupils. As a result, the majority of students who graduated from the school were able to obtain good jobs in business organisations in Shanghai. In 1905, the then Minister of Commerce visited the school, commended its educational philosophy, and presented it with a national award. Tang Jingchong, Head of Educational Affairs in Shanghai also presented the school with an inscribed board.*

*— An extract from
"Shanghai's Old City" authored by Xue*

1-26
21 世纪初期的民立中学
Old Minli School
in the early 2000s

进入民国时期，"民立上海中学堂"一边在老城厢区域迁址扩张，一边继续开门办学，并在1927年改名为"民立中学"。迁址后的新校舍一度可供数千学生入读，著名的"左联五烈士"之一殷夫也曾在此就读。

1937年"八一三"淞沪抗战爆发后，民立中学遭到日军炮火炸毁，学校无奈向西迁移进入租界，最终于1939年在目前的威海路上找到了新校舍，也就是前文提到的"邱氏大宅"。

As China entered the Republican Era, Minli Shanghai Middle School continued to accept students, even as it expanded into Shanghai's old city. In 1927 it changed its name to Shanghai Minli School (Minli School for short). At one time the school campus was capable of accommodating several thousand students. Yin Fu, one of the Five Martyrs of the League of Left-Wing Writers, studied there.

During the Battle of Shanghai, which began on 13 August 1937, the school's campus was destroyed by Japanese artillery. This forced the school to move into the Foreign Settlements. In 1939 it found a new campus on what is now known as Weihai Road – none other than the Qiu Mansions.

1 - 27
袖珍上海里弄分区精图 · 1946
Layout drawing of Shanghai lanes (1946)

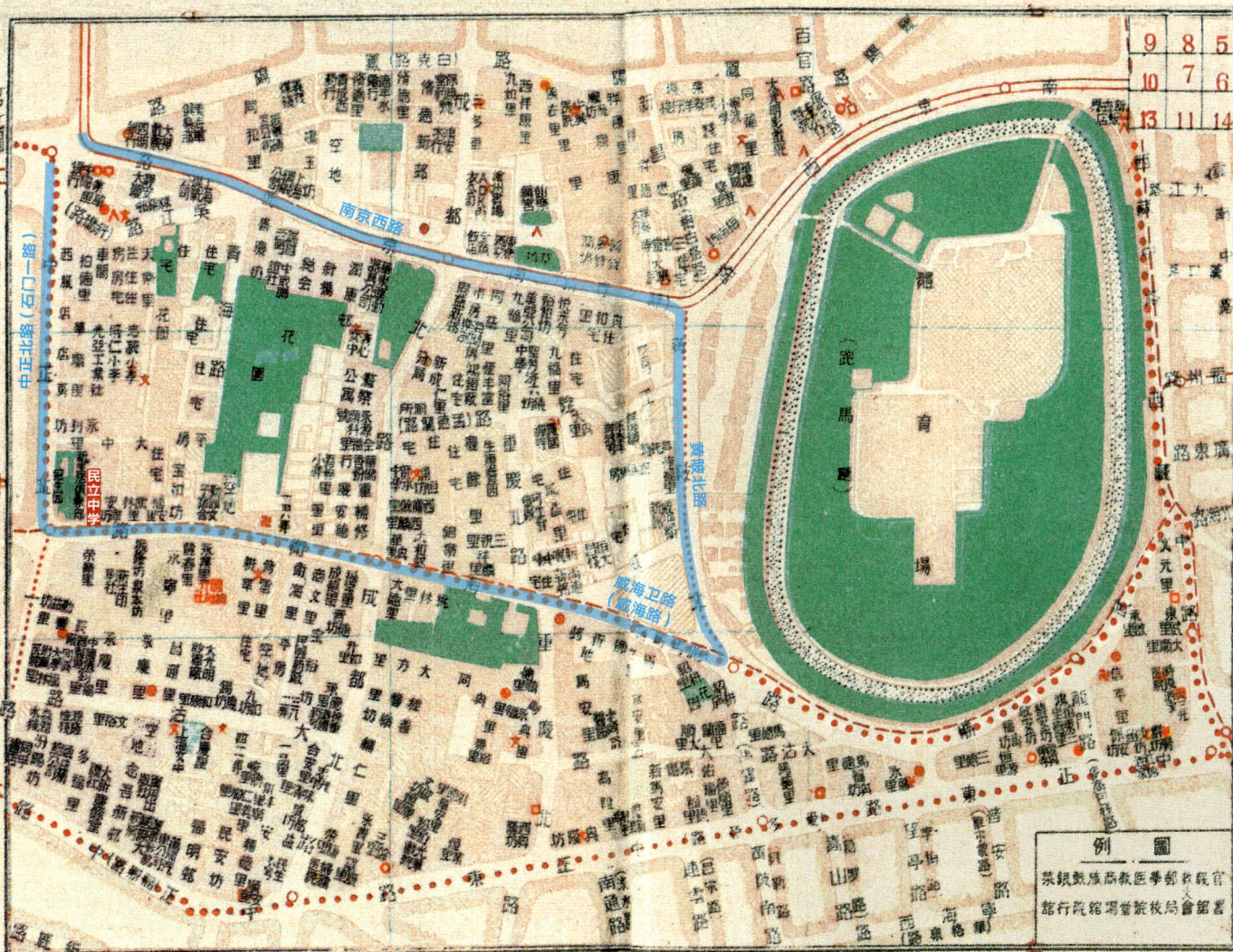

1-28
民立中学鸟瞰图
A bird's-eye view
of Minli School

1-29
原民立中学操场
The playground of
Minli School

根据民立中学老校友吴珏的考据，民立中学最初只租赁了东宅。随着中华人民共和国成立后学校性质由私立改为公办，规模逐渐扩大，才在上海市教育局的斡旋下同时获得了西宅的使用权。在这一过程中，"民立中学"一度更名为"上海市第六十一中学"，原校名直到 1985 年才得以恢复。

According to research conducted by a former student, Wu Jue, Shanghai Minli School originally rented only the east block. Following the founding of the People's Republic of China, the institution became a public school and gradually grew in size. With the help of the Shanghai Education Bureau, it obtained the right-of-use for the west block. During this time the school was renamed "Shanghai No. 61 Secondary School". It was not until 1985 that it resumed its former name.

Shanghai Minli School was the first choice for the vast majority of students living in Dazhongli. Shu Haolun recalled that when he was a student at the school, the east block housed not only classrooms, but also the canteen and gymnasium. Students would make the stairs and floorboards creak when they scampered over them between classes. Regrettably the west block, which was used mainly for teaching, was infested with termites and did not survive. It was demolished in 1990 and replaced by a brand-new four-storey teaching building.

During the 2001 Asia-Pacific Economic Cooperation (APEC) Conference, which was held in Shanghai, the then United States Secretary of State, Colin Powell, chanced upon the school's east block during a stroll. He immediately noticed its unique architectural style, and walked around for some time before asking for permission to explore the school's premises. His request was enthusiastically granted, and Secretary Powell thoroughly inspected the interior and decorative details of what he later found was "an outstanding heritage building in Shanghai".

At Minli School's 100th anniversary celebration in 2003, its administration arranged for alumni living in the United States to present Secretary Powell with a scale-model of the east block, together with a commemorative publication and a CD. Since then, the school has moved to a brand-new campus at No. 681, Weihai Road.

However, one thing has not changed. Dazhongli, which has already seen a century of transformation, continues to be an integral part of Shanghai's story.

作为区域内重点学校，民立中学是大中里片区内绝大多数适龄学生在中学时的选择。舒浩仑回忆称，他在民立中学读书时，东大宅不仅用作教室，也被分出了食堂、体操房等功能，课间时分的楼梯和地板都是"吱吱嘎嘎"的响声。遗憾的是，另一座以教学功能为主的西大宅保养不佳，白蚁成患，最终没能被保留下来，1990 年拆除后就被一座全新的四层制式教学楼所代替。

2001 年上海承办亚太经济合作组织（APEC）会议期间，东大宅的独特风格，无意间被在上海街头散步的时任美国国务卿鲍威尔所捕捉。他在校门前长时间驻足后，决定通过工作人员向校方提出入内参观，并在获准后饱览了这座"上海市优秀历史建筑"的内部空间和装饰细节。

2003 年，民立中学建校 100 周年之际，校方特意托常住美国的校友将东大宅的建筑模型连同校方的纪念册、纪念光盘，一道转赠给鲍威尔。也是在那一年，民立中学正式迁出了旧址，转入位于威海路 681 号的全新校舍。

历经百年沧桑的大中里区域，此时正处于大变革前夕的关键时点上。

# Chapter II
# A WITNESS TO EXTRAORDINARY IDEAS

第 二 章

见证

非同凡「想」

**无**论在经济、文化还是艺术领域，上海长久以来都在中国乃至世界的舞台上，占据着举足轻重的位置。

**I**n terms of its economy, culture and the arts, Shanghai has always occupied a pivotal position in China and on the world stage.

2-1
**20世纪90年代上海乍浦路桥和四川路桥航拍**
Aerial view of Zhapu Road Bridge and Sichuan Road Bridge in the 1990s

**能**够在经济全球化浪潮中赢得先机，源于中国在世纪之交的国际经济版图上重新校准了上海的定位，并采取了一系列富有远见的发展战略。这里，良好的投资环境和日益完善的市场功能，正对世界散发着独特的吸引力。

**T**he city's ability to capitalise on the rising tide of economic globalisation stems from the reinvention of its position on the world trade map at the turn of the century, and the adoption of a series of visionary development strategies. With its healthy investment ecosystem and increasingly sophisticated market, Shanghai presents a unique appeal to global trade.

**曾**经制约这座城市迈步向前的主要因素，就是空间的局限性。有人认为，上海最好的时光留在了20世纪二三十年代，因为当时的社会留下了优雅的社区肌理和路网血脉。但到了90年代，这座城市已处于超负荷运转的状态，面对未来，逐渐老态的社区显得左右为难。

**T**he primary factor that once constrained the city's development was its lack of space. Some consider Shanghai's best times to be the 1920s and 1930s, because the society of that time left behind such an elegant urban fabric and road system, which became the lifeblood of the city. But, by the 1990s, the city had become overloaded. Faced with a changing future, some aging communities were caught in a bind.

**出**于对美好生活的向往，各界有识之士很快开始
在上海的市中心聚集，这其中也包括对于家国
故土饱含殷切眷恋的归国华人。他们带来先进的城市
开发、设计与管理经验，正是这些智慧与努力，融会
交织成了上海全新的城市形象。

**T**he yearning for a better life saw capable and talented
people begin to gather in Shanghai's centre. They
included returned Chinese, who brought advanced
ideas for urban development, design and management
experience, as well as the love for the country they'd left
behind. Their wisdom and hard work created Shanghai's
new urban image.

**曾**将荒芜香港离岛打造为世外桃源般宜居社区的
查氏家族，也正是在这样的历史机遇中，获得
了重返吴越故地、参与上海市中心建设的机会。尽管
历经时局动荡，但其"尊人重土"的初心和极富洞见
的规划，已渗入了未来城市心脏的每一寸肌理内。

**T**he Cha family, which famously turned one of Hong Kong's barren outlying
islands into a blissful paradise community, took this historic opportunity to
return to their ancestral city and participate in the re-construction of Shanghai's
city centre. Despite the turbulent times, their resolution to respect the people and
cherish the land, along with inspired planning, seeped into every inch of the
urban space in what would become the future heart of the city.

{ 一 }

## "上海的心脏"

*The Heart of the City*

在国际级的大都市中，1843 年开埠的上海年岁不长。这座城市日常的运转节奏也如同年轻人一般，强健且轻快。但想要在 1930 年代建成的基础设施中长久地实现这一点，却是很不容易的。

城市的运转效率系于交通系统，而交通系统的效率，很大程度上又系于城市化的两大产物——私家汽车和公共交通。1949 年前修筑的许多"马路"，并没有考虑到其后中国城市的小汽车爆发潮；公共交通系统也随着城市人口激增和更大的流动性，出现了饱和现象。

自 1990 年代中叶，上海就着手规划"申"字形的高架快速路系统，以及覆盖面更广的地铁网络。在高架系统中，位于"申"字中心位置"一横"、"一竖"的十字形骨架，被视作当时的建设重点。这即是目前贯通上海市核心区域的延安路高架，以及南北高架。

Shanghai is still relatively young for an international metropolis. The city's day-to-day rhythm is youthful, strong and brisk. But it was not easy to sustain with the infrastructure and facilities built in the 1930s.

The efficiency of any city is tied to its transportation systems, which in turn are largely dependent on two major products of urbanisation: privately owned vehicles and public transport. Most roads built before 1949 weren't designed to handle the automobile boom in Chinese cities. Public transportation systems also became congested due to the surge in urban density and a growing population.

Inspired by the horizontal and vertical strokes at the heart of the character "申", in the mid-1990s Shanghai began planning a grid-shaped elevated expressway system and expanding its metro network. This eventually led to the construction of the Yan'an Elevated Road, which runs through the heart of Shanghai, and the North-South Elevated Road.

上海延安高架路航拍
Aerial view of Shanghai's
Yan'an Elevated Road

建设延安路高架的过程中，考虑了沿线许多中高层建筑和文保建筑的保护工作。例如1930年建成的上海音乐厅，就经历了一次史无前例的整体平移；至于南北高架，其动迁工作时间不过短短半年，沿线自主搬迁居民却有近10万之众，至今仍被视为中国城市建设史上的奇迹。

During the construction of the Yan'an Elevated Road, consideration was given to protecting many mid-rise, high-rise and historical buildings along its path. For example, authorities decided to physically move the entire Shanghai Concert Hall, which was built in 1930. The relocation of residents to make way for the construction of the North-South Elevated Road took just six months, but it involved the voluntary movement of nearly 100,000 people living along the route. It is still regarded as a marvel of Chinese urban construction.

在地铁网络中，与南京路及浦东大道这两条城市主干道走向一致的地铁2号线，亦是一场建设重头戏。这是一条从西至东连接虹桥和浦东两大机场的快速通道，并贯穿城市核心区域。1999年9月，地铁2号线一期工程建成试通车时，仅对外开放五座站点，其中就包括"南京西路站"。

上述这几条1990年代建成的交通"大动脉"，恰好将1930年代的"斜桥区域"包围起来，在21世纪初成为如同"城市心脏"一般的流量中枢。

Shanghai Metro Line 2, which lies beneath the main arterial thoroughfares of Nanjing Road and Pudong Avenue, was also a major construction undertaking. The line runs east-west through the core of the city and connects the Hongqiao and Pudong airports. When the first phase of Line 2 was opened to the public in September 1999, it stopped at only five stations, one of which was West Nanjing Road.

Built in the 1990s, these major transportation arteries surround the Xieqiao 'slanted bridge' areas constructed back in the 1930s. By the early 2000s, they had become the beating heart of the city.

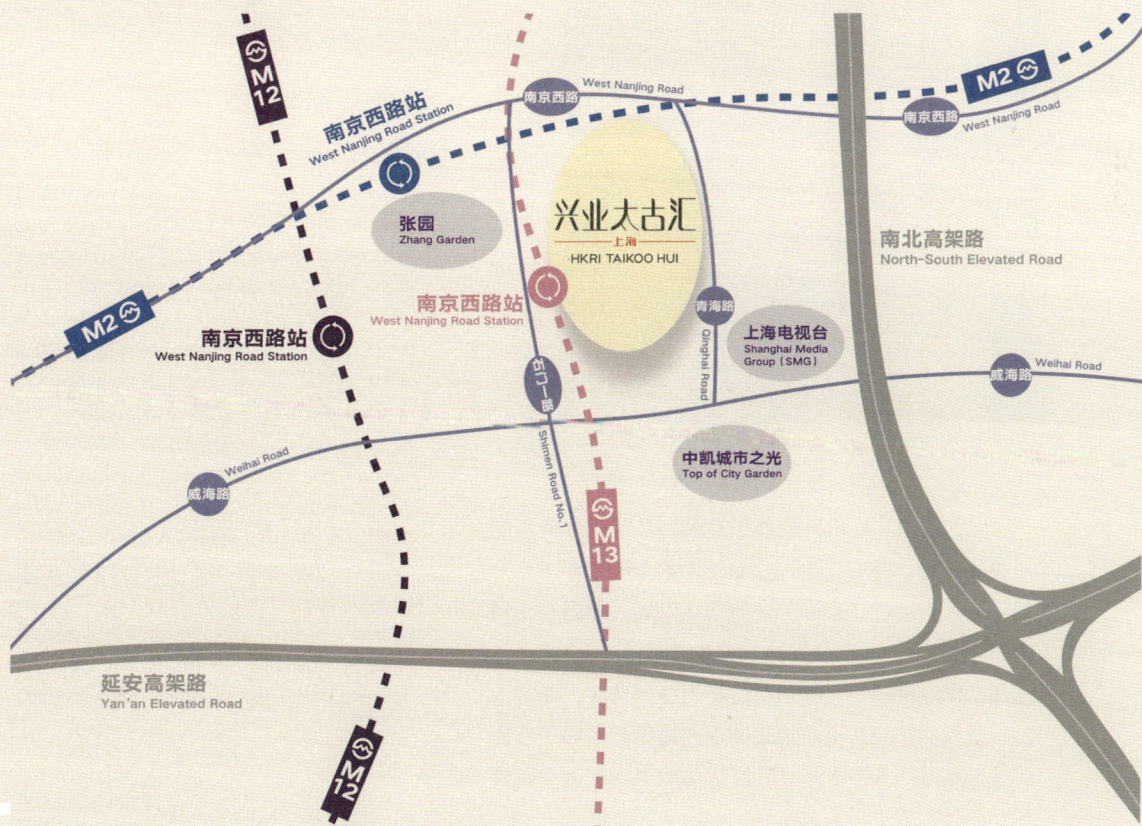

M12

南京西路站
West Nanjing Road Station

West Nanjing Road
南京西路

M2

南京西路 West Nanjing Road

张园
Zhang Garden

兴业太古汇
上海
HKRI TAIKOO HUI

南北高架路
North-South Elevated Road

M2

南京西路站
West Nanjing Road Station

南京西路站
West Nanjing Road Station

青海路
Qinghai Road

上海电视台
Shanghai Media Group（SMG）

威海路
Weihai Road

石门一路
Shimen Road No.1

威海路
Weihai Road

中凯城市之光
Top of City Garden

M13

延安高架路
Yan'an Elevated Road

M12

**查懋成** 香港兴业国际集团副主席兼董事总经理

原先的大中里、如今的兴业太古汇，位置正处在延安路高架与南北高架的交汇点左上方。这里如同人的心脏一般，能够连通周边所有道路的血脉。我们很幸运，当时能够受命开发这个上海市中心最好的地块之一。

**VICTOR CHA**
Deputy Chairman and Managing Director of HKR International

*The former Dazhongli, which is the present HKRI Taikoo Hui, is located at the north-west intersection between the Yan'an Elevated Road and the North-South Elevated Road. Like a human heart, it connects the blood vessels of the surrounding roads. We are fortunate to have been able to develop what is clearly one of the finest plots of land in the centre of Shanghai.*

Cardiac muscle cells are the strongest and longest-living in the human body. However, in the 1990s, a series of infrastructure projects exposed the poor urban conditions near the heart of Shanghai. Between the bustling commercial streets and tall buildings in Jing'an district, landmarks, such as the Zhang Garden and the Moller Villa, stood in stark contrast to many dilapidated and unsafe buildings and houses. Located on the edge of traditional residential areas and the foreign settlements, the average per capita living space in such places was less than 2.5 square metres. The yawning gap between these communities made the need to improve living conditions extremely urgent.

在人体内，心肌细胞属于最为强健、寿命最长的一类体细胞。但在 1990 年代的上海，伴随着一系列基建项目，靠近"心脏"处的糟糕肌理，却被更无情地暴露出来——在静安区繁华的商业街和幢幢高楼之间，既有张园、马勒别墅这样的花园洋房、深宅大院，也有原华、洋租界边缘的危棚简屋，人均居住面积甚至不足 2.5 平方米。社区之间的差距极大，改善居住条件的需求极为迫切。

2-5

**21 世纪初快速发展的静安地区与挣扎的石库门住宅区**
Jing'an, which saw rapid development at the beginning of the 21st century, compared to the struggling Shikumen area

由于建设时期规格较低，大中里区域没有像同期张园内的高级别墅那样配备马桶、浴缸等卫生设施，居民的日常生活仍有不便。经历过改革开放的移民热潮后，剩下的原住民安土重迁，选择与自家的房子一起老去。部分维护不善的老建筑，在 1990 年代后期迎来了身份背景复杂的新租客，社区的气质开始有所转变。

Low standards during construction meant that, unlike the high-class villas in Zhang Garden, buildings in Dazhongli were not equipped with sanitary facilities, such as toilets and bathtubs, which made daily life for local residents inconvenient. After an immigration boom caused by reforms, those who stayed opted to grow old with their houses. During the late 1990s, some poorly maintained buildings saw new tenants with a variety of backgrounds move in, causing the atmosphere in these communities to begin changing.

2-6

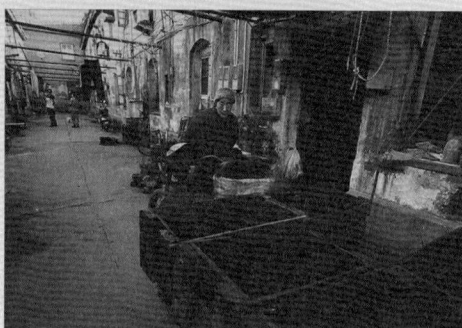

2-6
大中里生活旧貌组图
Life in old Dazhongli

舒浩仑早期在大中里为拍摄纪录片做调研时意识到，自己家所居住的大中里3号，最早仅有3户人家、共13人同住，都是宁波人。在"文革"结束时，作为"既成事实"被接纳登记的3号居民已经有35人。一个公用的水龙头，不够新来的浦东人、江苏人瓜分，曾经的银行高级职员和知识分子，要与产业工人乃至小商小贩一同吃喝拉撒。

外表看似风光的石库门建筑，实际也不如想象中那样容易翻新修复。查懋成还记得，自己实地考察大中里时发现，当年所用的建筑材料质量较差，加入海水烧制而成的砖块已经酥烂，直接架设在泥土地上的木头地基被白蚁严重侵蚀，"严格来说应该算是危楼了。"

When Shu Haolun began research for his documentary film about Dazhongli, he realised the building his family was living in – originally known as No. 3 Dazhongli – had in the past been home to three separate households totalling 13 people, all of whom were from Ningbo. By the end of the Cultural Revolution, the number of residents had increased to 35, and the situation was simply accepted as a fait accompli. The single public faucet could not handle the increased water needs of the newcomers from Pudong and Jiangsu. Those former senior bank staff and intellectuals had to live alongside factory workers and hawkers.

Shikumen buildings, which look beautiful from the outside, are not as easy to renovate as one might imagine. Victor Cha recalls that, during his onsite survey of Dazhongli, he discovered that the materials used in the old days were of poor quality. The bricks, which had been made with seawater, were crumbling. The wooden foundations set directly into the earth were severely damaged by termites, making the buildings dangerous.

2-7
石库门生活掠影
Shikumen living conditions

1995 年，静安区为各类"危棚简屋"定下了五年推进改造 39 万平方米的工作量——这为旷日持久、工程浩大的上海旧改拉开了序幕。逐步解决了这类"城市毒疮"后，形成街坊编制、规模更大的旧式里弄改造，以及更多新型住宅的建设，也被提上了政府改革日程。

In 1995, Jing'an rolled out a plan to refurbish 390,000 square metres of the district's "dangerous shacks and shabby houses" in the next five years. This represented the beginning of a long and complex period of urban renewal in Shanghai, including a number of massive engineering projects. After ridding the city of these "carbuncles", the government put the re-organisation of neighbourhoods, large-scale renovation of older Shikumen communities, and construction of new homes on its agenda.

2-8
21 世纪初期远眺城市天际线
21<sup>st</sup> century city skyline

2-9
大中里旧貌
The old look of Dazhongli

静安区政府曾创造性地提出，可以用土地批租制度吸引外商，共同参与旧改。1992 年，静安区政府就与香港美福房产公司签署了"劳动新村"地块的批租旧改合同，尝试缓解棚户区改造过程中，政府主导模式所常见的资金压力。

对外商的开放，也不仅限于旧改项目。1990 年代中叶，静安、卢湾两区政府对中国香港、新加坡商业地产开发商进行集中招商引资，使得上海的南京西路、淮海路两条大型商业街，一度看起来都像是大型建设工地。和记黄埔、恒隆、九龙仓、新鸿基、新世界、瑞安……这些长期占据"港交所"影响力前列的地产公司，都对日益开放且充满活力的上海市场展露浓厚兴趣。

不过，当时谁又能想到，斜桥地区这一上海市中心的"心脏"宝地，最后会交付给一家乍看起来貌不惊人的香港公司呢？

2-10
20 世纪 90 年代南京西路、西藏路大兴土木
West Nanjing Road and Xizang Road under massive redevelopment in the 1990s

2-11
20 世纪 90 年代人民广场航拍
Aerial view of People's Square in the 1990s

The Jing'an District Government boldly proposed using land leases to encourage foreign businesses to participate in the urban renewal project. To alleviate the financial pressures that government-led shantytown renewal projects commonly faced, in 1992 the District Government signed a lease renewal contract with a Hong Kong real estate company for the "New Labour Village" plot.

The offering of leases to foreign businesses was not limited to renewal projects in older parts of the city. In the mid-1990s, the Jing'an and Luwan districts made a concerted effort to attract Hong Kong-based and Singapore-based commercial developers. The goal was to transform the two main commercial streets of West Nanjing Road and Huaihai Road into large construction sites. The roster of real estate companies that showed great interest in the increasingly open and vibrant Shanghai market included some that have long dominated the Hong Kong Stock Exchange such as Hutchison Whampoa, Hang Lung Properties, The Wharf Group, Sun Hung Kai Properties, New World Development, and Shui On Land.

But, at the time, no one would have guessed that the treasured 'heart' of Shanghai – the Xieqiao area – would eventually be entrusted to a modest-seeming company from Hong Kong.

# 香江的来客

*From Hong Kong to Shanghai*

2000 年，查懋成坐上飞机，代表一家名为"香港兴业国际"的上市地产公司从香港来上海出差。落地之后，他觉得这一次自己确实来得有点晚了。

查懋成跟上海的缘分结得很早。他 1973 年首次造访上海时，内地还处于"文革"阶段。当时的上海，与经济正在井喷式跃进的香港，也确实太不一样了。

由于承接了大量欧美市场溢出的轻工业和制造业需求，韩国、新加坡、中国台湾、中国香港，这四个地方的城市形态，在 20 世纪下半叶经历了快速更迭，短时间内实现了经济腾飞，一跃成为亚洲发达富裕的"四小龙"。

如果往前追溯，如今以地产开发闻名的许多港资公司，其出发点也都来自劳动密集型的加工制造业和各类基础服务业。比如，和记黄埔和长江实业，背后是"塑胶花大王"李嘉诚；九龙仓以航运起家；新世界有百货和金店的基础。

In 2000, Hong Kong-born Victor Cha stepped onto a plane and headed to Shanghai as the representative of Hong Kong listed company HKR International. When he landed, he felt he was a little late.

Victor had actually formed a relationship with Shanghai much earlier. When he first visited the city in 1973, the mainland was still in the throes of the Cultural Revolution. The Shanghai of those days was very different from Hong Kong, where the economy was growing by leaps and bounds.

The tremendous demand for light industry and manufacturing from European and American markets meant that South Korea, Singapore, Taiwan and Hong Kong experienced rapid changes in the second half of the 20th century. Their economies took off in a very short period of time, and this led to them being known as the "Four Asian Tigers".

Many well-known Hong Kong real estate development companies can trace their roots back to being providers of labour-intensive manufacturing and basic services. For example, Li Ka-shing, the man behind Hutchison Whampoa and CK Asset Holdings, used to be known as the "King of Plastic Flowers". The Wharf Group started in shipping, and New World Development has its foundations in jewellery and department stores.

掌管着香港兴业国际这家公司的查氏家族，则与纺织业有着更为深刻的渊源。查懋成的外祖父刘国钧，曾是民国时期著名的民族工业家，其产业"常州大成纺织公司"所生产的纱锭、布匹行销东亚市场。抗日战争期间，大成公司产业大半毁于战火，刘国钧的女婿、查懋成的父亲查济民押送百台织布机撤往后方。此后，查济民在重庆将公司重组为"大明染织厂"，为抗战及日后中华人民共和国纺织工业的发展做出了重要贡献。

2-12
刘国钧先生
Mr Liu Kuo-chun

2-13
**1940 年摄于大明染织厂前，前排右五起：查济民、查母、夫人刘璧如**
At the front gate of the Daming Dyeing Factory in 1940. Cha Chi-ming, his mother, wife Liu Bie-ju (fifth, sixth and seventh from the right in the front row)

The Cha family, which heads HKR International, has deep roots in the textile industry. Victor's grandfather, Liu Kuo-chun, was a famous industrialist during the Republican Era, and the yarn and fabrics produced by his Changzhou Dacheng Textiles Company were sold all over the East Asian market. Although most of the company was destroyed during the Sino-Japanese War, Liu Kuo-chun's son-in-law, Cha Chi-ming – who was also Victor's father – carried hundreds of precious looms away from the conflict zones. He then reorganised the company into the Daming Dyeing and Weaving Factory, which made important contributions to the Textile Industry of the People's Republic of China during and after the war.

2-14
**1958 年的中国染厂**
The China Dyeing
Works in 1958

　　在"国共内战"期间举家迁往香港之后，查济民继续大力发展纺织工业。他将自己的"中国染厂"、"新界纺织公司"设立在尚处于发展期的香港新界地区；夫妇二人还带着年幼的查懋成和其他子女住在工厂里，日夜与印染织机的声音相伴。

Amidst the chaos of the Chinese Civil War, the family moved to Hong Kong, and Cha Chi-ming continued to develop his textile empire in earnest. He built the China Dyeing Works Limited and the New Territories Textiles Limited in Hong Kong's developing New Territories region. He and his wife lived in the factory with young Victor and their other children, accompanied day and night by the sound of dyeing and weaving machines.

2-15
**1970 年的中国染厂**
The China Dyeing Works in 1970

**查懋成** 香港兴业国际集团副主席兼董事总经理

中国实在是一个很大的国家，每一个市场有它的相似性，也有它的独特性。香港兴业国际讲究"尊人重土"的企业价值观，针对项目的背景、地理条件、人文历史等多方面特点，配置合适的开发模式。秉承父亲的教诲，我们情愿多花一点时间、投入多一点的资金，来把事情做好，而不是在短时间内复制许多千篇一律的产业。

## VICTOR CHA
Deputy Chairman and Managing Director, HKR International

*China really is a big country. And every market has similarities and their own unique characteristics. HKR International's corporate values are "respecting the people and cherishing the land." We shape our development models based on project background, local geographic conditions, history, and other considerations. Sticking to my father's teachings, we would rather spend more time and invest more money to do things right, instead of copying some stereotyped industry model to get things done within a short period of time.*

这种讲求实干、巧干的民族工业精神，最终使查氏家族的产业成为香港乃至全球最重要的纺织、印染生产基地之一。查济民还在 1960 年代亲赴非洲开拓市场，也因此有了"非洲纺织大王"的称号。谁想到这位"纺织大王"决心涉足房地产业，原来也是出于一桩事关民族声誉的交易。

1976 年，港英政府宣布了一桩面积达 650 万平方米、相当于香港岛面积 8% 的离岛土地交易案，卖家是王氏商人。此地块是全香港面积最大的单一私人开发土地，可谓空前绝后。王氏所创立的"香港兴业有限公司"原计划将这一位于大屿山东北畔的荒芜地块，从一张白纸开始，逐步开发成香港最大的度假胜地。亦因如此，公司的英文名称为"Hong Kong Resort Company Limited"。

2-16

愉景湾开发前旧貌
Discovery Bay before development

In the end, this kind of industrial spirit, which focuses on skills and hard work, made the Cha family's property one of the most important production bases for textile printing and dyeing in Hong Kong and the world. When Cha Chi-ming travelled to Africa in the 1960s to open up that market, it earned him the nickname "King of African Textiles". Who could have imagined that his determination to enter the real estate business would originate from another transaction involving national prestige?

In 1976, Hong Kong's colonial government announced an unprecedented 6.5 million square metre land transaction on the outlying Lantau Island. Equivalent to 8% of Hong Kong Island, the plot was the single largest private development in the territory. Hong Kong Resort Company Limited, founded by Edward Wong, originally planned to develop the barren area in northeast Lantau. Starting from scratch, it would turn the land into Hong Kong's largest resort.

2-17

1979 年查济民与夫人刘璧如主持中国染厂集团 30 周年庆典

Cha Chi-ming and his wife Liu Bie-ju, attending the 30th anniversary celebration of the China Dyeing Works Group

碍于对各类基础设施建设成本估算不足，王氏很快陷入财务危机，不得不将大部分公司股权抵押给莫斯科纳罗尼银行。1977 年，从纳罗尼借出的一笔贷款到期，王氏无力偿还，意味着这家苏联银行随时可以接收这块面积巨大的香港土地，这引起外界的广泛关注。

查济民了解到这一情况后，当即决定力排众议，支付 3,000 万港元从银行手中买下香港兴业股份，并承接了此前的所有银行债务。就这样，查氏家族成为香港兴业的新当家，也获得了此后享誉亚洲的著名社区——"愉景湾"的开发权，正式涉足房地产业务。

Unfortunately, Wong underestimated the construction costs and quickly ran out of money. He had to mortgage most of the company's equity to the Moscow Narodny Bank. When the loan fell due in 1977 and could not be repaid, the idea of a foreign bank potentially taking over such a large plot of Hong Kong land caused public concern.

When Cha Chi-ming learned of the situation he immediately decided, against all advice to the contrary, to buy the bank's HK$ 30 million share of HKR and take on all of the company's debts. This was how the Cha family became the head of HKR, acquired development rights to the famous community in Asia, Discovery Bay, and officially entered the real estate business.

# 敢为天下先

## *Dare to be the First*

　　查济民购入愉景湾股权后，随即从非洲召回正在当地主理纺织业务的长子查懋声。放眼荒芜山野，全无房地产开发经验的查懋声毫无惧色。他以超前的视野、创新的态度，从地块先天地理限制和后天政策规条中另辟蹊径，矢志将这片人烟零落的荒野打造成为亚洲第一个环保小镇。

After Cha Chi-ming bought Discovery Bay, he asked his eldest son, Payson Cha Mou-sing, to return to Hong Kong from the family's textile business in Africa. Looking at the barren rural land, with its natural limitations and the government's regulatory constraints, Payson Cha was determined. He set high goals for the Cha Family's first project in the property industry, hoping to create Asia's first eco-friendly town.

## 愉景湾的故事

　　20 世纪 70 年代末，经济腾飞，查懋声看到香港的独特战略位置，瞄准英治殖民地政府在产业升级的远景——把香港从制造业基地转型为环球贸易中心，进而迈向国际金融枢纽的目标。他摒弃了愉景湾作为度假村的原有规划，给出一个更远大的发展蓝图，决心在这离岛一隅建造一座可持续发展的综合住宅区，吸引海内外专才迁居香港，助力城市升级转型。

　　豪情壮志让人钦佩，但从零开始谈何容易。逢山开路，遇水架桥。查懋声带领团队铺设交通，搭建电网，开凿水库，建设码头，运营车船，以至后期打通行车隧道，每一项基础设施都是浩大复杂的工程，几乎没有先例可循。

　　当时香港的屋苑囿于空间，大多活力不足，更遑论对"品味生活"的追求。在考察各国经验后，查懋声为愉景湾确立了风格鲜明的南欧风情生活方式，以超低容积率的前卫规划，带出十足空间感。查懋声坚信，打造生活空间不应止步于房屋建造，更应聚焦于"人"。他引进开放式户型，花园大宅、小别墅和高层公寓依山而建，错落有致，满足不同人士的需求。同时，学校、会所、商业设施，一系列增加居民幸福感的项目也相继落成。居民倘佯在人造沙滩，极目远眺繁华的维多利亚港和壮丽的南中国海景致，身心舒畅。

　　愉景湾的故事成就一段佳话，是"兴业人"引以为傲的精神财富，它不仅回应了以查济民、查懋声为代表的第一代建设者的初心，也始终紧扣时代脉搏。今天的愉景湾以其独特魅力，吸引了来自超过 50 个国家的 20,000 多位居民。查懋声实现了当年的承诺，为香港打造出一个独一无二的多元文化小康社区，为亚洲综合住宅区奠定行业典范。止于至善的建设从未停步，这座动感之都的宁谧港湾，将持续以其独有的方式为新老香港人创造品味生活。

## The Story of Discovery Bay

*It was in the late 1970's, when Hong Kong's economy was about to boom, that Payson Cha saw Hong Kong's unique strategic position. He set his sights on the government's plan to transform the colony from a manufacturing base to an international trade centre, with the ultimate vision of making the city a global financial hub. Payson believed that Discovery Bay deserved to be more than a holiday resort destination, so he re-negotiated with the government to change the development plan. He decided to create a stylish and sustainable residential community – one which could help attract international talent to come and build Hong Kong together.*

*Fulfilling a vision of that scale is always easier said than done, but Payson knew Discovery Bay was much more than a property development. It was a huge, technically-sophisticated, ongoing building project designed to create a long-lasting, living community. Payson led his team in laying the foundations and establishing infrastructure before any houses and apartments were built. That included constructing a pier, amassing a ferry fleet, laying down roads and formulating a bus service network. The company also built an extensive power grid, and a reservoir - the first of its kind to be built by a private company.*

*Land scarcity in Hong Kong has long hindered quality-of-life in housing projects, particularly in the 1970s. However, Payson wanted something different. He made the most of the available space by creating a unique Mediterranean lifestyle. Eschewing traditional wisdom, Discovery Bay's low land ratio is unusual even by the standards of today's Hong Kong, with a design philosophy that prioritises people. To accommodate differing expectations for living spaces, he provided garden villas, small houses, both low-rise and high-rise apartments, and even introduced studio flats to Hong Kong. To make Discovery Bay a real living community, Payson also built schools, clubs, piazzas, parks and commercial facilities. Today, residents enjoy themselves on the idyllic man-made beach that looks out on the glamorous skyline of Victoria Habour and the open South China Sea.*

*Discovery Bay's story has become a legend, and every HKR International employee feels proud to be part of it. As a real multicultural community, with more than 20,000 residents from over 50 countries, it fulfils the promise of Dr Cha Chi-ming who made it possible, and the vision of Payson Cha who built it. Although the development is highly regarded as a property industry benchmark, the truth is that the Discovery Bay project will never be finished. It will continue to evolve and modernise. Whether you were born in Hong Kong or are new to the city, this unique community will always provide a tasteful lifestyle for residents and an attractive escape for the wider community.*

香港兴业国际集团执行董事邓满华
Jackie Tang, Executive Director
of HKR International

现担任集团执行董事的邓满华在 1985 年就加入集团，除了负责公司的日常管理工作之外，很多年都维持着另一份"兼职"，就是以形象大使及"导游"的身份，带领各界贵宾参观，介绍愉景湾项目的开发概念和建造过程。

2001 年的一天，愉景湾收到了一则来自上海的考察访问需求。邓满华一如既往，询问客人需要参观多长时间、有什么具体要求，以为贵宾"量身定制"介绍内容。这一趟格外不同的是，对方直接提出：希望全方位参观愉景湾，了解这个由香港兴业始于 1970 年代兴建，并持续运营、改造、升级的社区项目的详细理念。

顺利完成参观后，考察团才正式道明来意：他们来自上海市静安区政府，正为市中心一幅体量较大、位置十分重要的旧里社区"大中里"寻找合适的开发商。

对于中国商业发展的龙头城市上海，查懋成在 2000 年出差时看到了翻天覆地的城市变化。也正是因为静安区政府对愉景湾的愉快访问，香港兴业国际得到与其他开发商共同竞争上海"大中里地块"的机会。

2000 年初的上海静安，在经历了各类大型基础设施建设以及第一轮危棚旧屋的改造后，对于大型工程、社区动迁和各类新商业模式，已经有了基础的认知和实践经验，并开始试水更大规模的旧式里弄社区改造。位于上海"心脏"地带、诞生于 1920 年代的大中里区域，自然很快地进入了城市规划者的视线。

Jackie Tang Moon-wah, Executive Director of HKR International, joined the company in 1985. In addition to his role in day-to-day management, for years he had another "part-time job" as Discovery Bay's ambassador and tour guide for visiting VIPs. He briefed them on the concepts and construction processes used throughout the development.

One day in 2001, Discovery Bay received a tour request from Shanghai. As usual, Jackie asked the visitors how long they intended to spend, and whether they had any specific requests. Unlike other visitors, this group wanted to see Discovery Bay from every direction, learn in detail how construction started in the 1970s, and understand how the property operates and continually renovates and upgrades the community.

The delegation did not reveal their intentions until the visit was successfully completed. They turned out to be from Shanghai's Jing'an District Government and were looking for a suitable developer to undertake a large project in the middle of the city for the strategically located old Dazhongli community.

On a business trip in 2000, Victor Cha saw how Shanghai was leading China's economic development and ushering in an earth-shattering urban revolution. The Jing'an District delegation's visit to Discovery Bay gave HKR International an opportunity to compete with other developers for the chance to bid on the Dazhongli lot in Shanghai.

By the beginning of 2000, Jing'an had already seen various infrastructure projects. The first phase of renovations in the dangerous squatter housing area had given the authorities the basic knowledge and practical experience required for large-scale projects, community relocation, and exposed them to a variety of new business models. It began putting its ideas into practice on an even larger scale with the renovation of old communities. Built in the 1920s, and located in the heart of Shanghai, the Dazhongli region became a natural focus for urban planners.

经过详细评估，并与多家热切渴望参与这个重要项目的开发商沟通后，静安区政府决定与香港兴业国际集团签订整体开发协议。2002年底，后者以13.1亿元人民币的价格，拿下市中心这幅占地超过62,800平方米的土地。查懋成预计，这一项目的总投资成本高达45亿元人民币，是一项举足轻重的投资，在集团资产净值中占比不小。

After detailed evaluation, and speaking with a number of developers eager to participate in this important project, the Jing'an District government decided to sign an overall development agreement with HKR International. Towards the end of 2002, the company won the development rights for more than 62,800 square metres of land in the city centre for a price of RMB 1.31 billion. Victor estimated the total cost of the project might be as high as RMB 4.5 billion – a pivotal investment that accounted for a large part of the group's net asset value.

2-24
静安区46号、40号大中里地块土地使用权出让签约仪式
Signing ceremony for the transfer of land usage rights for lots No. 46 and No. 40 in Dazhongli, Jing'an District

**查懋成** 香港兴业国际集团副主席兼董事总经理

在签订协议前夕，我们与静安区政府实际都是既兴奋又紧张的。在议价阶段，领导提出了一个极高的价位，我估计他们是预留了一定的议价空间。但我一点价也没还，当场握手成交。这确实让领导有些意想不到。他们脸上的惊讶表情，至今我仍历历在目。当时区政府认为，整块土地的转让价创了历史新高；对于我们来说，这也是香港兴业国际在上海的首个大型投资项目，金额巨大。面对这么重大的决定，我觉得一定要把事情做好。

## VICTOR CHA
Deputy Chairman and Managing Director, HKR International

*On the eve of the signing, we and the representatives of Jing'an District were both excited and nervous. The officials proposed a very high price. I think they probably padded it a bit to give themselves some room to negotiate. I didn't bargain one bit and shook hands with them on the spot. It must have surprised them. I can still see the expressions on their faces. At the time, the transfer price for the entire plot of land marked a record high. It was also the first large-scale investment project for HKR International in Shanghai. It was such an enormous decision and a huge investment that I felt I had to do things right.*

抱着对这块珍稀土地的敬意，查懋成带领邓满华走访世界知名的地标建筑，拜访享誉国际的建筑设计师，从中取经。期间，更是有幸获殿堂级建筑大师贝聿铭接见，亲授锦囊。因此，在大中里的建设规划中，香港兴业国际贯彻了公司"尊人重土"的核心价值观，首先给出一个颇具前瞻眼光、兼容零售、办公、住宅和酒店的"混合型"开发方案。

Victor led Jackie on visits to renowned landmarks, famous structures, and respected architects to learn from them. They were fortunate to meet with master architect Pei Ieoh-ming (I. M. Pei) and receive valuable advice. At Dazhongli, HKR International followed the company's core value of "respecting the people and cherishing the land," and proposed a forward-looking, hybrid development plan that combined retail, office, residential, and hotel space.

Rocco Design Architects Limited, 2002-08

The Jerde Partnership International, 2003-04

Belt Collins, 2006-02

查懋成（右一）、邓满华（左一）
拜会建筑界大师贝聿铭
Victor Cha (right) and Jackie
Tang (left) pictured with Pei
leoh-ming

項目南部接近 12 万平方米的建筑面积，被划定为高端住宅和零售商铺。在社区建设上，查懋成放弃了当时香港流行的豪宅风格和户型设计，而是在设计环节上综合考量上海本地市民的使用、消费习惯；北部区域的16 万平方米建筑面积则被划定为商用物业，包括办公楼、酒店和服务式公寓，可以为整片位于"城市心脏"的社区提供多元化的配套服务。

这一开发思路，既参考了香港兴业国际在愉景湾长期开发中深耕细作的积累，以及从中摸索出来的社区营造和管理经验，也汲取了邓满华在做前期市场调研时，从上海本地"老法师"处听到的一句话——"房地产开发和设计，都是十分本地化的工程。香港或是愉景湾的模式不一定可以全盘照搬到上海来。"

In the first design, the southern part of the project that involved close to 120,000 square metres was designated as high-end residential and retail. During the community design process, Victor avoided styles and designs that were popular in Hong Kong at the time, and instead considered the preferences and consumption habits of local Shanghai residents. The 160,000 square metres in the northern part were designated as commercial property. This included office buildings, hotels, and serviced apartments, to support the community in the heart of the city.

These ideas were drawn from HKR International's long-term developments in Discovery Bay, and the community-building and management experience gained from them. They also benefitted from a piece of advice Jackie received from a local "master" when he was conducting preliminary market research in Shanghai: "All real estate developments and designs are essentially local projects. You cannot just copy models from Hong Kong or Discovery Bay and implement them in Shanghai."

查懋成（右二）与邓满华（右一）向时任上海市副秘书长沈骏（左二）介绍项目设计理念
Victor Cha (second right) and Jackie Tang (right) describing the project's design concept to Shen Jun (second left), the then Deputy Secretary-General of Shanghai

## {四}

# 共绘一份蓝图

## *Joining Hands to Draw a Blueprint*

　　俗语有云：好事多磨。在前期的动迁和开发准备过程中，大中里项目接连遇到亚洲金融风暴、"非典"、"东八块事件"、"双增双减政策"、金融海啸，和上海房地产市场动荡的多次影响，开发工作举步维艰。

　　但查懋成笃信，大上海是充满机遇的，大中里地块具有不可复制的区位优势和商业价值。他把市场环境的起伏不定，视作暂时出现的困难和障碍。面对逆境，反而让他可以多花一点时间把项目细节想得更清楚，同时也引发了他长期持有并运营这一项目的决心。

　　本着"站得高，看得远"的想法，查懋成主动与上海市、静安区相关部门商议，改变地块用途，完全放弃住宅部分。他的想法获得了市领导们的高度认可，变更手续很快获批。

As the saying goes, "nothing comes easy." That was certainly true at the beginning of the Dazhongli Project. It suffered through the Asian financial crisis and "SARS". Changes in construction and building regulations also created complications. The global financial crisis of 2007-2008 and fluctuations in the Shanghai real estate market also made development difficult.

However, Victor believed that Shanghai was full of opportunities, and that the Dazhongli plot had both an unbeatable location and huge commercial potential.

He regarded the ups and downs of the market as temporary difficulties, not permanent obstacles. In fact, facing such adversities gave him time to polish every detail of the project, and the determination to see the project through over a long period of time.

Taking a broad, long-term view, Victor negotiated with the municipal government of Shanghai and the Jing'an District government to change the usage of the plot and drop the residential part. His ideas were accepted by the municipal leaders and the changes were quickly approved.

2006 年，种种外在原因导致动迁费用大幅上升，但香港兴业国际董事会仍旧坚定接纳了查懋成的动议，宣布调整整体设计思路，将大中里项目变更为以购物中心、写字楼、酒店为核心，全部自持运营的商业地产综合体。对于当时已有多个项目在开发中的公司而言，这也相当于放弃了快速回笼资金的选择。

一直以来，查氏家族与多家国内外房地产公司老板都是好友，合作的例子很多。在物色同业伙伴上，首要考虑对方在商业开发和运营的能力，同时也看重双方在价值观上的契合，务求能发挥最大的协同效应。

In 2006, external factors caused resident resettlement costs to soar. However, the HKR International board still resolutely supported Victor Cha's decisions and announced adjustments to the overall design. The Dazhongli Project was transformed into a mixed-use commercial real estate complex, with shopping malls, office buildings, and hotels as core assets, which would be owned and operated by the developer. For an organisation with multiple projects under development, that meant giving up the option of a quick return on investment.

The Cha family has maintained good relations with the owners of many domestic and foreign real estate companies, and worked with them on many projects. When the family seeks out a partner in the same industry, the first thing it considers is the other party's development competence and operational capacity. Matching values and maximising synergy are also important.

2-28
2009 年民立中学 4 号楼平移暨项目动工仪式合影，（右起）香港兴业国际副主席兼董事总经理查懋成，原太古地产主席简基富，原太古地产（中国）行政总裁安格里，香港兴业国际执行董事钟心田
Group photo to mark the commencement of the relocation of Building No. 4 of Minli School and the ground breaking of the Dazhongli Project in 2009.（From right to left）Victor Cha, Deputy Chairman and Managing Director of HKR International; Keith Kerr, Former Chairman of Swire Properties; Gordon Ongley, former Chief Executive Officer, Mainland China of Swire Properties; Abraham Chung, Executive Director of HKR International

香港市场孕育的杰出地产开发商为数不少，成功运营了包括太古城、太古坊和太古广场的太古地产，更是其中翘楚。香港兴业国际与太古地产惺惺相惜，于 2006 年 11 月 25 日正式宣布成立合资公司，双方各占一半权益，共同开发大中里项目。

到 2010 年，双方组建的合资公司为大中里项目安排了一笔 80 亿元的银团贷款融资，推动项目发展。

The Hong Kong market has produced some outstanding real estate developers, including Swire Properties. HKR International has always respected Swire Properties, especially after observing the success of its Taikoo Shing, Taikoo Place and Pacific Place projects. On 25 November 2006, these two powerful and respected enterprises officially announced the formation of a joint venture, with each company owning a 50% stake in the development of the Dazhongli Project.

In 2010, the joint venture company arranged an RMB 8 billion syndicated loan to develop the Dazhongli Project.

**白德利**　太古地产集团行政总裁

自 1866 年在上海创立以来，太古集团一直认为上海是中国的现代化典范。无论在生活、工作还是营商环境方面，上海不但具备国际领先城市的增长动力和保持成功的实力，还拥有与时并进的应变能力，勇于汲取新理念的创新精神。

我非常欣赏上海市政府将保育纳入城市规划不可或缺的部分，以及在历史传承上所作出的巨大投入。我们乐见修复后的优质历史建筑分布全城，重焕新生的区域遍地开花。上海在保育重建的努力和创意，为这座城市带来无穷活力，增添独特个性。

## GUY BRADLEY
Chief Executive, Swire Properties

*Since Swire first established ourselves in Shanghai in 1866, we have found the city to be a paragon of modernity in China. It shares with other leading global cities the ability to grow and stay successful as places to live, work and do business in, with the culture and ability to adapt to change, to absorb new ideas and innovations.*

*I would also applaud that the Shanghai government has invested significantly in preserving heritage in the city, and to include conservation as an integral part of the planning process. I enjoy how all over Shanghai there are examples of quality restored and vibrant historic buildings and districts being reused in creative ways to add vitality and character to the city.*

**一个有趣史实**

太古集团早在 150 多年前就以上海为市场，除了专注中国航运生意外，与其他外资洋行一样，也曾觅地兴建物业，予驻沪员工居住。如今在南北高架路两侧，与大中里相距不远的新式里弄"润康邨"，原来是由太古洋行出售土地所兴建，旧称"太古弄"。

## An interesting historical fact

*Swire first entered the Shanghai market more than 150 years ago. In addition to focusing on shipping, like many foreign firms, it also acquired land plots to build staff quarters. Runkang Village, which is located not far from Dazhongli, and to the west of the North-South Elevated Road, was originally developed on land sold by the Swire Group. It used to be called Swire (Taikoo) Alley.*

2-29
润康邨（旧称太古弄）
Runkang Village（formerly Swire Alley）

110~111

香港兴业国际和太古地产集思广益，共同制定了大中里项目新的规划蓝图：商业综合体包括一座大型购物中心、两幢超甲级写字楼、三个酒店及公寓式酒店，大小商业建筑遍布整个地块。香港知名的"王欧阳"建筑设计事务所在整体设计方案中，给出了一个能够呼应历史与未来、融汇中西文化内涵的开放思路。

HKR International and Swire Properties developed a new blueprint for their joint venture Dazhongli Project. The commercial complex includes a large shopping mall, two prime office buildings, two hotels, and one serviced apartment tower. Large and small commercial buildings are positioned throughout the entire plot. The overall design plan, provided by the respected architectural firm of Wong & Ouyang Ltd., opened up ideas for a project that honours the city's history and future, with a focus on integrating the essence of Chinese and Western culture.

2-30
大中里项目整体规划设计图
Overall plan for the
Dazhongli Project

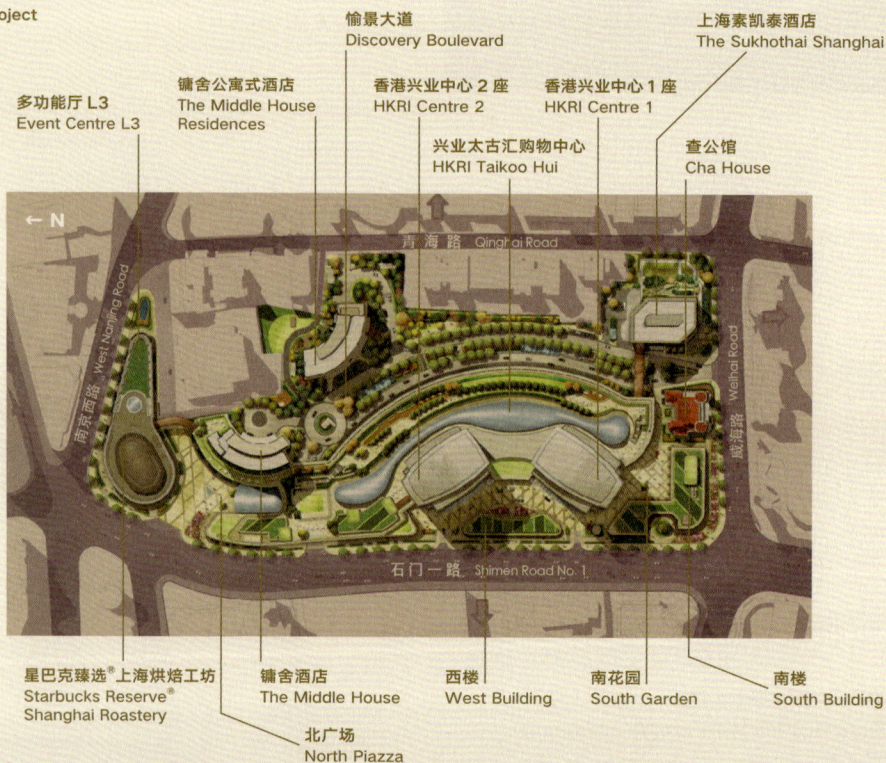

多功能厅 L3
Event Centre L3

镛舍公寓式酒店
The Middle House
Residences

愉景大道
Discovery Boulevard

香港兴业中心 2 座
HKRI Centre 2

兴业太古汇购物中心
HKRI Taikoo Hui

香港兴业中心 1 座
HKRI Centre 1

上海索凯泰酒店
The Sukhothai Shanghai

查公馆
Cha House

星巴克臻选®上海烘焙工坊
Starbucks Reserve®
Shanghai Roastery

镛舍酒店
The Middle House

北广场
North Piazza

西楼
West Building

南花园
South Garden

南楼
South Building

首先，购物中心的核心部分是一个贯通地块南北、气势恢宏的中轴商场；在沿街部分辅以切分为多幢二至三层楼高、低密度的沿街小型建筑；写字楼、酒店等塔楼或立于购物中心之上，或通过连廊相通。这样的布置令周边道路视野开阔，并回应了南京西路、吴江路传统逛街购物的商业街氛围。

First, the core of the shopping centre is a central mall of majestic proportions, which stretches from north to south. Two-to-three-storey high buildings are dispersed along the street. Towers, such as office buildings or hotels, are either located above the shopping mall or connected with corridors. The design leaves the surrounding roads open and views unobstructed, in response to the traditional commercial atmosphere of West Nanjing Road and Wujiang Road.

其次，在汇集多种业态的项目综合体中，人流可以在不同风格的建筑、街区和开放空间之间穿行，犹如旧日大中里居民在弄堂中穿梭一般，四通八达、移步换景。

再者，购物中心的外观参考了欧洲古典风格，商场主轴动线上方的设计采用了具有现代感的玻璃天幕，通透明亮；整个地块的沿街立面又巧妙结合了石库门元素，与周围的历史风貌浑然一体。

这样，以长达450米的购物中心为"轴"，零售、写字楼及酒店建筑群由南至北聚合成三个商业"节点"，整个项目体就以建筑群和设计风格构建出"一轴三节"的组织形态。这也巧妙地呼应了老上海里弄中的"前厅"、"中庭"和"后花园"的格局，以及石库门建筑群中常见的"北旺南静"状态，连绵不绝地激发顾客的好奇心和探索欲。

Secondly, in a portfolio which brings together multiple business types, people are able to flow unobstructed between different styles of buildings, neighbourhoods and open spaces. This is reminiscent of how residents of old Dazhongli shuttled through the alleys, travelling in all directions and enjoying different experiences in different neighbourhoods.

The shopping mall's design is a nod to classical European architecture, and a modern glass roof above the main traffic streams adds a clear and bright element to the space. The facade along the street merges naturally with existing Shikumen elements, integrating the structure with the historical features of the surrounding area.

The mall's 450-metre-long main axis features retail, office, and hotel complexes clustered into three commercial nodes running from north to south. The entire project is built around this "one-axis, three-node" design. It also subtly resembles the layout of old Shanghai houses, with the front halls, atriums, back gardens, bustling north-end, and serene south-end common to Shikumen building complexes. This encourages customer curiosity and motivates them to explore.

2-31
一轴三节布局：S形活动轴线、北广场、商办综合区、南广场
The "one-axis, three-node" design

2-32
大中里项目内部设计效果图
Interior design for the Dazhongli Project

### 百年老树现新颜

在项目设计进程中，靠近石门一路南段有一棵广玉兰古树，树龄已超过一百年。有关部门为该树"挂牌"记录，勒令保护。同时，有关部门亦为树根部分订立大范围保护区，不能有任何建筑结构。矛盾的是它的位置与项目及地铁站厅的设计方案都出现冲突；当时曾提出迁树方案，但不被接受。终于在开发单位、地铁项目部门及建筑师不断努力下，一切以原地保留该树为本，体现了尊人重土（树）精神的极致。

## A century-old tree shows off its new home

*A more than one hundred-year-old magnolia grandiflora tree near the southern section of Shimen Road No. 1 caught the attention of architects during the creative process. The tree and a large area around its roots were listed, with an order placed for their protection, and no structures were allowed on these locations. However, this caused conflicts for both the project and metro planning. Plans for moving the tree were proposed, but all were rejected. Ultimately, the efforts of the developers, the metro project department, and the architects paid off, and the tree was preserved safely in its original location, representing a genuine example of cherishing the land, and even the trees.*

2-33
被妥善保护的广玉兰古树新貌
The preserved tree's refurbished home

2-34
原大中里地块内广玉兰古树
Ancient magnolia grandiflora tree
in its former Dazhongli location

**林和起** 王欧阳（香港）有限公司首席顾问
兴业太古汇总建筑师

在巴黎、罗马等欧洲城市，很多商业项目都设在历史建筑群内，且都是开放步行式的。我们希望在兴业太古汇的设计中能延续这种空间的开放性，使人与人有更多互动的空间。

我们认为未来的商业发展中，体验式商业偏向于人群和商业之间的双向交流，而兴业太古汇提供的是一个多向的人群交流点。

## LAM WO-HEI

Principal Consultant of Wong & Ouyang Ltd.
Chief Architect of HKRI Taikoo Hui

*In European cities such as Paris and Rome, many commercial projects are located inside historical sites, allowing individuals to walk into them. We hope to continue the openness of space in our design for HKRI Taikoo Hui, so that residents have more room to interact.*

*We believe that, in the future, experience-oriented business will tend to serve two-way communication between visitors and brands. HKRI Taikoo Hui provides a place for multi-directional exchanges.*

至此，大中里项目拥有了新的定位和愿景：坐拥独一无二的核心位置——它是上海城市文化精神的集中体现；连接社区的历史与未来——它有着静安区特有的都会风貌；如同远离香港喧嚣的愉景湾，是精致、灵动的商业绿洲，融合香港兴业国际与太古地产的卓识远见——它将成为上海最耀眼的消费潮流地标。

虽然一幅全新的城市蓝图已经展开了，但大家未曾预见的是，为了"止于至善"的效果，大中里项目还要再经历一个长达十年的蛰伏期。

With a new vision and positioning, the Dazhongli Project is strategically situated in the heart of the city. It is a concentrated expression of Shanghai's urban cultural spirit - connecting the community's past with its future, and retaining Jing'an's unique style. And, like Discovery Bay far from the bustle of Hong Kong, it represents an exquisite commercial oasis that combines the distinct visions of HKR International and Swire Properties. In short, it has everything needed to become one of Shanghai's most dazzling and trendy consumer landmarks.

Yet, although a brand-new urban blueprint had clearly been unfurled, no one could have predicted that the search for perfection would mean the Dazhongli Project would have to wait for another 10 years.

2-35
大中里项目北广场设计效果图
Design rendering of the Dazhongli North Piazza

# Chapter III

# CONSERVATION OF CULTURAL HERITAGE

第 三 章

保育<br>与<br>文脉传承

2006 年，大中里项目正式展开动迁和建设工作。近百年历史的"深厚底蕴"和近在眼前的"未来规划"，在这片土地上以建筑群落的形式被保留下来。零售、办公、酒店、活动、艺术、服务、休闲、社交……更多崭新的功能也静候登场。

Relocation and construction work for the Dazhongli Project officially began in 2006. The city's deep-rooted heritage was retained in the form of architectural clusters, while functional spaces for retail, offices, hotels, events, art, services, leisure, social activities, and new uses were developed.

作为上海市中心罕见的超大体量工程，大中里项目的建设是一部繁复又鲜活的城市营造史。居民安置、基坑建设、地铁影响、区域联动、交叉作业、绿色施工……每个看似有法规可依、有技术可循、有案例可考的环节，落到现场都成了极富挑战的难题。

As an exceptionally large project in the centre of Shanghai, the Dazhongli Project is a microcosm of the city's rich and lively history. Each step brought its own challenges, including regulatory requirements, resident relocation, concurrent underground construction and the impact on metro services. Not forgetting the choice of which technologies to adopt and green construction techniques to employ.

越是复杂的工况、难解的疑问，越能吸引优秀的从业者为之持续倾注心血。在大中里项目建设的六年时间内，项目指挥部与各类合作单位始终倾心倾诚、迎难而上，以远超常规标准的要求推动施工，最终成为上海同类项目中的绝对标杆。

Complicated conditions often attract outstanding professionals. During the six years the Dazhongli Project was under construction, the project management team and other partners embraced the challenges and exceeded regular building standards, to create a new benchmark for this kind of development in Shanghai.

3-1
查公馆 Cha House

伴随着大中里地块历经风霜的邱氏大宅，也有幸交付至颇具古建筑保护及活用经验的团队手中。对整栋建筑"修旧如旧"的过程所费不赀，也动用现代工法为老建筑植入了重获生机的空间。现在，它不仅在风貌上重回 20 世纪的辉煌模样，功能上也为服务下一个百年做好了准备。

The Qiu Mansions had already withstood extensive changes in the neighbourhood. So, it was fortunate that a team with deep expertise in the preservation and revitalisation of old buildings was found to restore them. The process of returning the old structure to its original state was expensive, but modern technology allowed them to instil new life in the old building. It has now been restored to its former glory, and is equipped to provide the kind of modern services needed in the new century.

# { 一 }

# 从大局出发

## *The Big Picture*

考虑到建筑的实际情况，2000 年代初期，政府很快就将大中里区域的改造动迁提上日程。

香港兴业国际集团执行董事、兴业太古汇首任 CEO 邓满华忆述，鉴于大中里项目建成后，对静安区乃至整个上海而言，都将是一个重点地标，区政府理所当然十分重视，故成立了项目推进指挥部，由静安区重大办（指挥部下属办公室）全面协调处置项目建设全过程中诸如项目审批、安全生产、文明施工、施工扰民及需政府部门关心的问题。

根据项目建设的不同节点，静安区重大办有针对性地每周一次召集相关部门、建设单位及维稳小组、所在地街道、施工企业等，共同研判各类问题，预先提出解决方案，并制订时间节点。此类会议一共召开了 178 次，每次都留存文字纪要，从而有效提前化解了施工引发的居民矛盾，推进了项目建设。

Recognising the poor condition of many buildings, in the early 2000s the Shanghai government proposed a schedule for resident resettlement and the redevelopment of Dazhongli.

Jackie Tang, Executive Director of HKR International and the first CEO of HKRI Taikoo Hui, recalled that when completed, the Dazhongli Project would be a key landmark – not just for Jing'an District, but the entire city. The District Government noted its potential from the beginning, and set up a Project Implementation Headquarters in the earliest stages. Later, it brought in the Jing'an District Major Project Office to actively coordinate the construction process, including regulatory approvals, safety compliance, and the mitigation of disturbance to neighbourhood residents.

The Major Project Office organised regular weekly meetings and invited all the parties involved, including government departments, consultancy firms, neighbourhood officials, and construction companies to participate. They systematically anticipated and discussed possible issues, proposed solutions and formulated action plans with timelines. A total of 178 meetings were held, and they proved to be very effective in avoiding conflicts with residents. Meeting minutes were retained to help prevent future conflicts and ensure the project's success.

但在操作过程中如何能得到项目周边每一位居住者的理解、支持和配合，从而顺利推进后续工作，着实要费一番心思。加上社区内的上千户居民，以及复杂的人口流动状态，为整体动迁平添不少难度。

Relocating more than one thousand households in the community was difficult. It took significant effort to earn the understanding, support, and cooperation of each resident in Dazhongli and the neighbourhood in order to carry out the work smoothly.

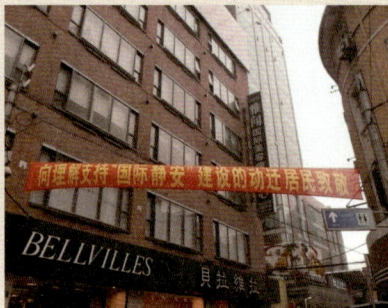

3-2
大中里项目动迁横幅
Dazhongli relocation banners

3-3
大中里拆迁过程（威海路方向）鸟瞰组图
A bird's-eye view of demolition in Dazhongli（Weihai Road）

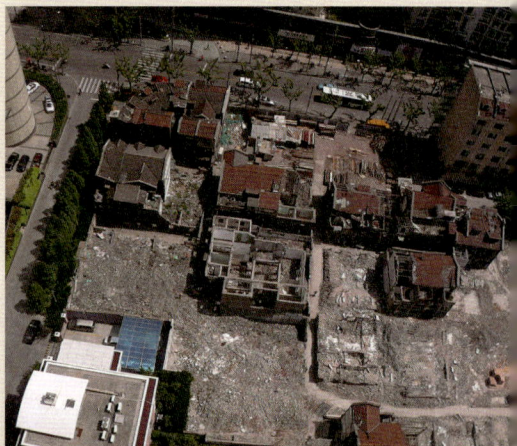

3-4
大中里拆迁过程（石门一路方向）鸟瞰组图
A bird's-eye view of demolition in Dazhongli（Shimen Road No.1）

面对相继出现的挑战，查懋成始终坚持"站高望远"，要求团队将日积月累的管理经验和理念，结合现场具体情况，贯彻在开发过程当中，披荆斩棘，保证整体工作的顺利实施。

为使动拆迁顺利进行，项目公司特别雇请有经验有资质的专业单位进行相关工作。除了给予原居民现金补偿外，更先后在静安、宝山、嘉定、普陀、闵行、浦东等多地寻找并购买适合的安置房源。要知道，当时上海房地产的价格在急速上涨，"浦西一张床"的价值，在一两日内就可能完全不同。能将上千户、超过九千名居民的诉求一一协调到位，难度不言而喻。

Despite facing continual challenges, Victor Cha held firmly to the ideal of maintaining "a higher perspective and focusing on long-term goals." He led the team to use their years of management experience and development ideas to overcome countless obstacles and ensure the project's ultimate success.

To smooth over the relocation process, the project company appointed professional partners with the experience and qualifications needed for each task. The team provided residents with financial compensation and housing for relocation in the districts of Jing'an, Baoshan, Jiading, Putuo, Minhang, and Pudong. It is worth noting that the price of real estate in Shanghai had been rising rapidly, and the value of "a bed in Puxi" could change from one day to the next. This added to the difficulty of coordinating the relocation of over one thousand households and more than nine thousand individual residents.

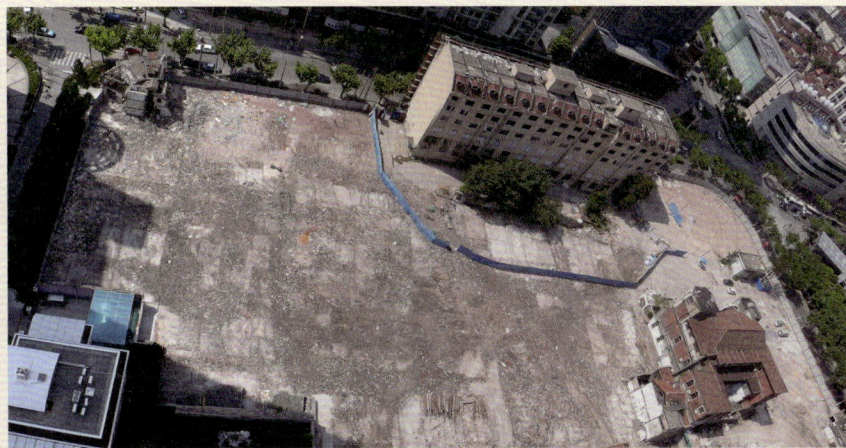

　　大中里位处上海市中心最优质的区域，多家开发商早已看中附近地块的区位优势，建设住宅区；地块的东、南、西侧先后建成了云海苑、中凯城市之光、静安四季苑等高档小区，再加上西南角的四季酒店和中邦酒店式公寓，东、西两侧的岳阳医院、公惠医院，以及与项目仅有一条小路之隔的上海电视台，即将开工的大中里工地相当于已被各类"高密度、严要求"的邻居团团包围了。

Dazhongli is located in one of central Shanghai's best areas, and developers had long appreciated the potential of nearby plots and residential developments. High-end communities, such as the Sea of Clouds Garden, Top of City Garden, and the Jing'an Four Seasons were built on the eastern, southern, and western parts of the plot. With the Four Seasons Hotel on the southwest corner, Yueyang Hospital and Gonghui Hospital on the east and west, and the Shanghai Television (Shanghai Media Group) building on the other side of the street, the Dazhongli Project site was surrounded by a forest of major buildings. It was also situated in the middle of a densely populated neighbourhood, with residents who paid close attention and monitored the project intensely.

3-5
大中里项目周边建筑示意
Dazhongli Project's neighbourhood

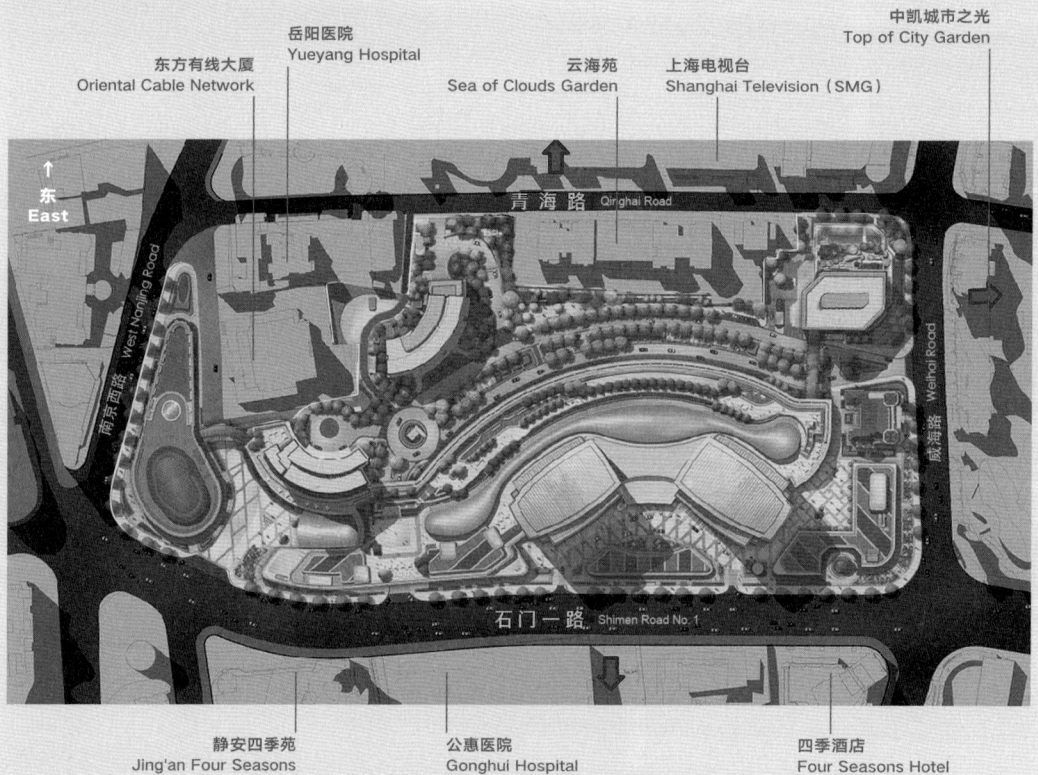

中凯城市之光
Top of City Garden

岳阳医院
Yueyang Hospital

云海苑
Sea of Clouds Garden

上海电视台
Shanghai Television（SMG）

东方有线大厦
Oriental Cable Network

东
East

南京西路 West Nanjing Road

青海路 Qinghai Road

威海路 Weihai Road

石门一路 Shimen Road No. 1

静安四季苑
Jing'an Four Seasons

公惠医院
Gonghui Hospital

四季酒店
Four Seasons Hotel

如何减少大型项目建设中常见的"施工扰民"问题？为此，项目公司连同上海建工一建集团和上海基础工程集团，开了大大小小上百次会议，制定了极为细致、远超常规的解决方案。此外，项目公司和施工单位更多次由领导人员亲自出席，与周边居民代表面对面沟通，解释和听取意见，优化方案，并建立定时联络会议，迅速回应邻居们的诉求，终于一步一步得到邻近居民的认同。

例子之一是针对常见的"麻烦源头"大型土方车，特别设计了不颠簸、噪声小的平坦入口；车辆进入时需要减速慢行，并冲洗轮胎；进入指定位置后，必须熄火。

切割钢材、搅拌混凝土、使用空压机的项目噪声都很高，规定仅限白天作业；在为周边居民区外墙安装隔音屏之外，还同时引进了机械静音切割拆除工艺等更多有效降低噪声、减少污染的技术。仅这些手段，就显著提高了施工成本。工地上产生的垃圾，是定时定点清运，日常管理时不仅会用绿网覆盖以减少扬尘，还会使用消毒水定期消毒……

这些"绿色施工"守则，使得大中里项目在建设过程中，连续多次被市民巡访团评为"上海第一"。更令上海市基础工程集团有限公司党委书记朱建明感慨的，是如何在建设过程中化解"民扰施工"这个老大难问题。

To minimise the impact of this large-scale construction on nearby residents, the project company, Shanghai Construction No. 1 Group, and Shanghai Foundation Engineering Group, formulated a number of unique solutions.

One example was the design of a flat site entrance – i.e. without bumps – which reduced noise from common sources of trouble, such as large trucks transporting soil. Vehicles were required to slow down and wash their tires upon entry, and their ignition had to be switched off after entering designated locations to reduce emissions.

Noise pollution caused by activities such as cutting steel or mixing concrete, and the use of loud equipment like air compressors, meant that much of the work could only be carried out during the day. In addition to installing soundproof walls to protect nearby residences, the project company also introduced silent cutting technology to make demolition work quieter. Waste produced on-site was stored at specific places and cleared away at regular intervals. Netting was used to cover the waste material and contain dust, and disinfectant was applied periodically. These measures significantly increased construction costs, but the results were well worth it.

Zhu Jianming, the Party Secretary of the Shanghai Foundation Engineering Group, which was in charge of building the foundations, was extremely concerned about minimising the impact of local residents on construction. Adopting these green construction principles helped the Dazhongli Project win the goodwill of local people, along with several consecutive "No. 1 in Shanghai" awards.

126~127

3-6
项目建设期间组图
Construction in progress

**朱建明** 上海市基础工程集团有限公司党委书记

在每一个大型项目中，"民扰施工"的问题都会比"施工扰民"更严重。怎样能做到互相理解、多方融洽？其实就是要从一开始就降低我们对于居民的影响。这中间涉及大量的、常态化的工作。

ZHU JIANMING
Party Secretary, Shanghai Foundation Engineering Group

*In large-scale construction projects, the issue of the "impact of residents on construction" has always been considered more severe than the "impact of construction on residents". How do we achieve mutual understanding and harmony among multiple parties? We must start by reducing our impact on the residents at the very beginning, which involves massive amounts of additional work.*

大中里项目立项之时，上海市基础工程集团就率先为周边居民搭建了一个设施和资料完备的沟通接待处，并有专职人员对接投诉与建议。

一方面，这使得施工方能够随时随地解答居民的疑问，并让他们逐渐意识到这类旧区改造和商业化建设，对于提升整个上海城市风貌和品质的意义；另一方面，在和居民的频繁接触中，施工方也发现了更多可以帮助疏导情绪的预防性措施——日常哪怕是帮老小区换个窗户、主动慰问，对于消解针对项目本身的怨气而言，都是物超所值的付出。

这套"细水长流、将心比心"的沟通思路，也被上海市基础工程集团延续到大中里之后的各类大型项目上，甚至将工程建设的"社区开放日"，设计成了一个以亲民方式讲解工程技术要点和未来价值的"科普活动"。倾心倾诚，方能将心比心。"民扰施工"的情况少了，居民与施工方之间的罅隙也随之逐渐消失。

When the Dazhongli Project began, the Shanghai Foundation Engineering Group took the initiative and built a fully equipped communication and reception area for nearby residents. It also assigned dedicated personnel to receive recommendations and respond to complaints.

Building a dedicated reception area allowed the construction companies to continually answer questions from residents. It also provided a way to gradually educate people on the importance of the renewal and introduction of commercial elements to old districts, and the role they play in improving the urban landscape and quality of life in Shanghai. The construction companies also took measures to reassure residents, such as replacing windows in old communities and sending greetings. These proved to be very effective in reducing discontent.

The Shanghai Foundation Engineering Group later extended the concept of building thoughtful long-term relationships to other large-scale projects. It even designed a Community Day for the Dazhongli Project, where experts made themselves available to answer questions from residents and explain the latest engineering technologies. This respectful approach helped to smooth tension between residents and the construction companies.

# {二}　"地铁上盖" 乐与苦

## *Metro Station Development Brings Mixed Blessings*

　　香港兴业国际在 2002 年底拿下大中里地块时，上海的地铁网络规划已经初现端倪。在当年修订完成的《上海市城市交通白皮书》内，有一则 "4 条市域快速轨交、8 条市区地铁、5 条市区轻轨线" 的地铁规划方案，规划有效期至 2020 年。

　　作为上海市中心最重要的交通流量节点之一，南京西路商圈内当时就有 "三线聚首" 的想法：已经建成的地铁 2 号线以市区通勤功能为主，沿途串联各主要活动中心，是交通流量的 "大动脉"；计划中的地铁 12、13 号线，则是将市郊新城与市中心直接连接，再以增设大型换乘枢纽的方式，"锚固" 整个地铁网络，支撑城市发展。

When HKR International took over the Dazhongli plot towards the end of 2002, Shanghai's metro network was still under construction. According to the "Shanghai Municipal Transport White Paper" published that year, the network would include four regional rapid railways, eight city metro lines, and five urban light railways by 2020.

The West Nanjing Road Shopping District was already one of the most important transportation hubs in central Shanghai. When the redevelopment of the district was planned, ideas included integrating and interconnecting district metro lines. Line 2 was already built and would be used for urban commuting, to connect main centres of activity along the route, and serve as the main transportation artery. Lines 12 and 13 were being planned and would directly connect new residential areas in the suburbs to the city centre. Large-scale interchange hubs would be added to "anchor" the entire metro network and support the development of the city.

3-7
繁忙的城市高架
Busy urban overpasses

3-8

**13 号线南京西路站站厅**

The concourse at the Line 13 West Nanjing Road station

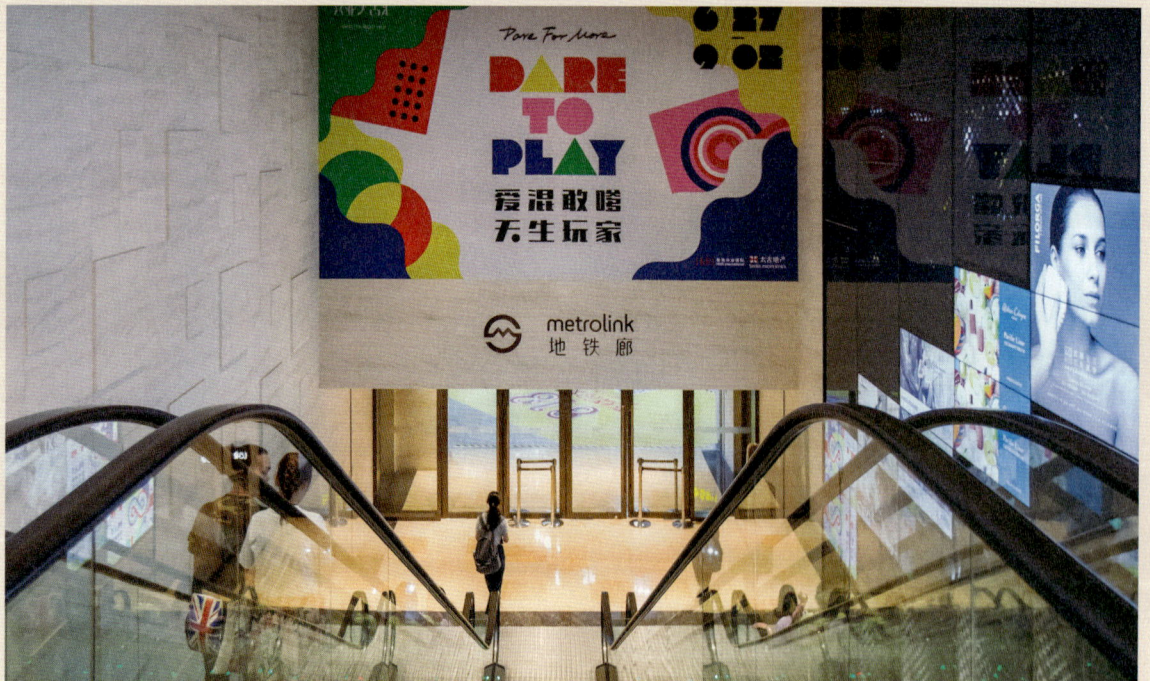

3-9

**兴业太古汇地铁廊连接地铁 2 号线、13 号线**

HKRI Taikoo Hui MetroLink connects to Line 2 and Line 13

在东京、香港等高密度、高强度开发的亚洲城市中，密集的轨道交通网络已经被证明是最佳的交通解决方案之一。伴随着轨道交通与房地产服务的联动开发，又有了所谓"地铁上盖"和"TOD"（Transit Oriented Development，以公共交通为导向的开发模式）这一说法。

"TOD"的关键，是以公共交通站点为枢纽，将周边的交通服务、社区住宅、商业服务乃至政务中心整合在一起，开发强度大大提升。对于住在地铁沿线的普通居民而言，这也是一种高效、安全、幸福感爆棚的生活体验。所以，港资、日资背景的地产开发商，都会争取开发"地铁上盖"项目的机会。

In dense, development-intense Asian cities like Tokyo and Hong Kong, rail networks have proven their value as transportation solutions. This has also led to the convergence of rail and real estate in a new public transport model that is known as transit-oriented development (TOD). It is especially visible in property developments that include metro stations.

The key to TOD success is to build interchange hubs that integrate public transportation stations, communities, residential areas, commercial premises and government offices. Done well, it provides ordinary residents living along the metro line with a pleasant, efficient and safe living experience. This is precisely why Hong Kong

在前期规划中，地铁 13 号线位于南京西路的站点及各类配套工程，正位于大中里地块之下的中心位置。这乍看起来是天赐良机，但 13 号线的走向，却着实让当时的项目负责人邓满华大大地犯了难。

and Japanese property developers have actively sought metro station opportunities.

In the earliest plans, the station and related facilities for Line 13 on West Nanjing Road were located directly under Dazhongli. However, what initially appeared to be a wonderful opportunity, ended up producing major difficulties for the project's then CEO, Jackie Tang.

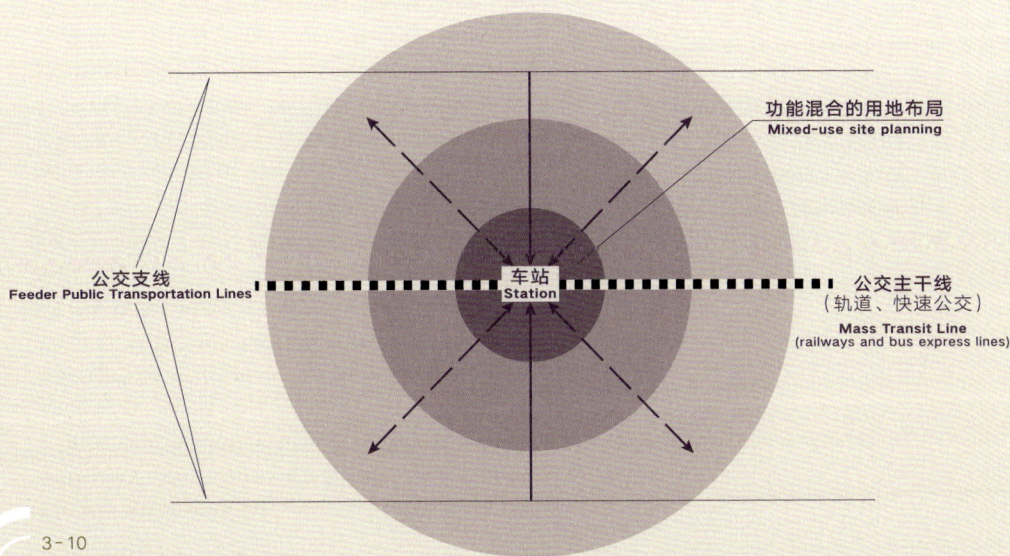

功能混合的用地布局
Mixed-use site planning

公交支线
Feeder Public Transportation Lines

车站
Station

公交主干线
（轨道、快速公交）
Mass Transit Line
(railways and bus express lines)

3-10
TOD 模式示意图  The TOD model

**邓满华** 香港兴业国际集团执行董事

当时地铁公司为地铁13号线给出的四个规划方案中，有一个共同点，就是地铁的走向都要从大中里的地下斜穿过去。即使是我们与地铁能够做到交叉施工，也会令项目的整体设计变得支离破碎，既不能保证施工期间不出问题、也不能保证竣工后地铁设施的绝对安全，唯一肯定的是，会大大影响项目的建设速度。还记得当时上海有一项同类工程，在施工期间出现附近地铁沉降的问题，需要将极大量的水注入整个地下开挖了的空间，犹如一个水库，才能稳住险情。期间施工需要停顿多月，动用巨资寻求解决方案。

大中里项目前期的动迁费用约80亿元人民币，每年的利息接近4个亿。打个比喻：如果工期拖延一天，就相当于把一台豪华房车推进黄浦江里去了，从公司角度来说风险很大。作为当时项目的负责人，肩上的压力不小。

我是学建筑设计出身，早年曾在港铁公司工作过。进入香港兴业国际工作之后，在香港东涌"蓝天海岸"大型住宅项目中，亦与地铁公司合作过，结识了不少地铁工程方面的专家朋友，让我可以向他们多多请教。此外，我们也聘请了设计英法隧道的国际知名工程顾问公司Arup共同参与。几经研究，终于做了一版能让地铁沿着地块一侧转出去的方案。虽然仍需将项目部分用地腾给地铁使用，但基本上保证了项目的整体设计不变，同时大大降低了施工的技术风险。在政府各部门的协调下，这个方案最后获得了认可，地基工程终于可以顺利展开。

## JACKIE TANG
Executive Director of HKR International

*The four development plans proposed by the metro company for Line 13 had one thing in common – the direction of the metro line passed diagonally below Dazhongli. Even if we synchronised construction with the metro, it would cause the entire design of the project to become fragmented. We could not guarantee that there would be no issues during the construction period, nor ensure the absolute safety of metro facilities after the completion of construction. All we knew for certain was that it would greatly slow down the construction of the project. There was a similar project in Shanghai at that time, where the metro began to subside during construction, and massive amounts of water had to be injected into the underground site to contain the hazard. Construction was suspended for many months and it cost a huge amount of money.*

*Preliminary resident resettlement costs were approximately RMB 8 billion, with interest of nearly RMB 400 million each year. To put that into perspective, each day of delay was the equivalent of pushing a luxury car into the Huangpu River. This posed tremendous risks for the company and, as the CEO of the project, I was under a lot of pressure.*

*I studied architectural design and I had previously worked for the Mass Transit Railway (MTR) in Hong Kong. After I joined HKR International, I worked with the MTR on the large-scale Coastal Skyline residential project in Tung Chung, Hong Kong. I became acquainted with many metro engineering experts and I learned a lot from them. In addition, we appointed the renowned engineering consulting company, Arup, which designed the Channel Tunnel between Great Britain and France. After researching the issues, the team produced a plan to construct the metro line along one side of the plot. Although part of the project's land had to be handed over to the metro, it essentially guaranteed that the overall design of the project remained unchanged, while significantly lowering technical risks during construction. With the coordination of various government authorities, the solution was finally approved, and the foundation plan set in motion.*

在 13 号线规划改道之后，交叉作业的难度虽然减小了，具体施工却依然是非常令人头疼的问题。首先，地铁及大中里项目两组施工单位需在同一个区域内进行大规模开掘，地下水位的控制十分关键。此外，要优先保障地铁的大型设备进场施工及安全，这大大压缩了项目方可以操作的空间。

使用打桩机，周边原有建筑密度高、个别楼龄老等问题，都影响 13 号线隧道掘进的速度，同时在铺设轨道时要慎防造成轨道沉降。为此，公司聘请了在上海享负盛名的同济大学建筑设计研究院地下工程设计院院长贾坚教授团队，为地基施工方案出谋献策。

面对上述错综复杂的技术问题，有关方面决定由上海市重大项目办公室牵头，按照时间节点"一步一动"联动管理，并就大中里地基工程与 13 号线地下维护工程制订"同步设计、同步施工、同步竣工"的"三同步"方案。

Although the difficulties posed by simultaneous construction were reduced after Line 13 was redirected, there were still issues. For example, when the metro and Dazhongli Project construction units had to operate on the same site, the control of groundwater levels became extremely important. In addition, allowing some of the larger pieces of metro equipment to enter the site from time to time and operate safely greatly reduced construction options.

The use of pile drivers, coupled with the density and age of nearby buildings, also affected the speed of tunnelling for Line 13. In addition, extra caution had to be exercised to prevent subsidence once the railways were laid. To address this, the Dazhongli joint-venture company appointed a talented Shanghai team. It was led by Professor Jia Jian of Tongji Architectural Design, who provided consultation on the construction of the foundation.

Faced with complicated technical issues, the authorities decided that the Shanghai Major Project Office would take the lead. It implemented an integrated, step-by-step programme, with strict schedules and detailed foundation plans for the Dazhongli Project and the underground sections of the Line 13 maintenance engineering project. The challenge was to achieve "Triple Synchronisation" which meant the simultaneous design, implementation and completion of the foundations between Metro Line 13 and the Dazhongli Project.

3-11
兴业太古汇购物中心与地铁 13 号线无缝接合
HKRI Taikoo Hui seamlessly connects to Metro Line 13

兴业太古汇　HKRI Taikoo Hui

南京西路站轨道十三号
Metro Line 13 -
West Nanjing Road Station

3-12
业主方、施工方项目协调会
A project coordination meeting
of the joint-venture company
and construction firms

3-13
兴业太古汇地铁廊
HKRI Taikoo Hui MetroLink

3-14
兴业太古汇有多个连通地铁的出入口
HKRI Taikoo Hui has multiple metro entrances

在此基础上，政府、顾问公司、施工单位和开发商项目管理部门紧密合作，在四个月的时间内经常是半夜开会，一份会议纪要能够写上十多稿。虽然耗费了大量精力，但朱建明认为，在他经历的此类合作中，大中里项目与地铁 13 号线的联动开发，是少有的对周边影响极小、对居民干扰也极少的成功案例。

建成后的 13 号线南京西路站，与大中里项目在多个地下位置无缝连接；上海地铁运营方"申通地铁"在设计及施工阶段，就与项目公司形成了良好合作关系。地铁 13 号线开通不久，申通地铁目睹开发单位在商业营运的强大实力后，同意双方联手开发地铁通道内的商业空间"地铁廊"。在上海市场的类似项目中，由专业购物中心运营方承办设计、招商及运营管理的项目绝无仅有，完美实现了兴业太古汇"地铁上盖"的开发优势。

The government, consulting firms, construction companies, and the developer worked together closely, and often held meetings until well after midnight. Just preparing summaries of the meetings frequently took more than ten drafts. However, despite the massive amount of time and energy required, Zhu Jianming of Shanghai Foundation Engineering believes that the coordination of the Dazhongli Project and Line 13 represents the rare case of a construction initiative that genuinely made a minimal impact on the surrounding area and its residents.

After it was built, Line 13's West Nanjing Road Station was integrated seamlessly with the Dazhongli Project. Shanghai's metro operator, Shentong Metro Group, formed a solid relationship with the project company during the design and construction stage. Suitably impressed, soon after the opening of Line 13, the metro operator Shentong Metro Group agreed to jointly develop the commercial spaces in the "metro connections" which were later named MetroLink. Among many similar projects in Shanghai, this is one of the few cases where a shopping mall operator has taken over the design, commercialisation, operation and management, to fully demonstrate the advantages of Transit Oriented Development.

# {三} "零敲碎打" 与 "小题大做"

## *An Innovative Approach to "Invisible" Challenges*

给大中里项目出难题的，当时还有另一条地铁线路——距离地面的埋深极浅、班次密集、客流量极大的"大动脉"地铁 2 号线。

根据上海建工一建集团副总裁、教授级高级工程师赵兴波回忆，大中里项目占地面积超过 6 万平方米，加上周边复杂的环境，地块首先紧靠运营中的地铁 2 号线，此外周边建筑群楼龄高、密度高，四面夹攻，困难重重。按照规模大小和周边线路走向，施工方划分出了 14 个平均挖深达 22 米的基坑，以形成整体多达四层的地下空间结构。上海建工集团纵然在上海建设历程中身经百战，但仍不得不认同这是难度最高的项目之一。

Another difficulty for the Dazhongli Project was Metro Line 2 – a main artery buried not far underground, with frequent trains and extremely high passenger volumes.

According to Zhao Xingbo, Vice President and Senior Engineer of Shanghai Construction No. 1 Group, the Dazhongli plot exceeded 60,000 square metres. With complicated surroundings, which included the Line 2 metro tunnel that passed right next to the site, along with densely packed older structures nearby, the project faced many difficulties. Although the Group had a wealth of experience, it recognised from the outset that Dazhongli was going to be one of its toughest projects. It began by carving out 14 foundation pits – each with an average depth of 22 metres – to support the four-storey underground structure.

面对这 14 个基坑，上海建工集团总承包部副总经理、时任大中里工程总指挥的周伟当时的判断是：在近似淤泥的土质上作业，必须讲究基坑开挖的先后顺序——既要保证 14 个基坑最终无缝地形成整体基础，又必须做到同步设计、同步施工、同步竣工的"三同步"。

其中，最难被"同步"的，当属原先是"天乐坊"、如今星巴克臻选®上海烘焙工坊所在地的 46 号地块。

Zhou Wei, the Vice President of the EPC Department of the Shanghai Construction Group, and former Chief Engineer of the Dazhongli foundation project, explained that the sludgy soil made the sequence in which the pits were excavated very important. In fact, the construction company had to "guarantee" that the excavation process would be completed successfully.

The most difficult was Plot 46 – the site of what was previously the Tianlefang housing estate, and is now the location of the Starbucks Reserve® Shanghai Roastery.

3-15
**2012 年 10 月，46 号地块底板完成**
The bottom slab for Plot 46 was completed in October 2012

地铁 2 号线在这一地块下横穿而过，而地铁隧道到地面覆土深度只有 9 米，这里平均每隔 3 分 30 秒，就能感受到一次地铁呼啸通行所产生的震动。在这里做基坑、建上层建筑，随时都可能严重影响 2 号线的通行和安全，甚至波及整个上海的地铁网络。

Metro Line 2 passes just 9 metres under the plot, and people feel the vibrations from trains passing every 3.5 minutes. It was clear that the construction of foundations and structures on the site could affect the operation and safety of Line 2, and possibly Shanghai's entire metro network.

3-16
如今的 46 号地块（现星巴克臻选®上海烘焙工坊所在位置）
Plot 46 today (now the Starbucks Reserve® Shanghai Roastery)

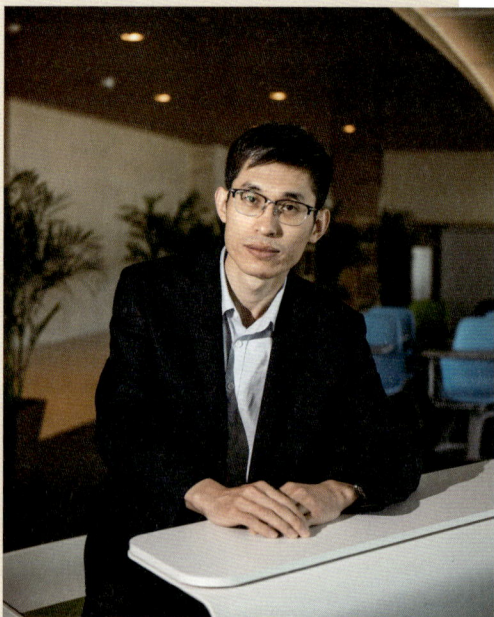

**赵兴波**　上海建工一建集团副总裁、教授级高级工程师

　　46号地块占地面积3,000平方米左右，按照以往的经验，如果不加PVC底板，建筑的底板浇筑也就在10天左右完成。但在大中里项目，我们从2013年6月到12月，耗费了整整半年时间。

　　为什么呢？因为我们只能利用地铁2号线每天停运的7个小时来作业，折算下来相当于每周只有不到两个工作日；如果有检修车路过，或有其他特殊情况，还要重新申请工作时间，折算下来，一个月里只有不到一周的时间。

　　按照作业工序，在有限的时间里是肯定完不成相关工作量。最后只能采取白天先做大量预制件，晚上清理好土方再吊进基坑的方法，但这种夜间作业，风险很大，必须胆大心细。

## ZHAO XINGBO
Vice President and Senior Engineer of Shanghai Construction No. 1 Group

*Plot 46 is approximately 3,000 square metres in size. Based on past experience, if the PVC sheet had not been required, the construction of the building's foundation would have been completed in about 10 days. However, for this particular project, the process took six months, from June to December 2013.*

*Why? Because we could only work during the seven short hours when Line 2 suspended operations each day. This meant that we only had 1-2 working days each week, or the equivalent of 6-7 days a month, to do the work. When inspection vehicles passed by, or when there were other special conditions, we had to re-submit application for more work time.*

*The construction could never have been completed in that time by following standard procedures. We came up with a plan to produce a large amount of pre-fabricated components during the day, and then placed them in the foundation pits at night. However, night operations incur higher risks, so we had to work smartly but carefully.*

　　最后，工程师和施工单位给出了一个"小题大做"的解决方案：避开地铁隧道，用50多米深的立桩，将建筑部分的荷载全部传导到大地深处；同时在做建筑部分之前，预先铺设一块厚度10厘米左右的PVC板，与建筑基础形成一个有"弹簧效应"的门梁结构，用来吸收地铁震动对于建筑本身的影响。

The engineers and construction units ultimately provided a scaled-up solution. Keeping their distance from the metro tunnel, they drove piles more than 50 metres deep to transfer the building's entire load into the ground. Before construction, a 10-centimetre-thick PVC sheet was laid out to cushion the foundation, absorb metro vibrations and reduce impact on the building.

另外，在项目规划过程中，石门一路与石门二路并非顺势相连，颇为曲折，由于 13 号线的建设需要，以及 46 号地块用地形态的变化，必须重新调整道路走向，并进行两次"道路翻交"。"道路翻交"是指划辟出临时道路，连同地面以下原有市政管线进行移动，地面上则以交通标示重新引导车辆。

周伟回忆称，这个将石门一路从大中里项目内"掏"出来的过程，同样难度颇大。大中里项目的全过程，充分展现了开发、设计、建设、管理单位都十分负责；这一项目也是政府指导、各方参与、共同维护社会安定的一次范例。

基坑建设、地铁影响、区域联动、交叉作业、道路翻交、绿色施工、安全管理……偌大规模的大中里项目，在六年主体建设过程中遇到的众多极富挑战的技术难题，全赖大批优秀的建设者为之倾注心血。

The original Shimen Road No. 1 and Shimen Road No. 2 had to be re-routed to accommodate the construction of Metro Line 13 and changes adopted for Plot 46. Doing so required traffic to be temporarily redirected while the new sections of road were built. Municipal utility pipelines running under the roads were also temporarily relocated, then restored permanently once the work was completed.

Zhou Wei recalled that the process of "moving" Shimen Road No. 1 out of the Dazhongli plot was also difficult. The developer, design, construction, and management units involved in the project proved themselves throughout the process. It was also a paradigm for governmental oversight, and participation by multiple parties while maintaining social harmony.

The support of so many outstanding professionals helped overcome the numerous challenges the Dazhongli Project faced, including building the foundations, the impact on metro lines, temporary traffic re-routing, green construction and safety management.

3-17
石门一路两次翻交示意组图（一）
**工程前期管廊施工阶段：车辆从石门一路通过**
Temporarily re-routing traffic on Shimen Road No. 1 during pipeline construction

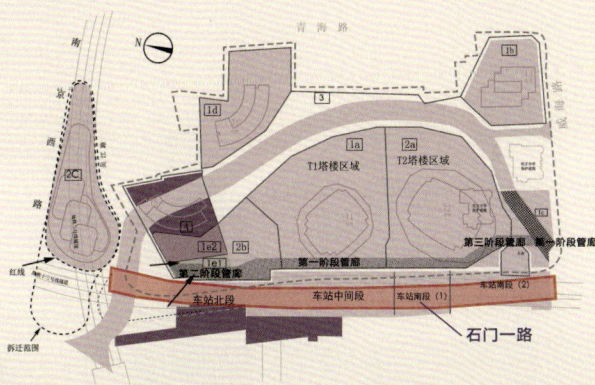

3-18
石门一路两次翻交示意组图（二）
**写字楼及 13 号线施工阶段：石门一路向东翻交**
Traffic was temporarily redirected to the east of Shimen Road No. 1 during the construction of the office towers and Metro Line 13

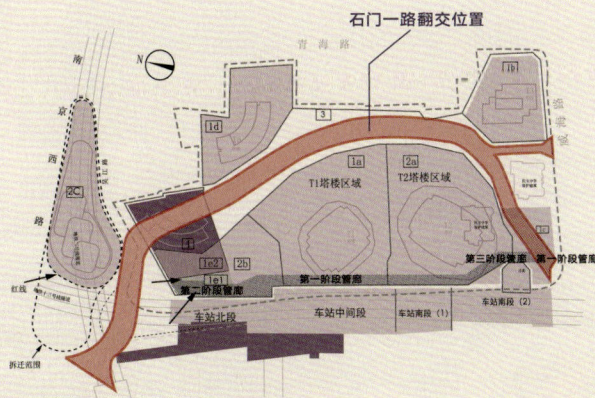

**144~145**

石门一路翻交前后实景图
Illustration of traffic re-routing on Shimen Road No.1

翻交道路

安全及临时措施工程

管廊工程

地铁 13 号线南京西路车站

2011/9/18

**周伟** 上海建工集团总承包部副总经理
第五管理部总经理兼大中里工程总指挥

石门一路下面有大量的市政管线，包括电路、煤气管、上水排水在内，大概有十几条。常规的做法是按各类管线逐一调整，费时费力。在大中里项目上，开发单位多花了超过1亿元人民币，研发安装了一个管廊桥，将所有的管线统一放进"隧道"里。这样在道路翻交时，就可以很方便地逐段调整。因此在大中里项目建设时，石门一路上没有出现"一修地铁就封路"的现象。

## ZHOU WEI

Vice President of the EPC Department of Shanghai Construction Group
Chief Engineer of the Dazhongli Foundation Project

*A large number of municipal pipelines, including the electrical grid, gas pipelines, water supply and drainage pipelines, were located beneath Shimen Road No. 1 – more than ten in total. The standard method is to move each pipeline one-by-one, but this would have taken time and effort. In the Dazhongli Project, the developer spent more than RMB 100 million in additional costs to research and develop a way to place all the pipelines in the same "tunnel". This approach made re-routing each utility pipeline a relatively easy task. Thus, there were no cases of road closures to facilitate metro repairs during the construction of the foundation for the Dazhongli Project.*

3-20
项目工程团队合影
Group photo of the HKRI
Taikoo Hui Project team

在查懋成的回忆中，大中里项目14个基坑的方案，背后就有多个技术课题研究作为支撑；刚毕业的大学生来这里工作六年后，基本已经轮转过所有岗位工种。如同多年前的愉景湾一样，大中里项目也从一个建设工程，转变成了"育人工程"。

According to Victor Cha, the Dazhongli foundation solutions represent multiple technical breakthroughs. In fact, a college student joining the project soon after graduation and staying for the six years during the HKRI Taikoo Hui construction work could have gained more experience than most engineers pick up in decades. Much like Discovery Bay many years ago, Dazhongli was also very much a talent cultivation project.

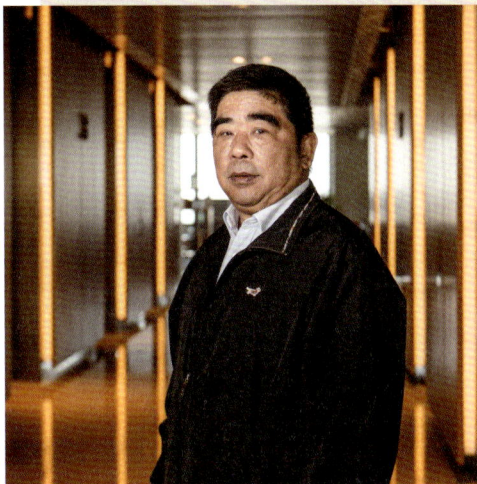

146~147

兴业太古汇的前期规划和地块平整耗费近十年光景。来到建筑工程启动时，邓满华明白必须快马加鞭。他一口气制定了一套为期五年的整体工程进度表，清楚列明每年的工作指标，推动工程团队有序地朝着共同目标全力奋进。

兴趣广泛、曾多次为大中里项目建设赋诗抒怀的邓满华，也常感叹工程之巨、耗时之长，以及开发过程之波折。回望长达15年的开发过程，全程参与大中里项目的他，感受最深的是得到两家股东的信任，合作伙伴和朋友的支持与帮忙，解决了大量棘手的问题。在2017年初竣工验收后，他长舒了一口气，在诗句中这样直抒胸臆——

3-21
2017 兴业太古汇 3、6、8 建设目标
Construction targets 3, 6, 8

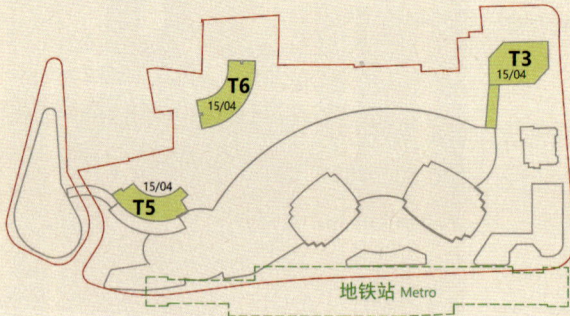

三包
3 exterior works done
T3, T5, T6

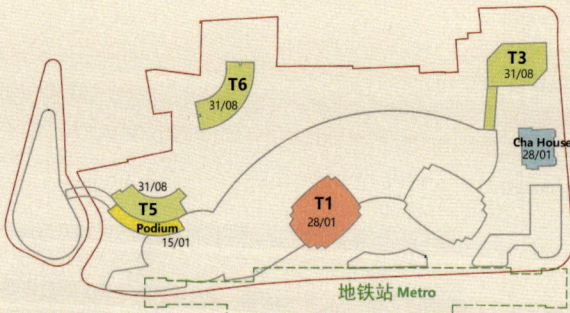

六竣工
6 buildings completed
T1, T5 Podium, T3, T5, T6, Cha House

八开业
8 commercial areas open to public
T1, T5 Podium, Shopping Mall, Cha House, T3, T5, T6, Plot 46

It took nearly 10 years to complete the initial project planning and resident resettlement. Jackie Tang realised the importance of conducting the construction work flawlessly and in a timely manner. He set up a five-year plan with clear annual targets. It helped motivate the construction team to move at full speed towards the goal.

Jackie Tang has a wide range of interests and has always drawn poetic inspiration from the Dazhongli Project. He often reflects on the immense amount of time spent on the construction, along with the challenges posed during the development process. As someone who participated in all 15 years of the development, from concept to completion, he is grateful for the support and assistance he received from partners helping to resolve difficult issues. When construction finished in early 2017, he gave a sigh of relief and composed a poem to convey his feelings.

一 山 跨 过 再 一 山
二 月 春 来 暖 寒 参
峰 高 登 过 苦 易 乐
忝 曾 功 建 上 海 滩

邓满华
写于二期竣工验收翌日
2017 年 2 月 28 日

One mountain after another
Spring in February warms our dinner
Over the mountains lies sweetness after endeavour
On the Bund we made our mark together

*By Jackie Tang*

*Written on the day after the official completion of*
*the second phase of the Dazhongli Project*
*28 February 2017*

# {四} 百年建筑的 57.3 米

## *A Century-Old Building Moves 57.3 Metres*

大中里区域启动整体动迁后，上海章明建筑设计事务所创始董事长、总建筑师章明就曾从她的两位老同事那里，听说这片石库门建筑群的故事与状况。

居住在大中里多年的这两位老工程师也提及：区域内有栋旧建筑，未来可能会涉及修缮，愿不愿意接手做做看？

针对各类优秀历史建筑的保护、修复、改造，是章明建筑设计事务所最为擅长的工作领域之一，公司还拥有国家文物局特许的"国家文物保护工程勘察设计"资质。章明经手修缮过的老建筑中，既有外滩建筑群、市百一店、武康大楼这样恢宏壮丽的大作，也有马勒别墅、丁香花园、建业里这样精巧别致的小品，行业内声望颇高。

After the Dazhongli resident resettlement, Zhang Ming, the Founding Chairman and Chief Architect of the Shanghai Zhangming Architectural Design Firm, learned about the condition of the Shikumen community from two of her former colleagues.

The two engineers, who had lived in Dazhongli for many years, mentioned that an old building in the area might be undergoing refurbishment in the future and said, "would you like to take over?"

The Zhangming Architectural Design Firm specialises in the preservation, restoration, and refurbishment of historic structures. It also obtains qualifications for "Survey and Design of Cultural Relics Protection Projects", with special approval from the National Cultural Heritage Administration. Zhang Ming is highly regarded in the industry and has refurbished many old structures. They include large projects, such as the exotic buildings on the Bund, the Shanghai No. 1 Department Store and Wukang Mansion, as well as smaller projects like Moller Villa, Lilac Garden, and Jianyeli.

3-22
上海音乐厅平移
Relocating the Shanghai Concert Hall

历史建筑修复是细致活，章明对事务所里年轻人的要求都是"上穷碧落下黄泉，动手动脚找材料"，不仅要去档案馆、图书馆尽可能收集齐原来的设计、施工图纸，还要实地走访当年的建设者和建筑的长期使用者，来搞清楚建筑本身发生过哪些变化。

The restoration of historic buildings is a delicate task. Zhang Ming expects young employees in the firm to "go to the ends of the earth to find the materials you need." They are not only required to collect the original design and construction schematics from archives and libraries whenever possible, they must also visit the builders and long-term users of the structures to learn about changes in the building over the years.

## 让上海音乐厅"走起来"的团队

上海音乐厅原名南京大戏院，建成于1930年，是当时上海最豪华的电影院；1959年"中华人民共和国成立十周年"之际，由于其混响效果出众，被改建为新中国第一座音乐厅。它由第一代留洋归来的华人建筑设计师范文照、赵深设计，也是上海现存为数不多的具有欧洲古典主义风格的建筑，厅内的罗马式廊柱、大旋梯、穹顶都具有文物价值。

2002年，由于延安路高架建设以及地铁施工的影响，上海音乐厅计划迁往宁海路、龙门路口的新址，与延安中路的旧址直线距离为66.4米。章明团队为其度身设计了从加固保护、整体顶升、沿轨道平移，到再顶升、落位、后期修缮等一系列环节；尤其是在平移阶段，仪器对每一毫米的移动，都会重新检测计算建筑各部位的位移和受力情况。这是上海乃至全国范围内，首个平移音乐厅这类高要求项目的案例。由于国内外均没有类似经验可供参考，技术难度可想而知。

## The Team that Made the Shanghai Concert Hall "Walk"

*The Shanghai Concert Hall was originally known as the Nanjing Theatre. It was built in 1930 and was the most luxurious theatre in Shanghai at the time. On the tenth anniversary of the founding of the People's Republic of China in 1959, it was converted into New China's first music hall due to its outstanding acoustics. It was designed by the first-generation of overseas-educated Chinese architects, Robert Fan and Zhao Shen. It is also one of the few classical European buildings to survive in Shanghai. The Romanesque arches, large spiral stairs, and ceilings are a valuable cultural heritage.*

*Due to the construction of Yan'an Elevated Road and the metro, in 2002 plans were made to relocate the Shanghai Concert Hall to its new site at the intersection of Ninghai Road and Longmen Road – a straight-line distance of 66.4 metres from its old site on Yan'an Road. Zhang Ming's team designed a series of measures for the preservation, elevation, transportation, re-elevation, foundation setting, and follow-up refurbishment. Instruments were used to monitor every millimetre of the move and calculate the load in every part of the building. It was a benchmark-setting relocation project for concert hall-type structures in Shanghai, and perhaps the entire country. There were no comparable case studies, in China or any other country that could be used as a reference, so one can only imagine the technical difficulties involved.*

2018 年 5 月 18 日，查懋成与章明于查公馆揭幕展合影
Victor Cha and Zhang Ming pictured together at
the opening of Cha House on 18 May 2018

**查懋成** 香港兴业国际集团副主席兼董事总经理

　　在民立中学时代，这栋建筑很多部分已经失修多年，肯定需要翻新。但到做项目总体规划的时候，发现校舍所处的位置，会影响到项目的整体布局，考虑了很多方案，效果都不理想。

　　我们听说了上海音乐厅平移的案例，探讨下来觉得可行。虽然平移这样一栋楼，成本会大幅提升，但整体布局上会好得多。

　　我们觉得要么不做，做就要做得好。一方面，尽可能地复古，不要将里面的东西全都换掉；另一方面，从内到外地修护，让这栋房子可以再维持 100 年。就这样，我们主动将维护费用增加了好多。

## VICTOR CHA

Deputy Chairman and Managing Director, HKR
International

*The structure had fallen into disrepair during its
time as Minli School, and renovations were required.
However, during project planning we discovered
that the building's location would affect the
overall plan for the project. We considered many
solutions, but none were entirely satisfactory.*

*Then we heard about the relocation of the Shanghai
Concert Hall, and concluded that such a solution
was feasible. Although relocating the building
would greatly increase the cost of the project, it
would provide for a much better overall layout.*

*We thought that, if we decided to do it, we should do it
meticulously. On the one hand, we wanted everything
to stay the way it was as much as possible, and without
replacing anything inside the structure. On the other
hand, we wanted to refurbish the house from inside out,
so that it could last another hundred years – even if that
increased the restoration fees by a significant amount.*

　　2002 年，查懋成与静安区政府签订土地出让协议时，了解到地块内有"民立中学 4 号楼"这栋历史保护建筑，因而在早期规划中，就将它的修缮再利用考虑在内，作为项目的亮点之一。

　　无独有偶，与香港兴业国际在大中里项目上携手的太古地产，不仅在香港有建筑和社区保育、活化的经验，也在成都以合资形式开发备受赞誉的商业综合体"成都远洋太古里"，成功将四川古建元素融入商业综合体的设计当中，其中，经修复的唐代古刹大慈寺等古建筑更为项目增添了独特的历史及文化韵味。

When Victor Cha signed the Land Use Rights
Transfer Contract with the Jing'an District
Government in 2002, he was aware of the existence
of Building No. 4 of Minli School on the plot. In fact,
restoring the building was included in the earliest
plans as one of the highlights of the project.

Good things come in pairs. Swire Properties, HKR
International's partner in the Dazhongli Project, had
experience in building conservation and community
revitalisation in Hong Kong. Swire Properties also
developed the award-winning Sino-Ocean Taikoo Li
Chengdu mixed-use complex, which was designed
and built in keeping with the neighbouring ancient
Daci Temple and traditional Sichuan architecture.
The Temple, whose lineage stretches back to the
Tang Dynasty, also contributed to the unique
historical and cultural value of the project.

3-24
成都大慈寺
The thousand-year-old
Daci Temple in Chengdu

　　从历史上看，"大慈寺"之于成都，不仅是一个宗教中心，自古以来也是商业和文化活动的集中地。"成都远洋太古里"的设计思路延续了川渝老建筑青砖灰瓦的风格，新旧浑然一体，成功地重塑了成都市中心的风貌。

Throughout its history, the Daci Temple has been more than a centre of worship in Chengdu. It has also been a place of commercial and cultural activities. The successful integration of new and old reshaped downtown Chengdu's urban landscape.

**彭国邦** 太古地产（中国内地）行政总裁

　　如何在历史传承和焕发新生中取得平衡，实非易事。我们在成都远洋太古里项目中汲取了不少宝贵的成功经验。过程中我们不但成功修复六座古旧建筑，保留其丰富历史价值，更通过创新思维，为建筑物注入新生命。通过与环球品牌和国际文化机构合作，我们将这些珍贵的古老建筑摇身一变，成为呈现世界顶级时尚艺术和文化活动的绝佳场所。

　　上海民立中学四号楼见证了大中里的历史变迁，现在它以"查公馆"之名肩负起历史传承和重焕文化内涵的新使命，在兴业太古汇延续其促进艺术文化发展的价值，并为更广泛的社群带来裨益。

## TIM BLACKBURN

Chief Executive Officer, Chinese Mainland, Swire Properties

*It is always a difficult balance, but we have learnt many valuable lessons from the successful Sino-Ocean Taikoo Li project where we were committed to restoring six ancient buildings and respecting their rich heritage, while embracing opportunities to explore innovative ways to bring these buildings to life. In collaboration with global brands and international cultural institutions, these historical buildings have provided excellent venues to showcase world class fashion, art and cultural events.*

*In Shanghai, the former Building No. 4 of Minli School (now named Cha House) is a valuable reminder of the history and the rich cultural heritage of the area. The restored building links HKRI Taikoo Hui with its past, while providing a focus for the promotion of art and culture for the benefit of a wider community in the future.*

3 - 25
成都远洋太古里
Sino-Ocean Taikoo Li Chengdu

154~155

3-26
邱氏大宅图纸资料
Drawings of the Qiu Mansions

SECTION A.B.

2007 年，大中里项目部针对民立中学4 号楼的移位修护工作，延揽了上海章明建筑设计事务所参与项目建设。章明接手后发现，这个"小房子"的问题，一点都不比当年那个体量庞大的音乐厅来得少。

In 2007, the Dazhongli Project team appointed the Shanghai Zhangming Architectural Design Firm to participate in the relocation and refurbishment of Building No. 4 of Minli School. After taking over the "little house", Zhang Ming discovered it had more issues than the immense Concert Hall that she helped to relocate five years before.

首先，邱氏大宅在历史档案中留下的资料不多，不仅建筑设计者和施工情况无从考据，而且这栋通高三层、局部四层的建筑，只能找到其剖面图、南侧立面图，以及其中两层楼的平面设计图纸。这些图纸与老建筑一样脆弱，档案馆工作人员展示时要非常小心翼翼。为免受损，也只能拍照，不能复印。至于其他的立面、楼面该如何修复，只能结合建筑现状和改造痕迹加以判断。

其次，在作为民立中学校舍使用期间，邱氏大宅经历多次改造，有很多缺失部分。其中，最大的变动是建筑西南角、带着德国式尖角盔顶的第四层凉亭消失了。至于台阶消失、木柱变砖柱、窗户封堵、烟囱缺失等各类其他大小改动，更是不计其数。

First, very little data on the Qiu Mansions could be found in the historical archives, and there was no way to obtain information on the designer or the construction. In fact, the only architectural references of this three-storey building, with four storeys in certain areas, were a cross-section drawing, a south elevation drawing, and plans of two floors. What's more, the drawings were extremely fragile, and archive staff had to be very careful with them. To avoid damage, photocopying was not permitted, so only photographs could be taken. Restoring the floor plans relied on studying the current state of the structure and examining signs of previous refurbishment.

The Qiu Mansions had already been refurbished multiple times when they were used as the Minli School building. The biggest change was the disappearance of the pavilion with a German finial roof design, which used to be on the southwest corner of the fourth floor. There were also numerous modifications, such as the removal of stairs, the conversion of wooden pillars into brick ones, blocked up windows and missing chimneys, along with other changes of various magnitudes.

3-27
历经沧桑的百年建筑
A century-old building that has witnessed lots of history

考虑到平移过程，要着重考量建筑的结构强度，特别是基础部分的状况。上海音乐厅在平移前，因为混凝土强度较低，就预先做了整体加固。在邱氏大宅的基础中，既有砖混结构又有钢结构，有部分还因为此前加建人防空间而受到破坏，平移前必须加固，且新位置需要重做包括地下空间在内的整个混凝土基础平台。

最后，建筑的外立面污损情况严重，原先的清水红砖墙、陶立克式门厅柱、中国江南风格的北部立面和各类精致细节都荣光不再；由于曾用作校舍，建筑内部也重新分隔过空间，需要拆除后重构。

The structural strength of a building is important in any relocation process, with the condition of the foundations being especially critical. Before the relocation of the Shanghai Concert Hall, its overall structure had to be fortified because the original concrete was relatively weak. The foundations of the Qiu Mansions included both brick concrete structure and steel. Certain parts were damaged during the construction of air-raid shelters. In addition, an entire concrete foundation platform, including underground spaces, had to be constructed at the new site.

The building's external facade had been severely damaged, and the intricate details of the original fair-faced brick walls, Doric columns and the Chinese Jiangnan-style northern facade, were no longer displayed in their full glory. Since the building had been used as a school, the interior had been repartitioned, and those had to be removed before reconstruction.

3-28
建筑整体加固
Structural reinforcement

为保证项目整体进度，民立中学4号楼新址所在的基坑率先开挖、最先完成，旧校舍也在整体加固、切断底基柱头后被移入轨道。2010年1月26日，这栋百年老校舍以每分钟两厘米的速度，开始了总长57.3米的"爬坡行走"过程。在移位过程中，工程团队实时监测变形、应力、荷载、动力特性及沉降数据，以及时发现移位过程中可能出现的结构变化。13天之后，老校舍最终落定到比原位高40厘米、安全稳固的钢筋混凝土基础上。

The first thing to be done, and also first to be completed, was the excavation of the foundation pit on the structure's new site. The old building was reinforced, with the foundations cut and separated before the structure was moved onto custom-built tracks. On 26 January 2010, the entire building was moved a distance of 57.3 metres at a speed of 2 centimetres per minute.

Throughout the relocation process, the engineering team conducted intensive real-time monitoring, looking for signs of deformation, as well as stress. Load, structural dynamics and sedimentation data was watched carefully to quickly identify any changes. After 13 days, the old building finally arrived at its new location on a secure and solid reinforced concrete foundation, 40 centimetres higher than the original site.

3-29
平移下滑梁制作
**Manufacturing the slide tracks**

3-30
新址地基建设
**Constructing the new foundation**

# 新民晚报

飞入寻常百姓家 / www.XINMIN.cn

国内统一刊号 CN31-0003 第 17187 期 文汇新民联合报业集团出版 文新传媒 www.news365.com.cn

2009年3月 **10** 日 星期二 今日48版 A叠新闻/B叠专刊周刊

农历己丑年二月十四

今天：晴天转多云，最低9℃（昨天最高18.0℃）
明天：多云，最高16℃，最低10℃

静安大中里保护建筑上午启动移位工程

## 90岁民立中学老校舍今"开步走"

本报讯（记者 宋宁华）今天上午，静安区大中里地块启动保护历史建筑移位工程，有近90年历史的上海市优秀历史建筑民立中学老校舍，将被平移到约50米外的威海路边。

民立中学老校舍是一幢中西合璧的花园洋房，建于1920到1930年间。为上海道著名颜料巨贾邱信山、邱渭卿兄弟所建，原为两幢，其中一幢于上世纪90年代拆除，被迁移的这幢曾是民立中学的办公楼，于1999年被评定为上海市优秀历史建筑。它檐带山墙为巴洛克式，二层中部设有欧式外廊，北立面附有中国江南建筑特色。

据介绍，今天启动的大中里项目位于石门一路及海路，毗邻南京西路，占地约6.3万平方米，将建设成包括商业购物中心、办公楼及酒店的大型综合性项目。民立中学老校舍，位于轨道交通13号线一出口处，经市、区有关专家反复论证，决定将老校舍平移。因为有上海音乐厅平移的成功经验在先，这一建筑保护技术已比较完善，一般是先将原有建筑切割加固保护，随后把地基整体移动到新架设的轨道上，再用千斤顶缓缓推移。这一平移工程预计在半年内完工。

此外，该地块内还有一棵百年玉兰树，也将在原址保护。

■民立中学老校舍位于石门一路威海路附近的"大中里"

首席记者 廉和 摄（资料照片）

进入修复环节后，上海章明建筑设计事务所团队以"修旧如旧"的形式复原已被破坏的墙面、烟囱、山花、门窗、线条等细部特征。所有的花式都按图纸和历史风貌进行修护，并采用了与原物质地相同的材料。此前被焚毁消失的露台和铜制尖顶也被修复完善，邱氏大宅恢复了漂亮的风貌外立面。

During the restoration process, the team from Shanghai Zhangming Architectural Design Firm restored the damaged walls, chimneys, bargeboards, doors and windows to their original state. Everything was done in accordance with old schematics and original images. Materials from the same source as the originals were used. A balcony that had burned down was also fully restored, as was the beautiful facade.

## 3-34
### 外立面清水红墙修复
### Restoration of the red brick north facade

## 3-35
### 风貌外立面修复
### Restoration of the south facade

## 3-36
### 两侧铜制盔顶修复前后对比
### The bronze roof before and after restoration

3-37
西班牙风格螺旋麻花柱式栏杆修复
The restored Spanish spiral banisters

3-38
精心修缮后的查公馆
Cha House after restoration

修复后的邱氏大宅并非只是一座"观赏建筑",而是要承担推动文化、历史、艺术发展的使命,结构上要考虑展览、活动、餐饮、会所等多功能需求。且加建了地下室后,垂直方向上的动线需要重新梳理,过去的内部结构并不能完全支撑新的需求。

对此,章明团队并没有刻板地在建筑内部维持原貌,而是根据新的需求,在不太牢靠的二楼增加了钢梁结构,同时在老楼里增加了两部具有古典风格但很现代化的小型电梯。

最终,上海章明建筑设计事务所为大宅撰写了一份详细的项目介绍和实施方案,上百页的厚度记录了几乎所有施工要点、难点及工法,以便后世借鉴。

After its restoration, the building became more than a decorative structure. It took on a new mission of promoting the development of culture, history and art. That meant it had to support multiple different functions, such as exhibitions, events, catering and club activities. After the construction of the basement, the rest of the building had to be reorganised to fully support the new requirements.

Zhang Ming's team did not follow the building's original design too rigidly. Sometimes changes were necessary. For example, they added steel beams to support the less structurally sound second floor, along with two small elevators, which are modern in function, yet feature a classical style.

The Shanghai Zhangming Architectural Design Firm put together a detailed project introduction and implementation plan, containing hundreds of pages of construction guidelines and methodologies, as a reference for future generations.

3-39
查公馆手绘图（南立面）
A painting of Cha House（South facade）

**章明** 上海章明建筑设计事务所创始董事长、总建筑师

城市更新在上海市中心是具有可操作性的想法。例如在石门一路上，建筑与街道的尺度，各类新、老建筑结合的效果都是很好的。而新建筑的交通又比较方便、功能更全面，对于整个区域的流量都有提升。

只要是根据需要设计的、不与外部风貌相冲突的功能，放到老建筑中都是可行的。相对需要警惕的，是那些需求不明确、最终没能发挥出建筑特质和风貌的情况。

### ZHANG MING
Founding Chairwoman and Chief Architect of Shanghai Zhangming Architectural Design Firm

*Urban renewal is a feasible idea in central Shanghai. For instance, the mix of various new and old buildings on Shimen Road No. 1 has achieved great results. New buildings provide for more convenient transportation and comprehensive functionality. They also help improve mobility and accessibility in the entire area.*

*New functions that are based on real-world requirements, and do not conflict with external appearances, are always acceptable when placed in historic structures. What we need to look out for are conditions where the requirements are unclear, and changes may alter the characteristics and appearance of these buildings.*

从大中里的更新改造，到邱氏大宅的规划、平移和修复，始终遵循着香港兴业国际创始人查济民博士倡导的"尊人重土"这一核心理念。为纪念查济民先生，也为了赋予这座历史保护建筑新的生命，修缮后的大宅被重新命名为"查公馆"。

2018年5月18日，查公馆举办"济世为民"揭幕展，暌违多年后首次对外开放。展览不仅详细介绍了查济民博士振兴民族工业、爱国爱港、福泽桑梓的生平经历，也展示了项目动迁及建设期间，保留下来的"大中里"印记。旧貌新颜交织之中，参观者大多由衷感慨着旧时光的情感和记忆，并热烈地畅想城市与生活空间的未来。

The renewal and renovation of Dazhongli, and the planning, relocation and restoration of the remaining building of Qiu Mansions was driven by the motto of "respecting the people and cherishing the land" embraced by Dr. Cha Chi-ming, the founder of HKR International. To commemorate Dr. Cha and instil new life into the protected historic structure, the renovated building was renamed Cha House.

Cha House opened for the first time in many years during a ceremony to unveil "The Cha's Spirit: Serving Society and People" exhibition on 18 May 2018. The exhibition detailed Dr. Cha's life work in developing national industries, his patriotism for the country and Hong Kong, and his contributions to society. It also showcased relics of Dazhongli that were retained during the relocation and construction. Many visitors reflected on their feelings and memories of the old days, while passionately discussing the future of the city and their living environment.

3-40

2018 年 5 月 18 日，时任静安区委副书记暨区长陆晓栋与香港兴业国际副主席兼董事总经理查懋成为查公馆揭幕

Lu Xiaodong, former Deputy Chief of the CPC Jing'an District Committee and Jing'an District Governor, and Victor Cha Mou-zing, Deputy Chairman and Managing Director of HKR International, officially open Cha House on 18 May 2018

3-41

查公馆揭幕展一楼部分场景
The first floor of the Cha House exhibition

3-43

查公馆揭幕展二楼部分场景
The second floor of the Cha House exhibition

3-42

百年大中里石匾及消防栓
Fire hydrants and a century-old stone plaque from old Dazhongli

166~167

# Chapter IV
# REVITALISING
# "URBAN INGENUITY"

第 四 章

时空交错的城市更新
Spanning Time and Space

文化与商业的共振魅力
The Charms of Culture and Commerce

复兴

都会匠心

大拆大建、完全推翻，曾经是中国快速城镇化进程中最为普遍的做法。上海作为商业文明的绝对高地，率先认识到历史积淀能大幅提升商业空间的品质，并带来独一无二、有形和无形的价值。所以，一批对海派文化理解深刻、有所担当的商业革新者，正引领越来越多的老建筑走上保育活化之路。

Large-scale demolition and construction used to be the most popular approach in China's rapid urbanisation. However, as the country's most recognised centre of culture and commerce, Shanghai was also the first to appreciate that respect for history can greatly improve the quality of commercial space and create unique, tangible and intangible value. That is why a group of business trailblazers, with a keen understanding of western culture and a sense of duty, are now taking the lead in conserving and revitalising more and more historic buildings.

从邱氏大宅、民立中学到查公馆，如今位于兴业太古汇最南端的这座优秀历史建筑，承载了上海的百年沧桑。它的整体保留改造，正顺应了留存城市肌理的城市更新大潮。修缮后的查公馆与兴业太古汇的购物中心、写字楼、酒店等业态，共同组合成了既具历史底蕴又有潮流活力的高品质魅力载体，为老牌商圈南京西路重新注入了文化和商业的活力。

The outstanding historic building at the southernmost tip of HKRI Taikoo Hui was originally known as one of the Qiu Mansions. Then it became Minli School, and today it is known as Cha House. It has witnessed over a century of turbulent history. And, its preservation and transformation are very much in line with a booming trend in urban renewal that focuses on preserving a city's context. HKRI Taikoo Hui's Cha House, its shopping mall, office towers, and hotels combine to produce a charming jewel imbued with both history and vitality – injecting cultural and commercial energy into the long established West Nanjing Road commercial district.

近年历史建筑、工业遗产和旧社区改造的项目越来越多，重新融入城市文化生活的速度越来越快。这些优质的城市更新项目，正以不同方式，唤醒城市空间的活力。如何让这些文化遗产踏上城市更新的浪潮，正是当今复兴"都会匠心"之路的核心命题。

In recent years, more historical buildings, industrial heritage sites and old communities than ever have been renovated. And, the speed at which they are being reintegrated into life and culture is rising. These quality urban renewal projects are awakening the potential of urban spaces in a variety of ways. Indeed, they have become a key factor in the rebirth of what is being called "urban ingenuity".

# {一}    时空交错的城市更新

*Spanning Time and Space*

早在 2000 年代初期，上海新天地、田子坊等石库门里弄的成功改造案例，就让上海这个中国商业触觉与艺术氛围最为发达的城市意识到，在大规模的拆建之外，还有一条名为"城市更新"的道路可选。

在城市规划专家的认知中，凡是在城市存量土地上进行开发的，通俗来说，就是在有房子、有人的土地上进行的再开发活动，都可称之为城市更新。这种以保留、修缮并活用历史建筑为核心的过程，不仅能够激发出项目的文化魅力，也能为商业需求带来极为稀缺的附加价值。

Shanghai realised some time ago that urban renewal was a viable alternative to other urbanisation models that were popular in China. Since the early 2000s, the successful transformation of old districts, like Xintiandi and Tianzifang, which featured Shikumen houses, has helped to define Shanghai as China's flagship commercial and cultural city.

In the minds of urban planning experts, any development of urban land, or the redevelopment of an area with existing houses and residents, can be called urban renewal. But that isn't the full picture. Carried out properly, the process of preserving, renovating, and finding new ways to use historic buildings does more than restore and enhance cultural appeal. It can also add value to something in danger of losing its relevance. However, while it may be a heartfelt goal, it is a rare outcome for any commercial project.

**郑德高**　中国城市规划设计研究院副院长

城市更新在中国已经演进出现了四种模式，也对应着中国城市化发展的不同阶段。

第一种是直接推倒重建，这是如今大多数中国城市面对旧城改造所选择的发展道路；第二种是保留一部分，更新建设一部分，典型的案例是上海新天地与兴业太古汇；第三种是保留片区中大部分原有建筑，比如自"哥伦比亚公园"改建而来的"上生·新所"文创园区；第四种是将"生态修复"和"城市修补"结合起来的"双修模式"，典型的案例是上海愚园路街道综合整治，通过提升街道空间舒适度，新增一些小的开放空间。

**ZHENG DEGAO**

Deputy Chief Planner, China Academy of Urban Planning & Design

*In China, urban renewal has evolved and four models have appeared, each corresponding to different stages of urbanisation.*

*The first is to demolish and rebuild outright, which is the development path chosen by most Chinese cities today when they face the issue of transforming their old neighbourhoods. The second is to retain one portion while upgrading the infrastructure in another. Examples of this include Xintiandi and HKRI Taikoo Hui in Shanghai. The third is to retain most of the original structures, such as in Shangsheng Xinsuo, a cultural-creative business district that resulted from the redevelopment of the old Columbia Circle. The fourth is the "double repair model" , which combines "ecological and urban restoration". A typical case is the comprehensive renovation of Yuyuan Road in Shanghai, increasing space at street-level to open it up for more lifestyle applications, and adding new, open areas so people can relax and enjoy the experiences the area has to offer.*

越来越多的城市遗产，在这股力量的推动下被重新唤醒。在近年来被行业内外津津乐道的成功案例中，就包括于2018年重新面世、现由香港兴业国际旗下上海素凯泰酒店负责运营及管理的"查公馆"。

An increasing number of urban heritage sites have been rejuvenated by this trend. In recent years the success stories have grown to include Cha House, which was re-launched in 2018, and is now operated and managed by the Sukhothai Shanghai, a hotel subsidiary of HKR International.

细腻的修缮过程，使查公馆这座文物建筑的深厚底蕴得以重现于世——历史的印记被保留下来，与活化后的空间交织融合。以身示范上海的旧时风韵之余，查公馆焕然一新的场地，同时还承载了包括艺术、文化和品味生活展示在内的多种功能。

The intricate renovation process has brought the rich heritage of Cha House to the world once more. The marks left by history have been preserved and integrated with the newly restored spaces. In addition to demonstrating Shanghai's old charm, the transformed Cha House also serves various different functions, such as holding arts, cultural and stylish lifestyle events.

4-2
2018 年 5 月至 7 月，"济世为民"查公馆揭幕展吸引近 3 万人次入内参观
From May to July 2018, an exhibition entitled "The Cha's Spirit: Serving Society and People" attracted nearly 30,000 visitors to Cha House

为了营造更高的开放性，查公馆在修缮过程中做了充分准备，先将现存保留完整的地砖切割下来，集中重新铺设于二层阳台，然后用更耐磨的材质按原样复制的地砖铺设到沿街露台等区域。为了适应多种文化活动的需要，除了加装空调，查公馆还模仿 20 世纪上海滩人工电梯的年代特色，增添了带有菱形格网栅栏的电梯。

In order to create an exquisite function space, the Cha House renovation process was extremely thorough. First, the existing floor tiles were taken up and re-laid on the second-floor balcony. Those tiles were then replicated with more durable materials and placed on the terrace and areas along the street. In order to meet the needs of various cultural events, air conditioning was installed. So was an elevator, featuring a classic lattice gate similar to the old manually-controlled lifts found in buildings on the Bund during the last century.

4-3
查公馆修缮后的楼梯和地板
The restored staircase and floor of Cha House

开业至今，查公馆所承载的各类文化展览或是创新零售案例，无一不是历史、文化、美学与体验的完美结合。爱马仕旗下香水 Twilly d'Hermès 在这里开出上海首家快闪店，俏丽玫红色灯光映照下的中式阁楼，一时成为城中时髦话题；Diptyque 也在这里举办过香氛艺术展，查公馆中西合璧的强烈时空交错感，为活动氛围大大增色。这栋历史建筑的艺术与商业价值，正逐渐被更多时尚生活方式品牌所认知。

Since the official opening of Cha House, the exhibitions and innovative business events held there have demonstrated a perfect combination of history, culture, aesthetics and experience. Lit by chic red lights, the stylish building has become a hot ticket on the city's fashion scene, where its artistic and commercial value has been recognised by lifestyle brands. For example, Hermès chose Cha House for its first Shanghai pop-up store, where it sold its classic Twilly d'Hermès perfume. Diptyque also held an immersive fragrance exhibition at the venue. The intense feeling of time and space being distorted by the interplay of Chinese and Western styles, greatly enhanced the atmosphere of these events.

4 - 4
**Diptyque 香氛艺术展**
**Diptyque Immersive Fragrance Exhibition**

仅在最近 5 年内，上海市中心就涌现出了超过 10 个由历史建筑、工业遗产或者旧式社区改造而来，并融合商业与艺术的"新晋地标"。

In the past five years alone, historic buildings, industrial heritage sites and old communities have helped to create more than 10 newly renovated, integrated business-and-cultural landmarks in the centre of Shanghai.

上海近 5 年城市更新地图（2014-2019）
**Urban renewal map of Shanghai over 5 years（2014-2019）**

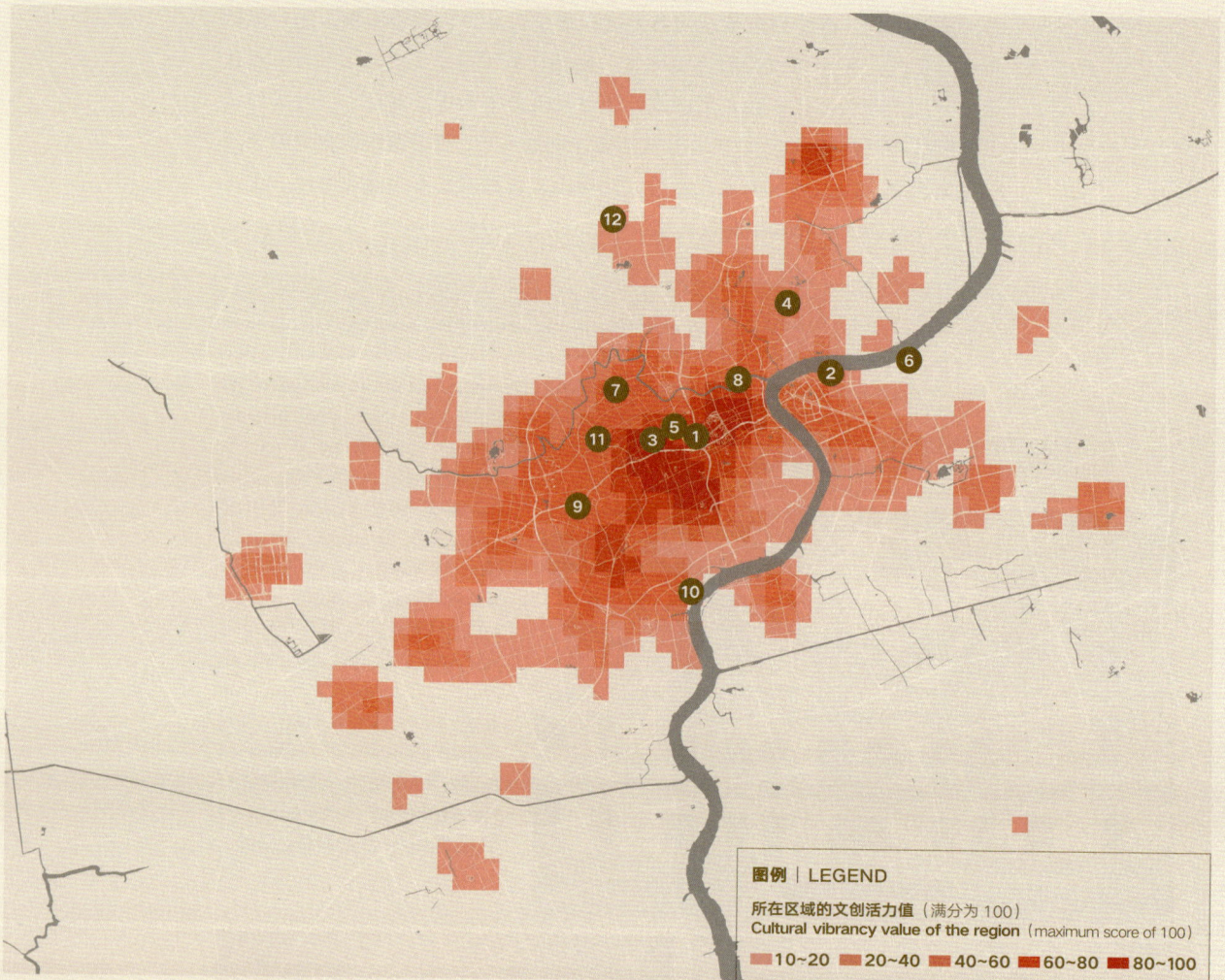

图例 | LEGEND

所在区域的文创活力值（满分为 100）
Cultural vibrancy value of the region（maximum score of 100）

10~20 | 20~40 | 40~60 | 60~80 | 80~100

| 序号<br>NO. | 名称<br>NAME | 所在版块<br>REGION | 原始用途<br>ORIGINAL USAGE |
|---|---|---|---|
| 1 | 查公馆 \| Cha House | 南京西路 \| West Nanjing Rd. | 颜料商邱氏兄弟住宅 \| Residence of the dye merchant Qiu Brothers<br>上海民立中学校舍 \| Shanghai Minli School |
| 2 | 船厂 1862 \| Shipyard 1862 | 黄浦滨江 \| Huangpu Riverside | 英商祥生船厂 – 上海船厂 \| British Xiangsheng Shipyard – Shanghai Shipyard |
| 3 | 荣宅 \| Rong Zhai | 南京西路 \| West Nanjing Rd. | "面粉大王"荣宗敬住宅 \| Residence of the "Flour King" Rong Zongjing |
| 4 | 瑞虹天地月亮湾 \| Ruihong Hall of the Moon | 虹口 \| Hongkou | 原上海中心城区最大棚户区虹镇老街<br>\| Previously the largest neighbourhood of dilapidated houses in the centre of Shanghai |
| 5 | 张园·丰盛里 \| Zhang Garden, Fengshengli | 南京西路 \| West Nanjing Rd. | 晚清富商张叔和花园 \| Zhang Shuhe Garden, late Qing Dynasty |
| 6 | 八万吨筒仓艺术中心 \| 80,000-Ton Silo Warehouse Arts Center | 民生码头 \| Minsheng Wharf | 民生码头存粮筒仓 \| Minsheng Wharf Silo |
| 7 | 上海西康 189 弄 \| 189 Xikang Road, Shanghai | 西康路 \| Xikang Rd. | 大自鸣钟广场 \| Dazi Mingzhong Square |
| 8 | 上海总商会 \| Shanghai Chamber of Commerce | 苏河湾 \| Suhewan | 上海总商会总部 \| Shanghai Chamber of Commerce |
| 9 | 上生·新所 \| Shangsheng Xinsuo | 愚园路 \| Yuyuan Rd. | "哥伦比亚公园"住宅区 \| Columbia Circle residential area<br>上海生物制品研究所 \| Shanghai Institute of Biological Products |
| 10 | 龙美术馆·西岸馆 \| Long Museum West Bund | 徐汇滨江 \| Xuhui Riverside | 运煤码头 \| Coal Pier |
| 11 | 静安 NEO \| Jing'an NEO | 静安寺 \| Jing'an Temple | 上海沪西纺织机械厂 \| West Shanghai Textile Machinery Plant, Shanghai |
| 12 | 静安·新业坊 \| Jing'an-Xinyefang | 汶水路 \| Wenshui Rd. | 上海冶金矿山机械厂 \| Metallurgy and Mining Machinery Plant, Shanghai |

所在地区文创活跃度
**Cultural activeness value of the region**

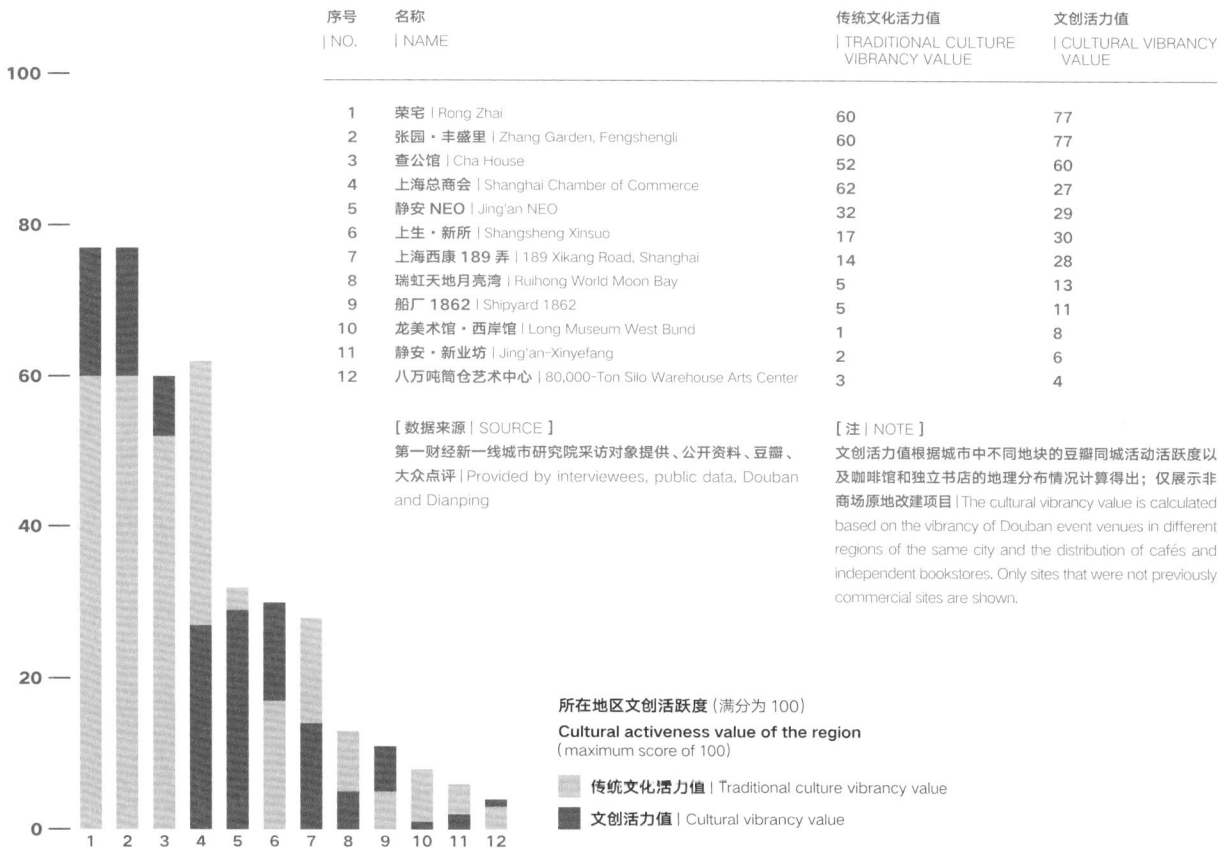

| 序号 \| NO. | 名称 \| NAME | 传统文化活力值 \| TRADITIONAL CULTURE VIBRANCY VALUE | 文创活力值 \| CULTURAL VIBRANCY VALUE |
|---|---|---|---|
| 1 | 荣宅 \| Rong Zhai | 60 | 77 |
| 2 | 张园·丰盛里 \| Zhang Garden, Fengshengli | 60 | 77 |
| 3 | 查公馆 \| Cha House | 52 | 60 |
| 4 | 上海总商会 \| Shanghai Chamber of Commerce | 62 | 27 |
| 5 | 静安 NEO \| Jing'an NEO | 32 | 29 |
| 6 | 上生·新所 \| Shangsheng Xinsuo | 17 | 30 |
| 7 | 上海西康 189 弄 \| 189 Xikang Road, Shanghai | 14 | 28 |
| 8 | 瑞虹天地月亮湾 \| Ruihong World Moon Bay | 5 | 13 |
| 9 | 船厂 1862 \| Shipyard 1862 | 5 | 11 |
| 10 | 龙美术馆·西岸馆 \| Long Museum West Bund | 1 | 8 |
| 11 | 静安·新业坊 \| Jing'an-Xinyefang | 2 | 6 |
| 12 | 八万吨筒仓艺术中心 \| 80,000-Ton Silo Warehouse Arts Center | 3 | 4 |

[ 数据来源 \| SOURCE ]
第一财经新一线城市研究院采访对象提供、公开资料、豆瓣、大众点评 \| Provided by interviewees, public data, Douban and Dianping

[ 注 \| NOTE ]
文创活力值根据城市中不同地块的豆瓣同城活动活跃度以及咖啡馆和独立书店的地理分布情况计算得出；仅展示非商场原地改建项目 \| The cultural vibrancy value is calculated based on the vibrancy of Douban event venues in different regions of the same city and the distribution of cafés and independent bookstores. Only sites that were not previously commercial sites are shown.

所在地区文创活跃度 (满分为 100)
**Cultural activeness value of the region** (maximum score of 100)

传统文化活力值 \| Traditional culture vibrancy value
文创活力值 \| Cultural vibrancy value

| 现运营规划 \| OPERATION PLAN | 具体用途 \| USAGE | 始建年份 \| YEAR OF START OF CONSTRUCTION | 改造完成时间 \| RENEWAL COMPLETION TIME | 改造方 \| RENEWAL IMPLEMENTOR |
|---|---|---|---|---|
| 索凯泰酒店活动空间 \| The Sukhothai Shanghai event space | 会所 / 品牌门店 / 展览 \| Club/Brand stores/Exhibitions | 1920s | 2018 | 兴业太古汇 \| HKRI Taikoo Hui |
| 文创商业综合体 \| Culture and creativity commercial complex | 剧院 / 商场 \| Theatre/Mall | 1862 | 2016 | 中信泰富等 \| CITIC Pacific |
| 艺术活动空间 \| Art and event space | 展览 \| Exhibitions | 1899 | 2017 | 普拉达 \| Prada |
| 音乐特色商场 \| Music-themed mall | 商场 / 音乐现场 \| Mall/Music performance space | 1960s | 2017 | 瑞安 \| Shui On Land |
| 商业街区 \| Shopping street | 餐饮 / 购物 \| F&B/Shopping | 1882 | 2017 | 静安置业 \| Jing'an Real Estate |
| 艺术空间 \| Art space | 展览 \| Exhibitions | 1900s | 2017 | 东岸 \| East Bund Investment |
| 音乐特色商场 \| Music-themed mall | 商场 / 音乐演出 \| Mall/Music performance space | 1926 | 2017 | 中信 \| CITIC |
| 宝格丽酒店会所 \| Bvlgari Hotel | 宴会厅 / 中餐厅 \| Banquet hall/Chinese restaurant | 1916 | 2018 | 宝格丽 \| Bvlgari |
| 文创商业综合体 \| Culture and creative commercial complex | 办公 / 餐饮 / 书店 / 展览 \| Office/Catering/Bookstores/Exhibitions | 1920s | 2018 | 万科 \| Vanke |
| 美术展览馆 \| Art museum | 展览 \| Exhibitions | 1950s | 2014 | 徐汇滨江建投 \| Xuhui Waterfront Development |
| 酒店及联合办公 \| Hotel and co-working space | 酒店 / 联合办公 \| Hotel/Co-working space | 1978 | 2018 | 华住 \| Huazhu |
| 影视产业园 \| Film industrial park | 影视文创 \| Film and culture | 1959 | 2018 | 上海电气置业等 \| Shanghai Electric Group Properties |

査公馆 —— 穿梭时光之旅

CHA HOUSE
— A JOURNEY THROUGH
TIME

4-7
查公馆组图
Photos of Cha House

## 六年修缮，"荣宅"令时光倒流

在上海市中心的陕西北路上，有一幢始于 20 世纪初期的花园洋房。1918 年，清末民初白手起家的著名企业家荣宗敬买下这座洋房，举家居住于此，故有"荣宅"之名。"荣氏家族"的名号乃中国近代民族资本家族之最，荣宗敬有"上海滩面粉大王"的称号。

中华人民共和国成立后，这里大部分时间是上海民主党派机关的办公地，亦曾用作美国新闻集团的驻沪总部。2011 年，Prada 集团 CEO 和创意设计总监在上海游览时偶遇这一宅邸，从此揭开了一场耗时六年的全方位修缮工程。

在修缮过程中，Prada 引入了此前在全球范围内参与历史文化遗产保护的经验，坚持维护旧宅所使用的各类传统工艺和材质，使其历史意义得以复活，也焕发出新的光彩。

自 2017 年重新开放后，"荣宅"如今常以"热门景点"的身份出现在地图软件上。这里曾举办上海时装周、Prada 新品发布会和私人晚宴，不定期对外开放的高端艺术展更是数次引发上海文化艺术市场的讨论。在 Prada 的设想里，这里会成为上海跨国界文化交流的标志性舞台。

Case *1*

## "RONG ZHAI"
## TAKES YOU BACK IN TIME

*On Shaanxi North Road in the centre of Shanghai, there is a Western-style house with a garden, that dates from the early 20th century. In 1918, Rong Zongjing, the famous self-made entrepreneur who started out in the late Qing Dynasty and early Republican China, bought the house and moved his family there – thus earning it the name "Rong Zhai" (Rong House). The Rong family was the greatest of modern China's "national bourgeoisie" families, and Rong Zongjing was known as "The Flour King of Shanghai".*

*After the founding of the People's Republic of China, the building was, for the most part, used as the office of the Shanghai Democratic Party. It later became the headquarters of News Corporation in Shanghai. In 2011, the CEO and creative director of Prada came across this old building during a visit to Shanghai, and kicked-off a comprehensive renovation project that would last for six years.*

*Prada brought all of its experience in the protection of historical and cultural heritage sites from around the globe to the renovation process. It insisted on using the traditional crafts and materials originally found in the house, preserving its historical significance, and giving it new splendour.*

*Prada's vision is to make the building an iconic site for cross-border cultural exchanges in Shanghai. Since its reopening in 2017, "Rong Zhai" has often appeared on map apps as a "popular destination". Shanghai Fashion Week, Prada's new product launches, and private dinners have all been held there, not to mention high-end art exhibitions, which are sometimes open to the public. This has sparked much discussion in Shanghai's cultural and art circles.*

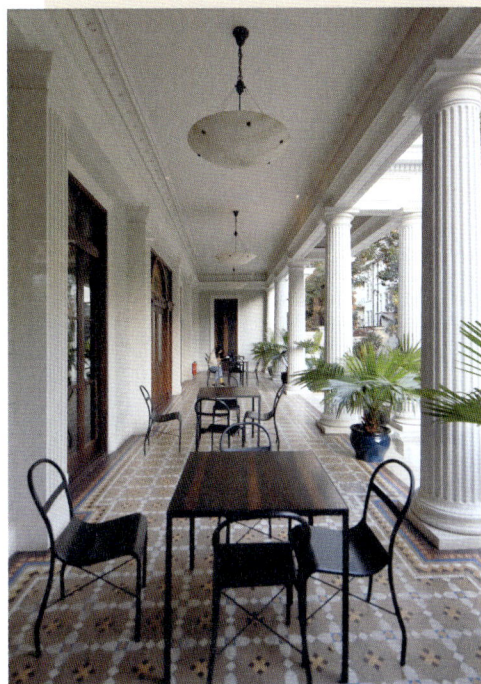

4 - 8
荣宅组图
**Photos of Rong Zhai**

*184~185*

## 复活邬达克图纸的"上生·新所"

　　如今，不少年轻旅行者会在上海城区的游览清单中，增加一个名为"上生·新所"的全新目的地。1920年代建成时，这里是由著名匈牙利籍建筑师邬达克担任总设计师的沪西高端休闲住宅区"哥伦比亚公园"。1949年中华人民共和国成立后，这里改作上海生物制品研究所的办公用地。当中"海军俱乐部"、"孙科别墅"等保护建筑大多被完整保存。

　　自上海生物制品研究所迁址市郊后，这一极富历史底蕴的空间曾闲置数年。2016年，万科集团以整体租赁开发形式接手"哥伦比亚公园"，并与知名建筑设计事务所OMA共同给出了活化设计方案。

　　这一方案不仅对景观广场和优秀历史建筑做出重点改造，还增设养老设施，并将项目体与附近社区内的邬达克纪念馆、上海交通大学法华校区等文化、教育设施更好地串联在一起，为周边居民增加了更有趣味的公共空间。

　　2018年5月，这一项目以"上生·新所"之名重新面世，成为集合了联合办公、买手零售店、生活方式书店、精品咖啡馆与精酿啤酒吧、展览馆和创意餐饮的文创商办园区。拥有白色欧式立柱环廊、铺满彩色马赛克的"海军俱乐部"泳池经修缮后，成为整个项目的亮点，也是社交网络上极具人气的本地景点之一。

## Case 2

## THE RESURRECTION
## OF COLUMBIA CIRCLE

Nowadays, many young travellers have added a new destination known as "Shangsheng Xinsuo" to their list of places to visit in Shanghai. When it was completed in the 1920s, it was called Columbia Circle – a high-end residential area in Puxi, designed by the famous Hungarian architect, László Hudec. After the founding of the People's Republic of China in 1949, the entire area was converted into office space for the Shanghai Institute of Biological Products. Most of the buildings, such as the Navy Club and the Sun Ke Villa were well looked after while they were in use.

After the Institute was relocated to the suburbs, this space which is rich in history, was left vacant for years. In 2016, the Vanke Group leased Columbia Circle, with the goal of redeveloping it. Together with the well-known architectural firm, OMA, it produced a plan to revitalise the area.

The plan not only made important renovations to the landscape, the plaza, and some of the many outstanding historical buildings, but also added new items, such as eldercare facilities. It built stronger links between the structures and cultural and educational resources in nearby communities, like Hudec Memorial Hall and Shanghai Jiao Tong University's Fahua Campus, creating popular public spaces for residents in the area.

In May 2018, the project was unveiled to the world as Shangsheng Xinsuo, which quickly became a culture-creative business district, where office buildings, retail stores, lifestyle bookshops, boutique cafés, craft beer bars, exhibition halls, and innovative restaurants congregate. The old Navy Club's swimming pool, with its European-style colonnaded corridor and colourful mosaics, was restored to become the highlight of the entire project, as well as a popular local attraction on social media.

案例 *3*

## "上海总商会"的下一个百年

作为如今中国最重要的商业中心城市，上海商界的大规模发展自清代晚期就已闻名海内外。1902 年，清政府在上海设立"上海总商会"，作为商界事务的关键协调部门。这一机构在民国时期被保留，并逐渐发展壮大，有"近代中国第一商会"之称；其位于苏州河畔的总部建筑在 1912 年启动建设时，也延揽了英商"通和洋行"进行设计，内部空间开朗，细节丰富。

中华人民共和国成立后，"上海总商会"大楼先后被上海电子管厂、联合灯泡厂、上海市电子元件研究所使用，并对建筑外观进行了一定改造。2011 年，项目所在地块的新业主华侨城正式启动"上海总商会"旧址修缮保护工作，后将这一空间交由中国内地第二家宝格丽酒店运营管理。

为了更契合 1920 年代"上海总商会"在苏州河畔所象征的社交地位，宝格丽酒店更倾向于把这个空间作为宴会和品牌发布会场来使用。为此，品牌方修复了总商会议事厅跨度 18.3 米的弧形穹顶，又重新挖掘出被封在砖墙里的花园露台。这里后来成为了宝格丽酒店的第一家中餐厅，是兼具现代性和私密性的聚会空间。

4-10
上海总商会组图
Photos of the Shanghai Chamber of Commerce

## THE NEXT 100 YEARS
## FOR THE SHANGHAI CHAMBER OF COMMERCE

*While Shanghai is China's most important financial centre today, the city has enjoyed a reputation as a major business centre since the late Qing Dynasty. In 1902, the Qing government established the Shanghai Chamber of Commerce, which became instrumental in coordinating business affairs. The institution retained its role during the Republican era. As its power grew, it became known as the "Number 1 Chamber of Commerce in Modern China". When it decided to construct its headquarters on the banks of the Suzhou Creek in 1912, it asked the British firm, Atkinson & Dallas Architects and Civil Engineers Ltd., to design the spacious and richly detailed building.*

*After the founding of the People's Republic of China, the Shanghai Chamber of Commerce building was used first by the Shanghai Electronic Tube Factory, then the United Bulb Factory, and later by the Shanghai Electronic Component Research Institute. During this time, the building's exterior was modified. In 2011, the new owner of the site officially launched a project to renovate and preserve the building. On completion, they transferred the operation and management of this space to China's Bvlgari Hotels and became the second hotel of the brand.*

*In homage to the building's social status back in the 1920s, and its location on the banks of the Suzhou Creek, the Bulgari Hotel has used the space as a high-class banquet hall and a luxury product launch venue. The brand owner repaired the 18.3-metre dome and also tore down a brick wall that sealed off the garden terrace. Later, it became the venue for the hotel's first Chinese restaurant, providing fine dining and privacy amidst a very modern décor.*

DARE FOR MORE

DARE TO DA

兴业太古汇
——上海——
HKRI TAIKOO HUI

# {二} 文化与商业的共振魅力

## *The Charm of Culture and Commerce*

在城市更新的浪潮中，涌现各类成功将文化与商业活动有机结合的项目，辐射出广泛的影响力。这也使各大商圈、城区看到了进一步协同提升的机会。

在中国城市规划设计研究院副院长郑德高眼里，一个好的城市更新项目，是要在保留历史建筑的同时，又赋予它更大的活力，比如引入多样化的文化创意活动、吸引越来越多的人来这个地方。"更进一步的是让这个城市更新项目持续地运营下去，有稳定的长期收益，这对开发商来说是一种挑战。"

并不是每个开业时看似成功的城市更新项目，都具有这样长期经营的潜质与实力。

The recent wave of urban renewal projects – especially ones that successfully combine culture with commercial activities – has alerted major business districts and urban areas to opportunities for further synergy.

In the eyes of Zheng Degao, Deputy Chief Planner at the China Academy of Urban Planning & Design, a good urban renewal project keeps the historic building, while adding new energy.

For example, holding cultural and creative events that attract more people to the site. "What is even more important is to make them sustainable and self-supporting by generating long-term profits. This can pose a challenge for developers," he said.

Some urban renewal projects may seem ideal when they first open. But, not all of them have what it takes to continue operating successfully.

过去很长一段时间里，因项目老化而显得有些沉寂的南京西路东段，在兴业太古汇投入运营后，就重新迎来了各类高品质、有格调的主题活动以及跨界合作。SIFS上海国际时装周、李宇春"菜市场"艺术展、英国V&A博物馆（Victoria and Albert Museum）"鞋履乐与苦"展览、爵士春天音乐节……品味、腔调、个性和活力，将年轻人带回到了上海浦西这条最重要的商业街上。

For a long time, the eastern part of West Nanjing Road looked like it had gone into a steep decline. Since HKRI Taikoo Hui began operations, the area has re-emerged. It has played host to a variety of tastefully themed events, including SIFS (Shanghai Iconic Fashion Showcase), pop musician Chris Lee's "Market" art exhibition, the British V&A Museum's (Victoria and Albert Museum) the "Shoes: Pleasure and Pain" exhibition, and the "JZ Spring". Along with cross-border cultural collaborations, they have brought young people back to the most important commercial street in Shanghai's Puxi region.

4-11
兴业太古汇丰富多样的活动
A rich variety of events at HKRI Taikoo Hui

4－12
新旧共存的兴业太古汇
*HKRI Taikoo Hui, where old and new coexist*

除了本身带来的多样化属性外，查公馆与兴业太古汇购物中心——这种新旧共存的空间，承载了独特的文化气息，两者的发展与构建相辅相成，在活化整个商业片区的同时，也为南京西路片区的整体更新改造和南京西路商圈的产业升级，提供了不一样的发展路径。

As spaces where the new and old coexist, Cha House and HKRI Taikoo Hui shopping mall have a unique cultural atmosphere. They complement each other, revitalise the entire business district, and have enhanced the renewal and renovation of the West Nanjing Road area and the local retail trade.

4－13
兴业太古汇独立市集品牌"敢·集"
*HKRI Taikoo Hui's Dare Mart*

4-14
兴业太古汇南花园航拍
An aerial view of HKRI Taikoo
Hui's South Garden

兴业太古汇引进的 250 家品牌中，有 27 家首次进入中国内地、37 家首次进驻上海。这其中包括了 15 家独特的品牌概念店，最广为大众熟知的是 2017 年 12 月开业的当时全球最大的星巴克臻选®上海烘焙工坊。如今，它已是全球星巴克销售额最高的门店之一，也成为上海的城市商业地标和旅游景点。作为老牌商圈，南京西路重新展现它对创新商业的孵化能力。

在上海的街头，还有许多体量虽小却极富代表性的"城市符号"：咖啡馆、DIY 手工坊、独立书店以及豆瓣同城活动地点。这些都是城市中能代表文创活力的第三空间；而那些代表上海城市海派风貌的历史建筑和具有烟火气息的小吃铺，则指向传统文化的独特魅力。

仔细观察这些城市符号的分布情况，以及近年来的脉络流动便可看出，各类更新改造项目正全方位地激活并重塑城市空间的文化活力。

Of the 250 brands that have been brought into HKRI Taikoo Hui, 27 of them were new to mainland China, and 37 were opening their first Shanghai store. The roster includes 15 unique concept stores, the best known being the then world's largest Starbucks Reserve® Shanghai Roastery, which opened in December 2017. As well as enjoying one of the best sales turnovers of any Starbucks outlet in the world, it has become a commercial landmark and a tourist destination. West Nanjing Road has once again shown its ability to cultivate innovative business opportunities.

On the streets of Shanghai, there are still many "urban landmarks" that are small in size but large in significance: cafés, DIY workshops, independent bookstores, and Douban event venues. These are the "third spaces" that cultivate the creativity of a city. The historic buildings along the Bund, as well as lively, down-to-earth snack shops, illustrate the unique charm of traditional culture.

A closer look at the distribution of these urban landmarks, along with changes in trends in recent years, shows that a variety of renovation projects are comprehensively reshaping and revitalising the culture of urban spaces.

4-15
2017 年 12 月，星巴克臻选®上海烘焙工坊开业
The Starbucks Reserve® Shanghai Roastery opened in December 2017

**徐岱雄** 仲量联行中国区战略顾问部总监

　　城市更新的主要目的，是在文化传承的基础上重塑这个区域的核心文化。通过各式各样的标签，重构整个区域，为在这里工作和生活的人们缔造一个全新的生活方式。这涉及产业、经济、文化等各个领域的提升。

　　相比单一项目的价值，城市更新更重要的是如何利用这些项目，打碎街区自身的区域特色，注入新的、未来的时代元素，引领城市发展。只有在更大范围上探讨人、产业、社会和物业之间的关系，才有可能真正实现整个区域的协同发展。

## XU DAIXIONG

Strategic Director, Jones Lang LaSalle China

*The main purpose of urban renewal is to reshape the core culture of an area based on its heritage. To restructure the entire area and create a new way of life for those who work and live there. This involves the promotion of various sectors, such as business, commerce and culture.*

*As opposed to focusing on the value of a single project, urban renewal is more about how to use these projects to inject new, futuristic elements into the zeitgeist, and lead the way for urban development. Only by exploring the relationship among people, business, society, and property on a larger scale is it possible to achieve coordinated development throughout the entire area.*

196~197

在上海的市中心，南京西路沿线以及属于原法租界的"衡复历史街区"，都是最具历史积淀的地带之一。查公馆、荣宅、"衡山和集"书店等文创地标的汇集，都在持续推动这里成为深具传统文化底蕴又兼具文创活力的商业魅力高地。

位于上海中北部的虹口地区，原本是五角场大学城和内环中心城区之间的"文创洼地"。以脏乱差闻名的"虹镇老街"，更是上海市中心最大的危棚简屋片区。现在，历经更新而建立起的瑞虹新城，以及引进了摩登天空 Livehouse 的"月亮湾"购物中心、加上近在咫尺的北外滩改造，为这一地区带来了大批热衷于音乐、美食和文化生活的年轻人。这片"洼地"逐渐填平，为城市北部和浦西中心连接起了更好的文创廊道。

传统文化氛围较弱的城市新区，被老一代市民视作"文化荒漠"。不过在上海浦东滨江，隈研吾由造船工坊改造而来的陆家嘴"船厂 1862"选择先把自己往戏剧地标培养，再建立起以艺术概念为核心的大型购物中心。

船厂原本的锻造车间被改造成一座可容纳 800 人的剧场，2018 年法国阿维尼翁戏剧节 OFF 单元、爱丁堡戏剧节 Fringe 单元、柏林戏剧节、东京戏剧节、伦敦默剧节的剧目在这里轮番上演，热爱浦西舞台的上海城市人，也渐渐适应前往浦东滨江看上一场戏。

这些项目的出现，正持续拓展上海市民的文化活动边界。但面对更长远的未来，"城市更新"的思路依旧有继续升级的可能性。

In the centre of Shanghai you can really feel the past along West Nanjing Road, and in the Hengshan Road-Fuxing Road Historic and Cultural Area in the former French Settlement. The mix of cultural and creative landmarks, such as Cha House, Rong Zhai, and The Mix-Place bookstore, continue to promote Shanghai as a leader in commercial appeal, cultural heritage, and creative energy.

At Hongkou in north-central Shanghai, the area between Wujiaochang University Town and the inner-city centre used to be known as a "cultural sinkhole". Called Hongzhen Old Street, it was infamous for being the bad part of town, and harbouring the biggest collection of dilapidated houses in the middle of Shanghai. After undergoing urban renewal, the area has risen in status, and it is now known as Rui Hong Xin Cheng. The Hall of the Moon Shopping Mall, with its Modern Sky Livehouse, plus the nearby North Bund renovation, attract a lot of young people interested in music and good food. What used to be a "sinkhole" has become a cultural and creative centre.

New urban areas are often regarded as "cultural deserts" by the older generation. But it isn't always true. On Shanghai's Pudong Riverside, an old shipbuilding workshop has been transformed into "Shipyard 1862" by Kengo Kuma. The project, which was originally intended to be a landmark for theatrical performances, has established itself as a major cultural-retail destination.

The shipyard's original workshop was transformed into an 800-seat theatre. The Festival OFF d'Avignon 2018, the Edinburgh Festival Fringe, Berliner Festspiele, the International Drama Festival in Tokyo, and the London International Mime Festival have all been held there. Shanghai urbanites who loved going to Puxi, have gotten used to the idea of going to Pudong Binjiang to see a show.

The emergence of these projects has continued the expansion of cultural activities for the people of Shanghai. That said, the idea of "urban renewal" still has plenty of potential and room for improvement.

**庞嵚**　Benoy 董事
上海公司负责人

　　每个城市更新项目背后，都有不同的目的和商业开发逻辑，很难一概而论。但是它要考虑的问题却万变不离其宗——创造并满足使用人群的未来生活方式。

　　在城市更新项目的运营方面，现在一般打出的标准组合是零售、餐饮、运动娱乐，特殊点的加上美术馆、书店等；但这些业态里面很大一部分是以考虑中产阶级的生活方式和文化取向为主要目标，但对那些相对购买力较弱，还挣扎在生存的边缘的人们来说，城市更新之后，干净的城市界面以及"高大上"的城市功能供应和他们的生活需求差距就相对很大，适合这些人的生活空间就被压缩甚至消失了。这就是城市更新导致"士绅化"的具体体现。所以这个问题绝不仅仅只是打造一个优秀的物理空间那么简单；物理空间的打造相对容易，把一幢楼、一个片区收拾干净也不困难，但之后的事，需要政府、开发商、设计师、各种各样的从业者，当地居民，大家一起来参与设计，一起想办法，这需要耐心和高超的协调技巧、实事求是的工作态度和设身处地的共情精神。

　　推动更多历史项目以新生之姿，唤醒城市文化空间肌理的活力重构，正是对城市发展有所担当的商业使命所在。而只有当各方都以更积极的姿态，主动融入城市文化活力的重塑过程，才能真正实现"都会匠心"的复兴。

**PANG QIN**
Director of Benoy and Head of Benoy Shanghai

*Behind every urban renewal project, there are different sets of objectives and business logic that make them difficult to generalise. But the core concept does not change, and that is to create and cater for the future lifestyle of the people the project applies to.*

*The standard portfolio in most current general urban renewal projects includes retail, dining, sports and entertainment, and perhaps an art museum and a bookstore in some special cases. While most of these businesses take a middle-class lifestyle and cultural orientation as their chief objective to a large degree. In the case of those people who have little spending power and are struggling on the margins of society, the sparkling-clean urban interface and supply of "high-end, elegant and classy" urban functions that result from urban renewal are far removed from their everyday needs. Living spaces that are suitable for them have been minimised to the point of disappearing. This is a tangible manifestation of "gentrification" caused by urban renewal. As a consequence, this issue does not merely involve the creation of outstanding physical spaces. It is relatively easy to create physical spaces, and neatening up a building or an area is not difficult. Government, developers, designers, businesses of all types, and local residents must participate in the follow-up, and jointly think of methods for achieving appropriate goals. This requires extreme patience and skilful coordination, a conscientious working attitude, and great empathy and consideration.*

Promoting more projects to give historical buildings a new look, and reawaken the spirit of urban cultural spaces, is the real mission of commercial urban development. Only when all parties take a more active approach to the process, can we truly realise the revival of "urban ingenuity".

# Chapter V
# REDEFINING A
# CITY LANDMARK

重释

潮流地标

第 五 章

动："爱混敢嗲"
Dynamism: "Dare For More"

静：居心之所
Serenity: A Home for the Heart

创：乐活无界
Creativity: LOHAS Has No Boundaries

变：止于至善
Change: The Relentless Pursuit of Perfection

上海市中心的心脏地带，肯定是中国市场中竞争最激烈的沃土之一。改革开放 40 年，无数野心勃勃的开发者携巨资与理想在此落子。他们无不怀抱着成就下一个地标性商业传奇的梦想。

Shanghai is one of China's most vibrant markets. In the forty years since economic reforms began, countless ambitious developers seeking to establish a foothold have invested heavily in the city, with the dream of building the next landmark.

2015 年，这片版图上的静安区最后一块大型拼图"大中里"项目，被香港兴业国际和太古地产联合命名为"兴业太古汇"。这一名称既体现了两家股东——香港兴业国际集团与太古地产——强强结合，也寓意各方宾客及能人汇聚项目之中。同年年底，兴业太古汇办公楼完成结构封顶，其余部分的建设也进入冲刺阶段。这个被业内称为"十五年磨一剑"的项目，正计划完成面世前的最后一跃。

In 2015, the last major piece in the central Shanghai jigsaw – the Dazhongli Project in Jing'an District – was named HKRI Taikoo Hui by its principals, HKR International and Swire Properties. The name recognises the collaboration of these two shareholders, and the efforts of the talented individuals who contributed to the development. The main structure of the office towers was completed in late 2015, and the remaining construction work was conducted at lightning speed, without cutting any corners or compromising quality.

2010 年当大中里建设工程正式施工，社会热点和商业机会波澜起伏、瞬息万变，兴业太古汇曾被赋予很多想象、期待，甚至质疑。它最终在 2017 年呈现给世界的，不单是一副亮丽夺目、大气谦和的面貌，还有一颗敢想敢做、创新开放的心。

When the Dazhongli Project officially began in 2010, its social impact and the related business opportunities became the talk of the town. HKRI Taikoo Hui stimulated imaginations, expectations, and even doubts. But, when it was finally presented to the world in 2017, it became a brilliantly stylish but relatively modest monument to those who dared to disrupt and innovate.

汇聚消费潮流的大型购物中心、吸纳业界精英的两栋写字楼、迎送八方商客的两座酒店与一座公寓式酒店，共同组成了这个都市中的商业绿洲——动静皆宜、创变自如。某种意义上来说，它也很好地诠释了商业的价值——用最符合需求的方式，描绘出生活、创意与未来的形态。

HKRI Taikoo Hui is much more than the sum of its parts. A large shopping mall that showcases all the hottest trends, two office towers occupied by leading global companies, and two hotels and a serviced apartment that welcome businesspeople from around the world. Together, they form a commercial oasis in the centre of the city that supports lifestyles, enables creativity, and facilitates the future in myriad different ways.

{ 一 }

# 动：“爱混敢嗲”

*Dynamism: "Dare For More"*

　　兴业太古汇融合了海派文化特点和国际潮流，打破了常见于传统商场的方盒子设计思路，强调宽敞开放的空间感。购物中心主体部分由南至北长达450米，贯穿了整个项目地块。S形动线重塑上海商业步行街的氛围，辅以灵活的中庭和通透光亮的玻璃天幕，步移景异，丰富了视觉上的享受和活动的韵律感，游走在其中并不会感觉疲惫，而是仿佛回到了商业街"逛马路"。

　　这种逛马路的感觉由内至外，渗透在兴业太古汇购物中心的不同角落。这里复刻了上海沿街树木茂立的都市特色，收纳了静安区少见的大面积屋顶花园，在繁华的城市中心打造鸟语花香的绿意空间，这不但冲击了人们的想象力，还为大家带来意想不到的无尽惊喜。

HKRI Taikoo Hui breaks away from the square-box design common in shopping malls by combining classic Shanghai style with international architectural trends. The main part of the new mall stretches 450 metres north to south through the heart of the project. The S-shaped design, flexible atrium and open spaces make exploring the various attractions an invigorating experience that feels very much like strolling along a bustling commercial street.

Visitors who find their way to the uppermost level will discover something special – an exceptionally spacious rooftop garden in the Jing'an district. A genuine green oasis, this hidden gem in the centre of Shanghai city is simultaneously a delight to the eyes and a tonic for the soul.

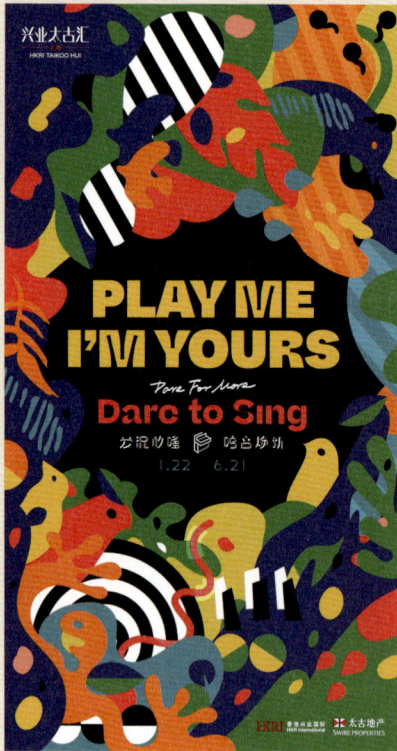

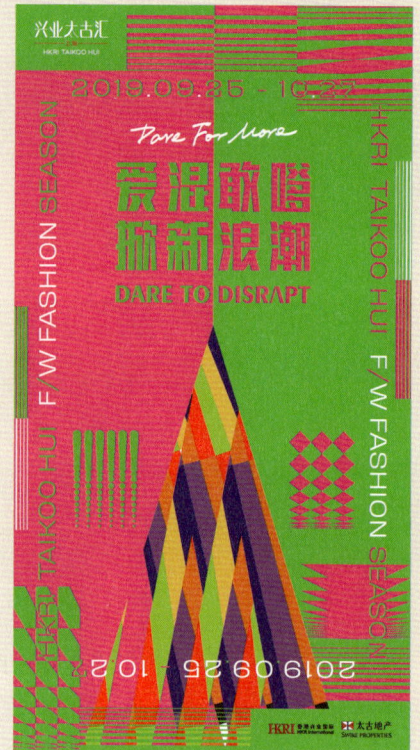

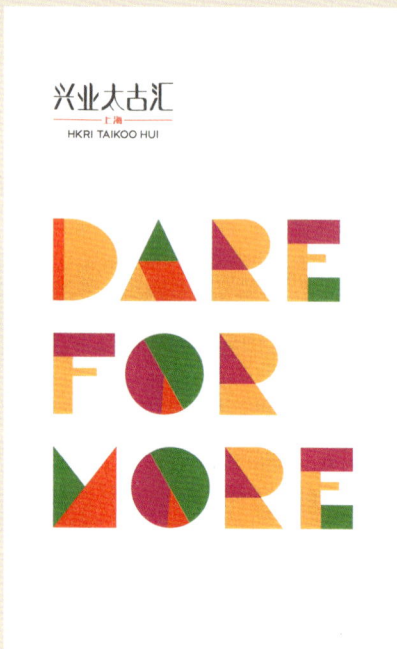

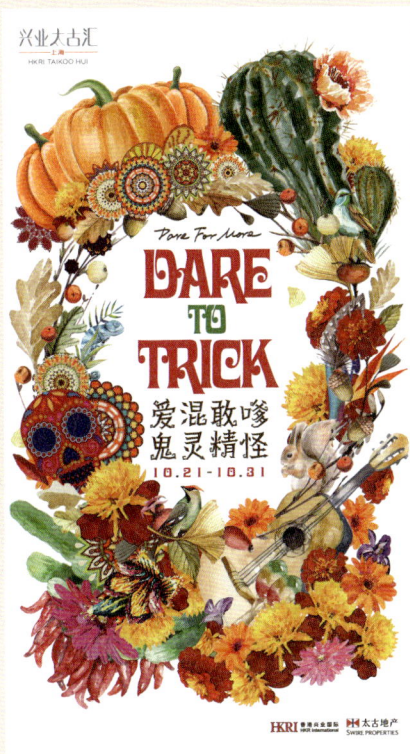

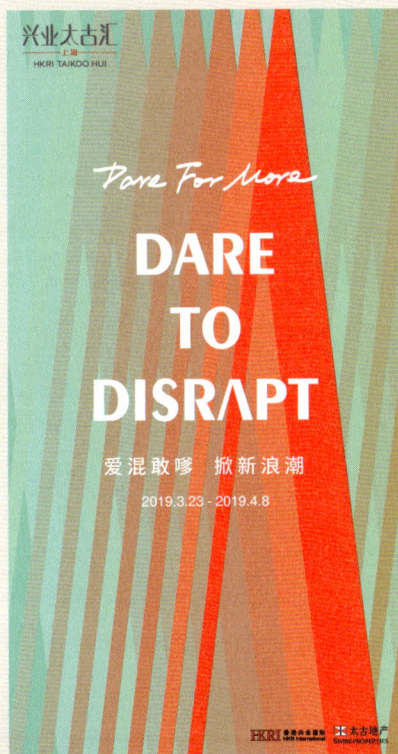

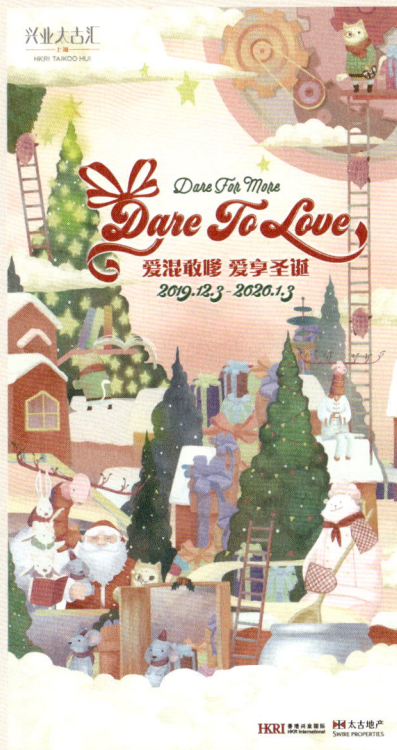

5-2

"Dare For More"体现了兴业太古汇购物中心的基调与活力

"Dare For More" embodies the spirit and vitality
of the HKRI Taikoo Hui shopping mall

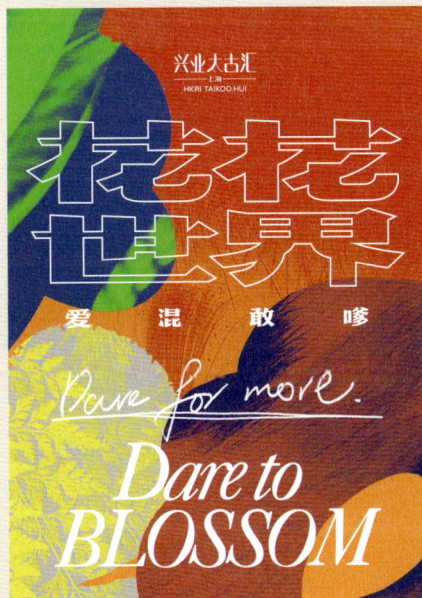

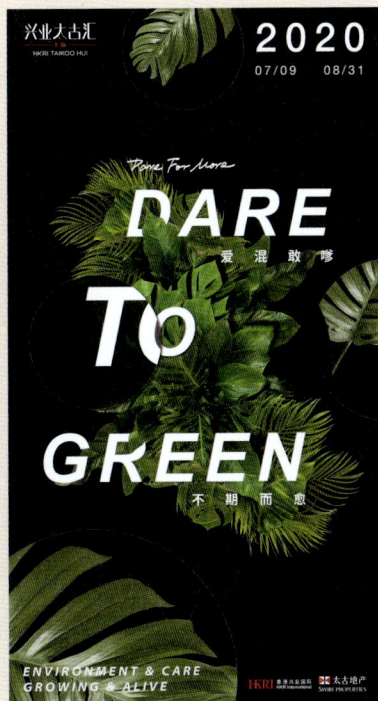

玻璃天幕为购物中心带来更多自然光
The glass roof allows natural light
to flow into the shopping centre

建筑设计中另一独具匠心的部分，是总长250余米的一体式玻璃天幕。自石门一路上方俯瞰，它宛若一条流光溢彩的飘带，落于项目体之上；自商场内仰视，它又能将自然光与彩灯效果，一起引入本已明亮通透的空间。

One of the most innovative aspects of the architecture is the integrated glass roof, which spans more than 250 metres. When viewed from above on Shimen Road No. 1, it looks like a shimmering ribbon shrouded in flowing lights. Inside the shopping mall, natural light and colour fill the already bright and airy space.

5-4

**活力的北广场与安静的南花园形成了
"动静皆宜"的平衡感**
**The lively North Piazza and the secluded
South Garden create a balance between
"dynamism" and "serenity"**

围绕商场主体以及南侧的"查公馆",另有多片形式灵活、设计流畅优雅的裙楼建筑,占据了商场沿南京西路、石门一路及威海路视野最好的位置。连通吴江路的开放式北广场较为热闹,隐藏在商场南端的南花园较为安静,构成了"一动一静"的平衡。

考虑到兴业太古汇地处上海心脏、不可复制的区位优势,以及南京西路商圈已形成的品牌氛围,招商团队对于商场可能呈现出的品牌配置颇具信心。

The main body of the shopping mall, and Cha House on the south side, feature elegantly designed podiums. They provide visitors with the best views of West Nanjing Road, Shimen Road No. 1, and Weihai Road. The open North Piazza that connects to Wujiang Road is lively, whereas the secluded South Garden is quieter. Together, they offer a balance between vibrance and serenity.

Considering HKRI Taikoo Hui's uniquely desirable location in the heart of Shanghai, as well as the commercial energy around the West Nanjing Road business district, the Leasing team was confident the mall would attract a wide range of quality brands.

5-5

**PUMA X MCFC 球迷嘉年华**
**PUMA X MCFC Carnival**

据香港兴业国际集团租务及管理总经理、兴业太古汇联席总经理杜一莉回忆称，按照当时市场普遍流行的高端商场租户配置，商场的一楼将云集各大奢侈品品牌；二楼属于各类国际品牌和大牌副线；三楼以运动品牌、设计师品牌为主；地下部分则交给潮牌及大型超市。餐饮食肆分布在所有楼面，随时满足消费者的需求。

但2015年前后，对于上海的商业社会而言，又是如此波谲云诡的时期——"重奢品牌"因品牌老化、团队更迭及消费者需求的升级，在全球市场都出现销量增长趋缓，中国市场一度也被认为已经饱和，甚至有所收缩。当已入市的商业项目都进入白热化的运营竞争阶段，留给新品牌和项目体的机会并不多；以年轻人为代表的下一代消费者又显得多变、善变，潮流转瞬即逝。

商业是为满足人的需求而生。顺应这条最核心的行事逻辑，兴业太古汇团队重新审视租赁的方向后，得出的结论是：在过去10年间，上海的零售业经历了翻天覆地的变化。随着购物中心越开越多，越开越大，市场竞争日趋激烈。若要突围而出，除了取决于能否有效落实"首店收割机"的策略，更须捕捉千禧一代对优质和健康的多元需求。千禧一代消费者追求体验，促使购物中心运营商不断通过潮牌快闪店、沉浸式市场营销活动等形式，为他们打造更趋个性化的解决方案。与此同时，品牌租户也要在产品和服务上不断升级迭代，才能赢得消费者的青睐。

团队很快就意识到，这座商业综合体必须突破创新，把重心转移到关注全新的消费者、全新的需求和全新的品牌变化，以期更好地服务于整个静安区商圈内总数多达20万、消费能力亦不断增长的白领群体，并让他们"从早到晚"都留在这里。

Susan Du, General Manager of Leasing and Management at HKR International, and Joint General Manager of HKRI Taikoo Hui, remembers that the team originally stuck to the popular leasing profiles for high-end shopping malls at the time. The first floor was earmarked for major luxury brands, and the second floor for international brands and the sub-brands of major players. The third floor was mainly aimed at sports and designer brands, and the underground level reserved for supermarkets and street fashion brands. Restaurants would be located on every floor for convenient access.

However, 2015 brought some sudden and unexpected challenges in the form of rapidly changing consumer behaviour, a worldwide slowdown in luxury brand sales and fierce competition. The China market was also described as saturated, or even shrinking, which left little opportunity for new brands.

Businesses are created to meet people's needs. With this core principle in mind, the HKRI Taikoo Hui team quickly realised that the new commercial complex had to prioritise innovation. The retail scene in Shanghai has become increasingly competitive over the past decade, with more and bigger shopping malls opening apace. The critical success factors range from realising a debut-shop strategy to catering to the diversified needs of the millennials who are more conscious about quality and wellness. Their relentless quest for a variety of experiences, ranging from luxury brand pop-ups to immersive marketing campaigns, has pushed mall operators to devise more personalised offerings. Tenants are also expected to reinvent their products and services more often, to compete and gain customers' attention.

They shifted their focus to new consumers, new needs, and new brands. The goal was to provide more relevant services to the more than 200,000 white-collar shoppers throughout Jing'an district, whose buying power is steadily increasing. A successful commercial complex would encourage these shoppers to remain in the district from early in the morning until late at night.

因此，在最终的招商策略上，兴业太古汇回应了一系列前期市场调研中发现的需求与挑战，给出了一个"以小博大、以快打慢、以变制变"的"非常规"思路。

首先，"不做大店做小店"——整个购物中心中最常见的主力店型是面积在 150 至 200 平方米、轻巧好逛的中型店铺。这也使得近 10 万平方米的空间中，可以容纳整合超过 250 个品牌，形成极为丰富的组合。包括国际品牌、轻奢、潮牌、生活时尚、餐饮等在内，原计划中的大部分品牌配置得到了实现。

其次，在最为重要的一楼空间，大胆地放弃了重奢，转而引入了包括 Cha Ling、La Mer、Jo Malone、Dior、Chanel 等中高档护肤美妆香氛品牌的体验门店，辅以空间上的勾连，形成了一条概念化、精品化、也更符合白领日常消费需求的"美妆大道"。

Guided by market research, the Leasing team adopted an unconventional strategy, designed to disrupt the trade mix and business model in the shopping mall. In practice, that meant going after emerging names, rather than established luxury brands.

The team prioritised small stores – those with 150-200 square metres of floor space – over big stores. As a result, smaller outlets are now the most common stores in the mall, and account for a sizeable proportion of sales. As well as being cosy and easy for visitors to shop in, prioritising small and medium stores allows a space of less than 100,000 square metres to accommodate more than 250 different brands, which massively increases variety and choice. The HKRI Taikoo Hui shopping mall includes a broad mix of international names, affordable luxury brands, street fashion brands, lifestyle brands, and food and beverage options.

The original plan of locating super luxury brands on the all-important first floor was abandoned. Instead, experience stores, such as middle- and high-end skincare and beauty brands were introduced. They include Cha Ling, La Mer, Jo Malone, Dior and Chanel. Together, they form a sophisticated "Beauty Avenue" that comprehensively meets the demands of white-collar consumers.

5-6

"美妆大道"上的绿化皆由店铺自行设计维护，尽显缤纷创意与趣味
The greenery on "Beauty Avenue" was designed and maintained by the stores themselves, providing a fun way to demonstrate creativity（2018-2019）

**杜一莉**　香港兴业国际集团租务及管理总经理
兴业太古汇联席总经理

　　此前在与全球各大奢侈品集团沟通的过程中，兴业太古汇的招商团队发现，位于南京西路与石门一路交叉口的独栋建筑，在设计上并不特别适合奢侈品品牌。因为在这些品牌的既有认知中，他们的客户抵达方式主要为私家车，消费要不受打扰。但受地铁 2 号线的影响，这里无法设计地下车库——这也促使我们转而寻找另类客户。

　　最终落户于此的星巴克，原先只计划在商场内打造一个 300 平方米左右的旗舰店。在多方努力和协助下，最终促成了其将当时全球面积最大的"烘焙工坊"引入中国市场。星巴克臻选®上海烘焙工坊不是一家传统意义上的"主力店"，而是一个非常有意思的首店项目。

## SUSAN DU
General Manager of Leasing and Management at HKR International
Joint General Manager of HKRI Taikoo Hui

*In the process of talking with worldwide luxury brands, the Leasing team realised that the design of the stand-alone building at the intersection of West Nanjing Road and Shimen Road No. 1 wasn't particularly suitable. These brands understood that their customers mostly arrived in private cars, and demanded an uninterrupted shopping experience. However, due to the proximity of Metro Line 2, underground parking was not an option. This also prompted us to look at other types of customers.*

*Starbucks originally planned to set up a 300-square-metre flagship store inside the shopping mall. With the help and encouragement of multiple parties, the company eventually decided to use HKRI Taikoo Hui to introduce its "Roastery" concept to the China market. The Starbucks Reserve® Shanghai Roastery isn't an "anchor store" in the traditional sense. It is a very interesting "first store" and was the biggest in the world at the time.*

　　店铺变小，品牌变多，商业组合的更迭速度也会变快。针对几处顶级品牌都心仪的优质点位，兴业太古汇最终决定大胆将其"留白"，用作快闪店和展览活动空间；过去签约就落定三年乃至更久的品牌门店租约，也变得灵活起来，可根据运营数据反映的情况，随时调整更换。

　　在这个思路下，某些先前困扰招商团队的问题，也因此迎刃而解。比如，这家购物中心需要一个什么样的"主力店"？

Smaller stores mean more stores, which also speeds up changes in the business mix. HKRI Taikoo Hui took the bold step of leaving several prime locations favoured by upscale brands empty, so they could be used for pop-up shops and exhibitions. Property leases, which in the past were for at least three years, also became flexible, and could be adjusted at any time according to business operations.

This concept helped the Leasing team to resolve other issues, such as what sort of "anchor stores" does this shopping centre need?

一座总面积超过2,700平方米、集咖啡烘焙、存储、包装、饮品生产、周边零售等所有环节于一体的超大"星巴克"，某种程度上说要比一个"重奢品牌"的门面有更强的"吸睛"能力。根据品牌自身的规划，这样的星巴克臻选®烘焙工坊未来只会出现在全球的20至30个核心城市。它们也代表了星巴克对于全球咖啡饮品及零售市场的终极蓝图。

为保证这一项目的成功落地，兴业太古汇团队多次与品牌方共同深化具体的内部动线、大型设施和设计需求，一起研究符合中国消费者未来需求的"新零售"解决方案。

2017年12月6日一早，这家被星巴克创始人舒尔茨称为"咖啡奇幻乐园"的超大门店，面向石门一路的厚重木门终于缓缓开启。无数消费者在畅游星巴克臻选®上海烘焙工坊的过程中，真正理解了咖啡文化的魅力，也对承载它的兴业太古汇有了更浓厚的兴趣。

The massive Starbucks location, with a total floor area of more than 2,700 square metres, integrates coffee roasting, storage, packaging, beverage production, and the retailing of related products. Because of its exclusivity, its attraction is even more powerful than a super luxury brand. Starbucks plans to launch no more than 30 Reserve® Roasteries in key cities around the world.

The HKRI Taikoo Hui team worked closely with Starbucks to ensure the success of the project. This involved delving deeply into details, such as design requirements, equipment needs and customer flow. They also conducted research into "new retail" solutions aimed at meeting future demands from Chinese consumers.

On the morning of 6 December 2017, this massive store's elegant, solid wooden door facing onto Shimen Road No. 1 slowly opened. Starbucks' founder, Howard Schultz, called it a "coffee wonderland". As consumers toured the premises, they began to appreciate coffee and Starbucks' culture much more and develop an even deeper interest in HKRI Taikoo Hui.

5-7
犹如"咖啡奇幻乐园"的星巴克臻选®上海烘焙工坊
Starbucks Reserve® Shanghai
Roastery: An immersive
"coffee wonderland"

5-8
2017年12月6日,星巴克臻选®上海烘焙工坊开门营业,吸引广大消费者关注
The opening of the Starbucks
Reserve® Shanghai Roastery on 6
December 2017, which attracted
tens of thousands of consumers

# 〔二〕　静：居心之所

## *Serenity: A Home for the Heart*

　　中国城市对于顶级酒店管理品牌的认知，几乎与整个商业社会的开放高度同步。作为上海最成功的商务区域之一，南京西路商圈自1990年代后期，就成为高星级外资酒店项目的聚集地。从昔日明星云集的四季酒店、曾是城市天际线的波特曼丽思卡尔顿、中国第一家全外资五星级的希尔顿，再到如今正在重装换新的锦沧文华，不一而足。

　　自2002年开始，上海又迅速发展成了著名的精品酒店试验场。行业调研表明，在目前全国范围内知名的精品酒店项目中，上海独占其中的1/5；高峰期平均每年都有三至四家新的精品酒店开业。

　　在喧闹的商业综合体中配置一座优质的酒店，常常能在以商场和写字楼为绝对重心的项目内，形成自然、舒适、静谧的"缓冲地带"。它的作用绝不仅局限于满足外来消费者和商旅客户的短期住宿需求，更可被视作整个项目体在品味、风格、细节把控和服务能力上的集中体现。

The ability of Chinese cities to accommodate upscale hotels is linked closely to their innate business sense and overall openness. As one of the most successful business districts in Shanghai, the West Nanjing Road area has been a hotbed of overseas hospitality industry investment since the late 1990s. This includes the former Four Seasons Hotel, which had been visited by many celebrities; the Portman Ritz-Carlton, which was once the most prominent edifice in the city's skyline; the Hilton, China's first fully foreign-owned five-star hotel; the JC Mandarin Hotel, which is under renovation, and many more.

Since 2002, Shanghai has seen an explosion of boutique hotels. Industry research suggests that Shanghai is now home to one-fifth of China's boutique hotels. On average, 3 to 4 new luxury boutique hotels open each year in Shanghai alone.

A top-quality hotel in a vibrant commercial complex can create a pleasant and naturally quiet "buffer zone". However, a hotel's utility is certainly not limited to satisfying the short-term accommodation needs of travellers. It can also be seen as an indicator of the entire project's taste, style, eye for detail and service quality.

As a very hands-on person who travels year-round on business, Victor Cha has developed a deep understanding of what makes a quality hotel. However, he notes that a lack of relevant experience can make selecting optimal hotel partners a daunting task for many developers. Creating a distinguishably stylish boutique hotel brand is equally difficult.

Fortunately, the two main owners of HKRI Taikoo Hui – HKR International and Swire Properties – have a wealth of relevant experience. It was really just a matter of waiting for ideas to collide and spark something amazing.

In the 1990s, the success and expansion of its Hong Kong flagship, Discovery Bay, introduced HKR International to a new investment area with strong growth potential: quality hotel brands and vacation estates. Its luxury residential buildings in Tokyo, and hotel projects in Thailand, have been praised by customers for their high standards and outstanding quality.

亲力亲为、常年出差的查懋成，深谙优质酒店项目的商业价值。但如何挑选优秀的酒店合作伙伴，乃至从零开始、打造出浓郁风格的自有精品酒店品牌，对于未有相关产业布局和经验的开发商而言，常是个难题。

所幸在兴业太古汇这一项目中，香港兴业国际及太古地产两大股东都有相关经验，只待灵感碰撞爆发之时。

在 1990 年代，愉景湾项目进入稳定运营和后续扩展阶段，香港兴业国际在亚洲市场上找到的下一个潜在增长型业务，即是投资各类优质的酒店品牌和度假物业。位于日本东京的豪华住宅以及在泰国市场开业的酒店项目，都受到对生活品质要求严苛的客户赞许。

5-9
香港愉景湾酒店海滨礼堂
The Pavilion at the Auberge Discovery Bay Hong Kong

5-10
位于泰国曼谷的豪华公寓
The Sukhothai Residences in Bangkok

5 - 11
曼谷素凯泰酒店内部设计与细节
The Sukhothai Bangkok features
exquisite interior design

5 - 12
曼谷素凯泰酒店
The Sukhothai Bangkok

　　其中，一个名为"Sukhothai（素凯泰）"的精品酒店品牌，更是香港兴业国际在泰国市场自行开发的"掌上明珠"。

　　与上海类似，泰国首都曼谷近年来亦是亚洲炙手可热的精品酒店必争之地。开业于1991年的曼谷素凯泰酒店，凭借其淡雅脱俗的泰式设计风格，至今仍被公认为当地最值得到访的豪华酒店之一。

The Sukhothai hotel brand is a treasured pearl for HKR International in the Thai market.

Like Shanghai, Bangkok has become an Asian hotspot for boutique luxury hotels. Opened in 1991, The Sukhothai Bangkok is still considered a top-notch luxury hotel, featuring elegant and cultured Thai-style design.

### 曼谷素凯泰酒店："幸福之始"

　　Sukhothai 是泰国历史上首个王朝之名，泰文原意为"幸福之始"。该王朝处于泰国发展历史上的黄金时期，对泰国文化有着深远的影响。香港兴业国际以"Sukhothai"为酒店项目命名，亦是希望将泰国的建筑、艺术及文化的精髓带给每一位宾客。

　　因安缦酒店成名的 Kerry Hill 和 Edward Tuttle 两位设计师，在这一酒店各处装点了大量水元素：仿造泰国皇宫护城河而建的如镜池水，优美的花园和水景别具禅意；再加上融合古典泰国皇室风格的艺术品和古董，以及现代摩登的雕塑和建筑，使其成为曼谷市中心令人难忘的花园天堂，收割了《漫旅 Travel+Leisure》2020 世界旅行奖曼谷最佳城市酒店的冠军宝座，在亚洲和全球酒店排名中，分列第四名和第 37 位。

## The Sukhothai Bangkok: "Dawn of Happiness"

*Sukhothai was the name of the old Thai kingdom. Its original meaning is "the dawn of happiness". The Sukhothai period is often seen as a golden time in Thailand's history, and it has profoundly influenced Thai culture. HKR International named its hotel project "Sukhothai" to pay homage to Thai architecture, art, and culture.*

*Kerry Hill and Edward Tuttle, two designers famous for their work on the Aman Resorts, have adorned this hotel with countless water elements. The mirror-like effect is intended to be reminiscent of the moat at the Thai Royal Grand Palace, with beautiful gardens and water scenery creating a Zen-like atmosphere. With classical royal-style, Thai artworks and antiques, as well as modern sculptures, the hotel has become an unforgettable oasis in Bangkok's city centre. It is ranked the Best City Hotel in Bangkok, the 4th in Asia and the 37th in the world by Travel + Leisure World's Best Awards 2020.*

5-13
上海素凯泰酒店
The Sukhothai Shanghai

自曼谷 Sukhothai 项目大获成功之后，香港兴业国际一直在寻找将这一精品酒店品牌推广至更大市场的机遇。在 2017 年正式开业的兴业太古汇项目南侧，其品牌姐妹店"上海素凯泰酒店"终获落地。

上海素凯泰酒店承袭了 Sukhothai 品牌对于设计风格、艺术元素和服务细节的重视，有着"繁华闹市中的唯美桃源"之称，并在开业第一年就斩获了包括"2019 年悦游金榜中国酒店 Top 10"在内的多个行业大奖。

5-14
上海素凯泰酒店店内部设计与细节
Exceptional interior design and attention
to detail defines The Sukhothai Shanghai

Following the success of The Sukhothai Bangkok, HKR International was looking for an opportunity to expand the brand into other markets. It realised its ambition when it created a sister hotel, The Sukhothai Shanghai, located on the south side of the HKRI Taikoo Hui project, which officially opened in 2017.

The Sukhothai Shanghai reflects the original Sukhothai brand's focus on design styles, artistic elements, and service details. It is designed to be "an elaborate haven in the centre of bustle". In its first year of operation, it won several industry awards, including being named in the Condé Nast Traveler Gold list 2019 as one of China's Top 10 Hotels.

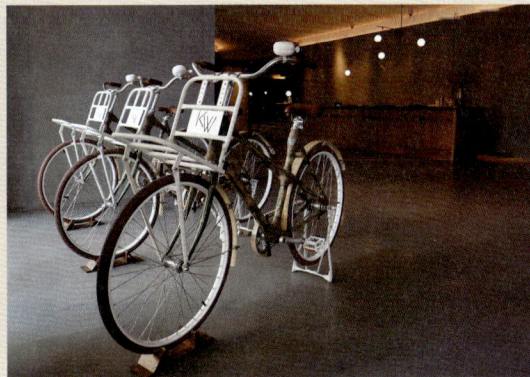

**李泓熙** 香港兴业国际集团酒店业务行政副总裁

　　上海素凯泰酒店是专为繁忙的现代都市人设计的酒店。客人不分国籍、年龄，但都有独特的生活品味。他们大多崇尚别具一格的设计风格和舒适自然的生活方式；其中也不乏工作节奏紧凑的职场人士，他们思想积极、乐观，懂得并享受生活，欣赏不同的群体、场所和体验，并期望精致贴心的服务。无论是在商务还是休闲旅行中，他们会在寻求灵感和放松的同时，探索城市的脉搏。

## IVAN LEE

Executive Vice President of Hospitality Operations, HKR International

*The Sukhothai Shanghai is specifically designed for today's busy urbanites. Its guests vary by nationality and age, and are common only in their uniqueness. Most of them appreciate classy design and a comfortable and natural lifestyle. Some of them are working people on tight schedules. They have a proactive and optimistic mindset; they know about life and how to enjoy it. They are able to admire different people, places, and experiences, and they expect sophisticated and thoughtful services. Whether travelling for business or leisure, they explore the pulse of the city as they search for inspiration and relaxation.*

　　对于在都市内寻找悠然之所的酒店爱好者而言，兴业太古汇的回馈不仅限于上海素凯泰酒店。在项目的北侧，另有两栋外立面风格低调、进门后却呈现复古美感的酒店及公寓式酒店，由太古酒店集团管理。这两栋建筑共用一个品牌"镛舍"。这一名称的出处，即是取自项目旧址大中里"中"字的历史余韵。

For hotel enthusiasts looking for "a place apart" in Shanghai, HKRI Taikoo Hui's offering doesn't stop at The Sukhothai Shanghai. On the northern side of the project stand two buildings with modest exteriors. However, behind the doors, their interiors exhibit a beautiful antique aesthetic. These are a hotel and a serviced apartment managed by Swire Properties under the "The Middle House" brand. The Middle House is derived from the Chinese character "中 (Zhōng)" – meaning middle – which is part of the location's old name, Dazhongli.

5-15
镛舍酒店大堂
**The lobby at The Middle House**

**霍柯南** 太古酒店集团营业及分销总监

"镛舍"是太古酒店旗下"居舍系列"之最新一员。"居舍系列"锐意脱离传统奢华和商务酒店的套路，为消费者创造不一样的选择，填补现有酒店未能满足的需要，符合追求新一代奢华观念的要求。我们致力通过舒适宽敞的房间、精心细致的设计、活泼灵动的团队、个性化的贴心服务，为客户营造一个像"家"一般的理想居停。"镛舍"蕴含上海现代化的精神面貌，提供当代和传统交融的生活神髓。

## MICHAEL FAULKNER
### Head of Sales and Distribution, Swire Hotels

*The Middle House is part of our House Collective brand. The brand steps away from the traditional notions of luxury and business hotels, offering another option to those that do not fit or relate to existing offerings and are seeking a new concept of luxury. For these people, we strive to provide a place they can call home, from our spacious and thoughtfully designed rooms to our personalised service, delivered by our fun and spontaneous team members. The Middle House captures the spirit of modern-day Shanghai, offering a way of being that is both contemporary and classic.*

在推出镛舍之前，太古酒店已在大中华区成功打造两个屡获赞誉的酒店品牌，旗下拥有多个酒店项目。居舍系列中的酒店各具特色，包括北京的瑜舍、成都的博舍和香港的奕居。太古酒店旗下还有两家时尚生活品牌酒店——东隅。每一家都独一无二，唯一不变的是独具匠心的美学设计和卓越服务。

Before it launched The Middle House, Swire Hotels already had several hotel projects under two award winning brands in Greater China. These are The House Collective of highly individual hotels, which includes The Opposite House in Beijing, The Temple House in Chengdu, and The Upper House in Hong Kong. It also includes two EAST branded lifestyle hotels. Each of these hotels are exceptionally unique yet joined by a shared appreciation for aesthetics and service excellence.

5-16
**镛舍酒店客房**
**Guest room at The Middle House**

5-17
**镛舍糅合了意大利风格、本土元素与当代美学**
**The Middle House adopts an Italian vision blended with a local twist and modern aesthetic**

# {三}

# 创：乐活无界

## *Creativity: LOHAS Has No Boundaries*

　　上海商业市场的"寸土寸金"，不仅仅适用于零售和酒店空间，亦适用于每天让都市白领停留八小时乃至更久的办公空间。以陆家嘴、南京西路等为代表的顶级"CBD"，往往又以每年少量的新增供应、高出新一线城市近一倍的租金水平以及超低的区域空置率，交叉掌控着"上海最贵商圈"的称号。

　　伴随全球实体经济行业的业绩震荡、数字化转型等市场变化，一度极为紧俏的上海核心商圈供应，也曾出现许多租户外迁的案例：原先位于核心商务区的罗氏、默沙东等药企分别迁到了漕河泾和闵行；WPP等原先最讲究"跟客户在一起"的广告公司，则从市中心的静安搬到了火车站附近的"新静安"。

In Shanghai's red-hot property market, an inch of land is often said to be worth an ounce of gold. This applies not only to retail and hotel spaces, but also to offices, where white-collar employees spend at least 40 hours a week. The upscale CBD, namely Lujiazui and West Nanjing Road, holds the title as Shanghai's most expensive business district. Limited supply has seen the average rental rate rise to nearly double that of any first-tier city, and vacancy rates are low.

However, in recent years global and local market fluctuations have seen leases in Shanghai's CBD move away. Pharmaceutical companies like Roche and MSD have moved to Caohejing and Minhang. WPP and other advertising companies that always promoted "being close to clients", have moved from Jing'an in the city centre to the "New Jing'an" near the train station.

驱动上述这些大公司行动的，不只是来自市场和报表的直接财务压力，年龄与观念都越来越年轻的主力员工需求，亦是参考因素。他们既是企业内的重要生产者，也是全社会的关键消费者。日常工作与生活间越来越模糊的界线，也会令他们质疑，自己的办公空间是否真正做到了"以人为本"。

作为兴业太古汇第一任 CEO，邓满华在项目建设竣工前，很早就启动了招租工作。

2016 年年底至 2017 年年中，兴业太古汇项目内的两栋超甲级写字楼"香港兴业中心"一座及二座先后投入运营，一口气在上海市中心释放了超过 17 万平方米的顶级办公空间。

由于项目本身在设计、建造之处的高品质以及贴近市场承租能力的租赁策略，一座写字楼在取得竣工备案时，整体出租率已达 52%，多家世界 500 强企业以及行业顶尖知名公司确定入驻；到 2019 年第一季度，两栋写字楼的总出租率已经稳定在 97% 以上，可以说是"一位难求"。

The drivers aren't purely financial. The needs of workforces, which are becoming younger in terms of age and attitude, is also a critical factor. Youngsters are now much more than key contributors within a company – they are also crucial consumers in the economy. In addition, the line between work and personal life is becoming increasingly blurred, which makes people question whether their office environment is truly people-oriented.

As the first CEO of HKRI Taikoo Hui, Jackie Tang started the work of leasing out space before construction was complete.

Between the end of 2016 and mid-2017, HKRI Taikoo Hui's two grade-A office towers – HKRI Centre 1 and 2 – opened amidst much fanfare. More than 170,000 square metres of top-grade office space in Shanghai's city centre were made available all at once.

The project's high-quality design, prime location, and a leasing strategy aligned closely with the market, contributed to a high occupancy rate of 52% by the time the first office building underwent its final construction inspection. Many Fortune Global 500 firms and other well-known companies confirmed their intention to move in. By the first quarter of 2019, the overall occupancy rate had exceeded 97%.

5-18
**香港兴业中心写字楼**
**HKRI Centre office towers**

针对灵活办公、开放空间等市场上讨论热度极高的办公楼变革话题，兴业太古汇也抱持开放态度。例如，从南京西路上另一超甲级写字楼搬迁而来的仲量联行，即在自己的办公空间里试行了"联合办公"的理念，减少固定工位、放大开放空间，鼓励工作时间的协作、分享、共赢，以增强公司的整体开放性、创造性。

值得一提的是，至 2019 年 5 月，兴业太古汇项目内所有新建建筑均获得了由美国绿色建筑委员会颁发的 LEED（Leadership in Energy and Environmental Design）认证。其中，香港兴业中心一座、二座更是获得了 LEED 体系内最高的"铂金级"认证。这可谓是对兴业太古汇在新一代办公体验与环境影响控制上的"双重"认可。

让人兴奋的是，凭借在专业性、团队合作、创新与技术、成果及成就等四个维度的卓越表现，兴业太古汇于 2020 年再下一城，荣膺英国皇家特许测量师学会评选的"中国年度商业地产项目"。

HKRI Taikoo Hui is keeping an open mind about office transformation. For example, JLL, a firm that moved in from another grade-A office building on West Nanjing Road, has experimented with the concept of "co-working" within its own office space. By reducing fixed workstations, enlarging open spaces, as well as promoting collaboration and sharing, it encourages people to create mutually beneficial situations that enhance the firm's overall openness and creativity.

It is worth mentioning that, by May 2019, all of the newly constructed buildings in HKRI Taikoo Hui had been awarded Leadership in Energy and Environmental Design (LEED) certification by the U.S. Green Building Council. HKRI Centre One and Two also won the "platinum" certification, the highest-level within the LEED system. This represents a double recognition for HKRI Taikoo Hui in creating next-generation office experiences with minimal environmental impact.

Professionalism, teamwork, innovation and technology as well as results and achievements have also earned HKRI Taikoo Hui the "Commercial Project of the Year" in the RICS Awards 2020 China by the Royal Institution of Chartered Surveyors.

5-19
日常忙碌的写字楼大堂
The lobby of the busy office towers on a regular day

5-20
香港兴业中心写字楼获美国绿色建筑委员会颁发的 LEED 铂金级认证
HKRI Centre One and Two achieved LEED Platinum certification by the U.S. Green Building Council

# 〔四〕　变：止于至善

## *Change: The Relentless Pursuit of Perfection*

世上哪有完全无拘无束的创新者。在框架、条件乃至运气的重重制约下推动发展，才是常态。

对于兴业太古汇而言，不断变化的商业潮流、消费者需求和地产行业自身的破局难度，始终没有动摇兴业太古汇作为上海新一代潮流地标的决心。而在背后支撑这些创新理念乃至突破制度天花板的，正是一股"止于至善"的精神。

以星巴克臻选®上海烘焙工坊这一项目为例，尽管有着绝佳的设计方案和商业预设，但想要在短时间内完成项目落地，实际面临着一系列体制层面的限制。

Completely unrestrained innovators don't exist. In most cases, prevailing circumstances, and even luck all play a role.

Ever-changing business trends, consumer demands, and the real estate industry's inherent resistance to innovation did not shake HKRI Taikoo Hui's determination to become a next-generation landmark in Shanghai. Its ideas, and efforts to break through the "institutional ceiling" in the back-end, are supported by a spirited pursuit of perfection.

Consider the Starbucks Reserve® Shanghai Roastery case as an example. Despite excellent design plans and a sound commercial set-up, it faced a series of regulatory restrictions that threatened to delay its opening.

5-21
体验性与观赏性俱佳的咖啡豆烘焙业态
Roasting coffee beans offers great
experiential value

比如，体验性与观赏性俱佳的咖啡豆烘焙业态，此前在市政规范中，并不允许以半开放空间的形式出现在咖啡馆内；位于门店视线中心、刻满文字印章的巨型铜罐，按照海关要求，需要破开罐体或是耗费巨资复制一套以用于检测。若是品牌方、项目方、政府及有关机构之间缺乏紧密配合和协商推进的眼光、共识与机制，星巴克臻选®烘焙工坊在全球落地的第二站，可能就不会是上海。

For example, although watching coffee beans being roasted can be a great experience for customers, Shanghai municipal government regulations forbade it being conducted in a semi-open space like a café. In addition, the centre of the store featured a copper cask adorned with engravings of Chinese characters. To meet customs requirements, the cask, or an identical replica, had to be provided for destructive testing – an expensive proposition. With close cooperation and consensus among Starbucks, HKRI Taikoo Hui, the municipal government, and relevant organisations, these obstacles were overcome, and Shanghai became the second city in the world to host a Starbucks Reserve® Roastery.

兴业太古汇运营团队也曾为购物中心另一个租户"法国娇兰"的新概念精品香水店出谋划策。

入驻兴业太古汇时，诞生于1828年的娇兰曾想在这里完美复刻法国巴黎"娇兰之家"的装修风格及特色服务，其中一项就是由顾客挑选喜爱的香水和彩色蜂印瓶，实现个性化挑香选瓶服务。但在国内，由于监管法规存在空白或需创新等原因，顾客只能在门店购买原装进口香水，无法实现新型的香水购买体验。

目前，在各级政府部门、行业协会和试点企业的共同努力下，项目已经争取到了相关部门支持，有待落地实施。顺应消费升级的发展趋势，今后将会涌现更多创新商业服务新模式。

在兴业太古汇的购物中心、写字楼和酒店空间内，这样因需进行的协调、改进和适应几乎每日都在进行。配合日程表已经近乎排满的品牌快闪店、都市市集、展览演出等推广活动，从商场预开业时算起，运营超过三年的兴业太古汇，时常让人有"常逛常新"之感。

**杜一莉**　香港兴业国际集团租务及管理总经理
兴业太古汇联席总经理

很多品牌在兴业太古汇的落地，背后都是不断协调、磨合的成果。我们不希望品牌只是抱持着"多开一家店"的心态进驻，而是真正做出有特色、不一样的品牌概念店。我们的工作正是全面配合，促成更多具创新意义的新零售消费体验。

## SUSAN DU
General Manager of Leasing and Management at HKR International
Joint General Manager of HKRI Taikoo Hui

*Attracting so many brands to set up at HKRI Taikoo Hui has been the result of constant behind-the-scenes and go-the-extra-mile negotiation and coordination. We don't want brands to come in with the sole intention of "opening one more store." Instead, we want them to develop a truly unique and different concept store. Our job is to cooperate in all aspects, creating more innovative retail experiences.*

The HKRI Taikoo Hui Leasing team worked on ideas for another lessee at the shopping centre – Guerlain – which developed a new-concept luxury perfume store.

Guerlain was established in 1828. When it moved into HKRI Taikoo Hui, it initially intended to replicate the decorative style and special services of "The House of Guerlain" in Paris. One of these special services was to offer The Bee Bottle selection, allowing customers to match the fragrance they prefer with the bottle design they like. Due to regulatory restrictions in mainland China, customers were only allowed to buy original imported bottles of perfume, making the creation of a brand-new perfume purchasing experience impossible to achieve.

Government departments, industry associations and pioneering enterprises are now trying their best to gain support from the nation's industry authorities, in the hope of implementing plans like Guerlain's as soon as possible to satisfy demand for innovative new service models.

Such negotiations, improvements, and adaptations take place almost every day all over the HKRI Taikoo Hui shopping mall, in the office towers and in the hotels. In its third year, the mall's daily schedule is packed with branded pop-up stores, market bazaars, exhibitions, performances and other promotional events that make people feel that they will find something new every time they visit.

5-22
兴业太古汇丰富多彩的展览与活动全年不断
A wide range of exhibitions and events take place all year-round at HKRI Taikoo Hui

　　越来越多的消费者肯定了兴业太古汇"爱混敢嗲"的品牌定位：文化和时髦混搭，美味和品位融合；敢于冲破循规蹈矩，宣誓新潮格局；用全世界最好的一切，混搭出上海最独特的"嗲"。

Consumers are increasingly recognising HKRI Taikoo Hui's "Dare For More" brand positioning, where culture mixes with fashion, and delicacy blends with taste. By daring to break the rules and set new directions, it enables consumers to take the best things in the world and use them to create Shanghai's most unique brand.

**查懋成** 香港兴业国际集团副主席兼董事总经理

对我们而言，商业项目的提升空间是没有尽头的。因为项目进入某一个阶段，或是达到某一个目标，往往就是下一个阶段目标的开始，永远可以做得更好。很多人会将精力花在表面上、大家都能看得到的东西；但在看不见的部分，我们所能做的改进其实更多。

除了这些"看得见的美好"，兴业太古汇的运营团队，目前还在许多少有外人知晓的领域，对自己提出更高的要求。

As well as delivering these highly visible achievements, HKRI Taikoo Hui is working on many new ideas that most outsiders do not have the faintest inkling of.

After HKRI Taikoo Hui opened, whenever Victor Cha visited Shanghai on business, he would ask the project management team to show him some of the less glamourous parts of the project – logistics areas, the central control room, refrigeration plant rooms, and even the back kitchen and staff rest areas. Following that lead, one of the goals for the project team is to improve the management of HKRI Taikoo Hui's back-of-house operations.

Victor Cha believes it won't be long until these behind-the-scenes activities attract their own visitors – people from various specialist fields – who will visit them just like other people tour the public spaces of the shopping mall, office towers and hotels.

## VICTOR CHA
Deputy Chairman and Managing Director of HKR International

*To us, business project improvement knows no bounds. When a project enters a certain stage or achieves a particular goal, that is usually the time to start the process of achieving the next goal, because we can always do better. Many people will put effort into things that everyone can see. But there are actually more improvements for us to make in areas that people can't see directly.*

兴业太古汇落成投入使用后，查懋成每次前来上海出差，都会要求项目管理团队带他去看整个项目的后勤区域、中央控制室、冷冻机房等等，甚至是酒店后勤厨房、员工的临时休息区。项目团队的日常工作目标之一，就是持续提升后勤空间的管理水准。

查懋成相信，兴业太古汇里这些"看不见的美好"，很快也能像购物中心、写字楼和酒店的公共空间一样，直接迎接各界参观。

232~233

The Next Chapter

# WE CREATE A
# LIFESTYLE

创造  品味生活

未终之章

在撰写本书的过程中，我们走访了众多与大中里和兴业太古汇结缘的人士，进行了广泛的调研，深入了解上海的过去、现在与未来和城市中的人们，收获了许多关于历史、关于付出、关于创造力以及关于生活本身的真知灼见。正是上述这些元素的不断交融和汇聚，塑造了上海这座城市的生活品味之源。

同时让人好奇的是，究竟是繁华都市的魅力，吸引和聚集着有识之士，还是人们期盼将城市建设为文化、商业或创意中心的雄心壮志，成就了一座又一座国际大都会？

对于上海而言，或许两者都有。但不可否认的是，当你徜徉在上海车水马龙的街道或狭窄的弄堂时，总会感到一种神奇的引力，仿佛脑海中有个坚定的声音在悄声说：不要轻易放弃梦想，必须砥砺前行，脚下的路将带你走向更美好的前方。

In writing this book, we interviewed a great many people and conducted extensive research. As well as helping us gain a deeper understanding of Shanghai's recent history, it taught us an incredible amount about the background, devotion and attitudes of the people who have brought this unique city to life.

However, it has left us wondering whether it is the world's great cities that attract such special people. Or, if the aspirations and ambitions of individuals who want to make their cities into centres of culture, commerce or creativity, puts them on the map.

In the case of Shanghai, it is probably a little of both. Nobody can deny the magical feeling one gets walking along its busy streets and narrow lanes. Or it might be the tiny voice you sometimes hear in the back of your mind, telling you not to be too quick to give up on your dreams, because they're the path to a better life.

6-1
兴业太古汇航拍
Aerial view of HKRI Taikoo Hui

　　无论哪一种说法更符合上海，有一点毋庸置疑：在过去的一个多世纪里，上海从未掩饰过它的雄心壮志。细细回溯历史，你会惊奇地发现，除了在特殊的动荡时期，上海从未失去其宝贵的城市精神，正是这种精神让人们创建美好未来的愿望真正成为可能。

　　道路两旁，公共大楼与私人宅邸、商业楼宇与住宅建筑竞相耸立，构成日新月异的城市景象。如今的上海，估计连 20 世纪初奠定城市格局的老一辈人都难以辨认。确实，城市彷佛在一夜间天翻地覆，若不是长居于此，即使是离开十年八载的人也会随时迷路。

　　然而，在生长发育并逐渐自我更新换代的过程中，适当的保育与传承、合理的兴替与活化、无可避免的拆迁和重建……这些有机结合，正是维持城市长久生命力的方程式——在新旧交融，更新不止的过程中得以不断升华，并与城市内核逐渐紧密相连，焕发出上海独特的魅力。

Whatever the answer, one thing is undeniable – over the course of more than a century, Shanghai has never concealed its ambitions. When you examine its history more closely, it is all the more astonishing that, despite periodic upheavals, Shanghai has never lost the extraordinary urban spirit that provides the kind of environment where building a better future is a genuine possibility.

What has changed tremendously is the mix of public and private, commercial and residential buildings that line the city's streets. Today's Shanghai would be unrecognisable to the residents who transformed its layout at the start of the last century. Indeed, even visitors familiar with the city of just a few decades ago, might be hard pressed to find their way around a metropolis that has undergone so many profound changes in such a short space of time.

Yet, it is this process of demolition and re-construction, combined with an eye for conserving, refurbishing and restoring some of the most exceptional historic structures, that has underpinned Shanghai's metamorphosis into one of the world's most iconic cities.

6-2
兴业太古汇 2019 圣诞装饰
Christmas decoration in
2019

## 幕后功臣

无论是外滩饱经沧桑又历久弥新的万国建筑群，还是不断刷新城市天际线的超高写字楼，抑或是魅力四射的现代化购物中心和层出不穷的精品酒店，这座城市的美随处可见。而那些贡献奇思妙想，让这一切成为可能的设计师和开发者们呢？遗憾的是，不少幕后功臣至今仍不为众人所知。

我们希望借本书来弥补这个遗憾，向那些为上海城市发展贡献了汗水、泪水与辛劳的机构和个人致敬。

商业世界为城市发展贡献了许多明亮与惊喜，继而为城市持续升华更多高品质的佳作和饶富品味的优质生活体验，它们的功勋值得抒写。兴业太古汇便是一个很好的例证。

## Recognising excellence

It is easy to admire historic buildings along The Bund, appreciate the magnificent new office buildings that have transformed the skyline, and enjoy the vibrant modern shopping centres and myriad boutique hotels that are popping up all over the town. But what about the achievements of the imaginative designers and developers who made it all happen? Sadly, the majority of them have gone unnoticed … at least until now.

We hope that this book will help to reverse that oversight, by recognising some of the sweat, tears and resources which many individuals and organisations have invested in creating outstanding developments.

Frankly, many of the brilliant ideas that have come from the world of business, and which are continuing to contribute tasteful, high-quality experiences to the city, deserve to be showcased - not only in Shanghai, but on the world stage. And that definitely includes HKRI Taikoo Hui.

## 着眼未来

上海仍在续写新的篇章。说起兴业太古汇的未来发展，香港兴业国际集团副主席兼董事总经理查懋成总是抱着一份审慎的乐观。

## Looking forward

Shanghai's story isn't over. In fact, whenever he talks about the future of HKRI Taikoo Hui, Victor Cha is always cautiously optimistic.

6 - 3
兴业太古汇的多彩活动营造活力社区
A mix of activities creates a vibrant community

他相信真正的行业领袖应当有能力，在不断变化的市场环境中，创造出独特的东西，独树一帜，无论是产品、业务还是生活方式，总能带来惊喜。作为一座城市心脏的综合商业体，兴业太古汇早已超越其商业职能，成为城市新景点。

2020 兴业太古汇新年美陈
New Year decorations at
HKRI Taikoo Hui

He is convinced that real industry leaders are those who can create something
unique – whether it's a product, a business or a lifestyle – in a changing
market environment. HKRI Taikoo Hui ticks all of those boxes and more.

查懋成坚信一个理念：企业不应将视野局限于自己的短期利益，而应当为社会作出更多贡献。例如，丰富人们的生活和工作，为城市注入更多活力。在过去的数十年里，他一直致力于践行这一理念，从香港大屿山畔的愉景湾，到上海市中心的兴业太古汇，初心不变。

香港兴业国际选择的不是易走的路。天道酬勤，在推陈出新（Pioneer）、尊人重土（Respect）、不同凡"想"（Innovation）、坚守诚信（Integrity）、倾心倾"诚"（Devotion）、止于至善（Excellence）——"PRI$^2$DE"——核心价值的驱动下，其在亚太地区取得的成就足以让人羡慕不已。而这一切的背后，香港兴业国际始终不忘初心，"真诚"与"尊重"的价值观最终收获的是永葆鲜活的骄傲和独树一帜的生活风格。

在这样的背景之下，兴业太古汇将继续立足过去、着眼未来，抓住新机遇，成为这座魅力之城品味生活的灯塔，带领千万人，共谱上海历史的崭新篇章。

正如上海这座城市一样，兴业太古汇蓄势待发，一切正是"未艾·方兴"之时。

The road that HKRI follows has never been an easy one. But, driven by its core values of Pioneer, Respect, Innovation, Integrity, Devotion and Excellence – PRI$^2$DE – it has created a track record of achievements across Asia Pacific that any developer would envy. And it has done so without compromising its principles of sincerity and respect.

Victor Cha believes that businesses should always look beyond their own short-, medium- and even long-term interests, and focus on the benefits they provide for society. Things like enriching the lives and work of people, and revitalising the city they are in. As the Deputy Chairman and Managing Director of HKRI, he has stuck to that philosophy for decades, from Discovery Bay on Hong Kong's Lantau Island, to HKRI Taikoo Hui in the heart of Shanghai.

Against that background, HKRI Taikoo Hui has every chance to open a new chapter in Shanghai's history by continuing to move forward, harnessing new opportunities, and being a beacon of tasteful living in the centre of this timeless metropolis.

Like the city in which it is located, HKRI Taikoo Hui is clearly on the rise.

俯瞰兴业太古汇
**Overlooking HKRI Taikoo Hui**

# 对城市的尊重
# 就是对自身的尊重

赵嘉

《第一财经》杂志总编

由于工作的原因，这两年我经常到上海出差，频率之高，让我对上海几乎不再有旅行者的新奇感。

取而代之的，是对这个南方城市的逐步熟悉，和一种介乎存在与不存在之间的眷恋。从酒店走到办公室需要十几分钟，我习惯穿一双轻便的鞋，在错落的小路间随意步行。早晨，便民菜场的生意正红火，周遭会飘来小馄饨和生煎包的香味，老弄堂门口常有艰难出行的家用汽车，公交车站儿位神色焦急的上班族不时拿起手机刷两下，我混在等待绿灯要过马路的人群里——尽管在我们北京人看来，马路窄小到也许没有必要设置红绿灯。

等过了马路，这个市井家常气息的上海便消失了。我们办公室附近，石门一路和威海路的结合地带，崛起一片新的商业区域，你很难用简洁的词汇来明确定义它：外饰精美的海派洋房"查公馆"，使人很想推开那扇紧闭的门进去一探究竟，同时，全球最大的星巴克臻选® 烘焙工坊为这里增添了时尚氛围，低调的上海素凯泰酒店矗立一角，再往里走，则是不动声色的镛舍酒店，旁边一个个动感雀跃的品牌门店，朝向一座购物中心延伸开去——这便是站在时代前端又嵌入历史栅格的兴业太古汇。

在香港兴业国际看来，这是一块历时15年方才建成的"南京西路商圈最后一块拼图"。兴业太古汇的前身为大中里，曾是上海最大的石库门建筑群之一，也曾是中国现代城市最早探索社区营造的区域之一，这奠定了整个街区的文化肌理。所谓最后一块拼图，只能以此为基础。

2002 年，香港兴业国际确定这个项目的时候，无法预料改造的具体难度。但能够肯定，香港兴业国际入场的时机恰逢其时，这一年，是中国正式加入 WTO 世贸组织的第一年，大部分城市进入经济快速增长的轨道，上海全年 GDP 达到 5,741 亿元，同比增长 10.19%。在此后将近十年的时间里，几乎每个中国城市都在拼命建造更高的建筑，以直观而迅速的方式表达对繁荣、财富，以及现代生活方式的渴望。

高层商品房、现代居住小区、新的商圈、地铁，人们把城市变成尘土飞扬的工地，急于改变它们的面貌。最常见的改变方法，便是拆除原有的老旧建筑，按新的设想修建理想之城。拆旧建新的思路就此贯穿了此后数十年的中国城市建设。

承接大中里地块的开发责任后，摆在香港兴业国际面前是机会，同时也成了一个考验：到底该如何面对渗透肌理的城市传统，保留还是推倒重来？如果保留，该以何种方式？

读完这本书之后，最令我印象深刻的，恰是香港兴业国际在处理新旧这对矛盾过程中的细节。2010 年 1 月 26 日，位于大中里地区的百年校舍民立中学以每分钟两厘米的速度，开启了历时 13 天，总长 57.3 米的"旅程"。工程团队实时监测移位过程，民立中学高了 40 厘米，在钢筋混凝土的基底上等待重生。

墙面、烟囱、山花、门窗、线条，残破的细部特征在"修旧如旧"的思路下被修复，这座宅院也向公众完美诠释了民国建筑风格的美感——它被命名为"查公馆"，以纪念查济民先生。正是通过这样的细节修整，香港兴业国际将上海的城市建筑传统延续下来。

我们建造城市，是为了更好的生活，而城市的伟大也早已超越了个体生命。城市，是人类生活的聚集地，也是人类文明天然的博物馆。它忠实地记录了我们以往生活的痕迹，也见证了曾经的悲喜。某种意义上，对于城市的尊重，也是对于我们自身的尊重。

写于 2020 年 9 月

# Respecting a City is
# Respecting Ourselves

**ZHAO JIA**

*Editor in Chief, YiMagazine*

In the past two years, I have made a lot of business trips to Shanghai. In fact, they were so frequent that I stopped viewing Shanghai with the usual curiosity of a traveller.

What replaced this curiosity was a gradual familiarity with the city and a kind of attachment. It takes me less than twenty minutes to walk from my hotel to the office. And I have developed a habit of wearing light shoes and sauntering around the streets of Shanghai. The food market is always busy in the morning, and the delicious scent of wonton and pan-fried buns spreads from the surrounding areas. Private cars are often seen having difficulty getting out of traditional housing estates. A few nervous-looking office workers at the bus station swipe their phones from time to time. I am part of a crowd that waits for a green light to cross the road.

Old Shanghai, with its quaint hometown atmosphere, disappears after crossing the road. A new swath of commercial property was built near our office at the intersection of Shimen Road No. 1 and Weihai Road. It is difficult to describe this area in simple words: The grand western-style "Cha House" has a beautiful external facade that makes you want to open the door and explore, while the largest Starbucks Reserve® Roastery in the world injects a sense of fashion into the area, and The Sukhothai Shanghai stands in one corner. Further inside lies The Middle House. A series of dynamic brand stores stand by its side, and extend towards a shopping mall. This is HKRI Taikoo Hui, a place at the forefront of the modern era, yet still embedded in the heritage of history.

The HKRI Taikoo Hui project was the last jigsaw piece in the West Nanjing Road business district puzzle, and it took 15 years to complete. Formerly known as Dazhongli, it was one of the largest clusters of Shikumen buildings in Shanghai, and one of the first areas in a modern Chinese city to explore the concept of community building. Its heritage determined the cultural landscape of the entire community.

When HKR International confirmed the project in 2002, nobody could have foreseen the difficulties in development. What we could be sure of was that HKRI entered the market at the perfect time. 2002 marked the year of China's entry into the WTO, and rapid growth had begun in most cities. Shanghai's annual GDP reached RMB 574.1 billion and grew by 10.19% from the previous year. For nearly ten years thereafter, almost all Chinese cities raced to build taller buildings and adopt new ways to express their thirst for prosperity, wealth and a modern lifestyle.

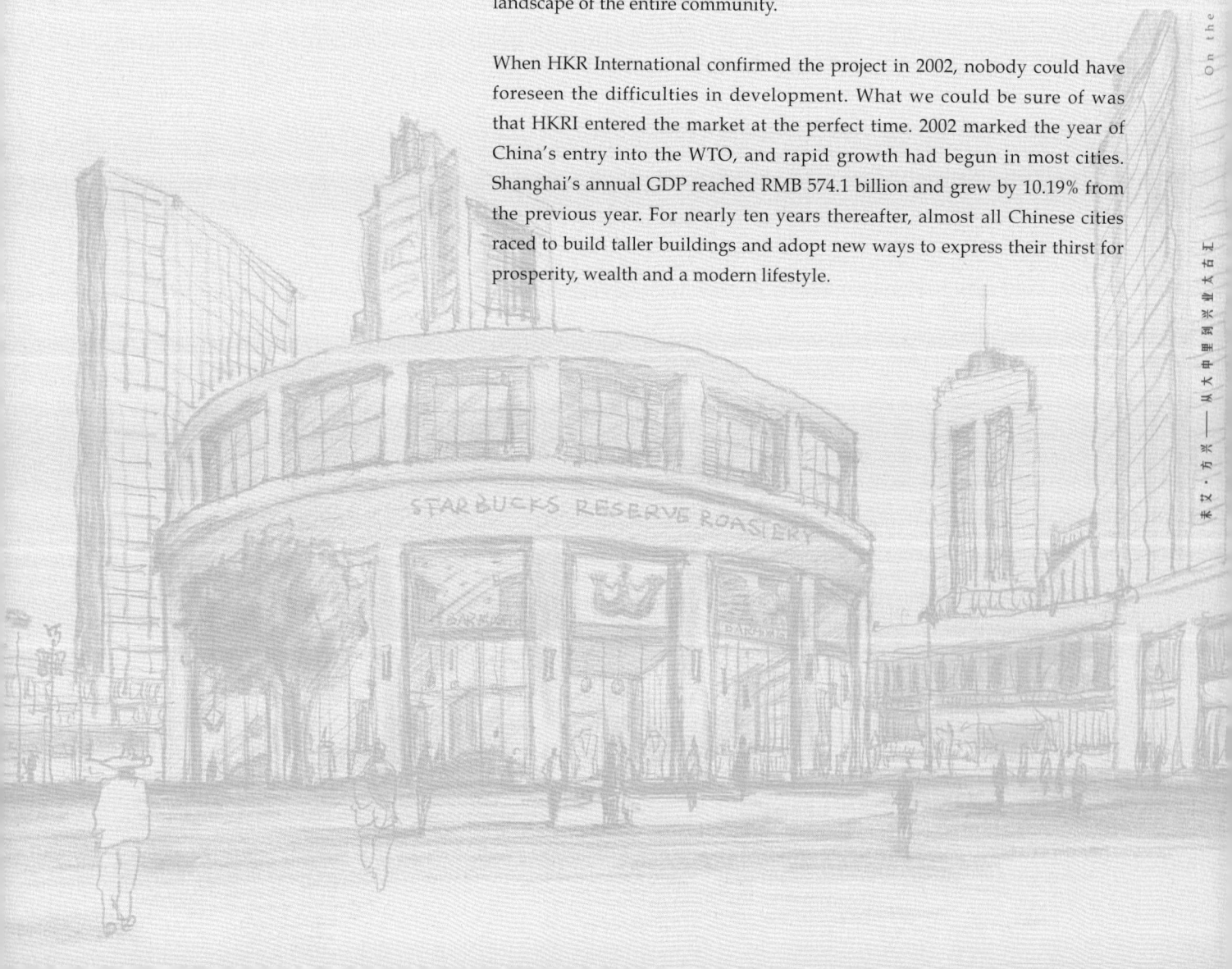

With high-rise residential buildings, modern communities, new commercial districts, and subways, people transformed the city into a dusty construction site as they rushed to change its appearance. The common method of change was to demolish old buildings and build an ideal city based on new concepts. It became a popular way for urban construction in China for decades to come.

The opportunity presented to HKRI also became a challenge. It tested the company's ability to handle urban traditions that had been thoroughly embedded into the city, and forced them to decide whether to keep or rebuild them. And, if they were to be kept, how should it be done?

After reading this book, what impressed me the most was how HKRI responded to the conflicts between new and old. On 26 January 2010, Dazhongli's old Building No. 4 of Minli School began its 13-day and 57.3-metre "journey" at a speed of 2 centimetres per minute. The construction team monitored the relocation process in real-time and even elevated the structure by 40 centimetres onto a solid, reinforced concrete foundation for its rebirth.

The walls, chimneys, bargeboards, doors, windows, contours, and other broken details and features were restored to their original state. The residence became the perfect exemplification of Republican-era architectural styles. It was renamed "Cha House" in memory of Dr. Cha Chi-ming. Through these details, HKRI passed down Shanghai's urban architectural traditions.

We create cities to enjoy better lives, and the longevity of great cities has long surpassed the lifespan of individuals. Cities are where humans congregate, and cities are also natural museums of human civilisation. They faithfully record traces of our lives and bear witness to our joy and sorrow. In a way, respecting a city is respecting ourselves.

Written in September 2020

# 心怀感恩·志存高远

邓 满 华

香港兴业国际集团执行董事
兴业太古汇首任 CEO

20 世纪 80 年代初，因缘际遇，我加入了香港兴业，参与开发位于香港大屿山东北侧的愉景湾项目。彼时，这座占地 650 公顷的亚洲环保小镇初现雏形，一如当时所料，这里成为我之后几十年奋斗的中心。其实，我与愉景湾的缘分更早于此。从香港大学建筑系毕业后，我进入一家建筑师事务所，第一个参与的项目就是愉景湾。

当愉景湾奠定亚洲环保小镇标杆地位时，集团开始转战上海。2002 年除夕，查懋成先生代表集团与上海市静安区政府签约，正式拿下南京西路大中里黄金地块的使用权，由那一天开始，我工作的重心便由香港转移到了上海，开启与这座城市的不解之缘。

21 世纪伊始，中国内地大兴土木，城市建设风风火火，商业经济高速腾飞。香港兴业国际拿下这块占地 62,800 平方米的地块，并不仅仅出于投资回报的考虑，更是怀抱热血雄心，矢志在中国经济的火车头——上海这块热土上再创一个堪与愉景湾媲美的经典传奇。

没想到的是，原先估量在三至五年内建成的商住混合地产项目，却历经了 15 年的耕耘，成为商业综合体。过程中，我们与这片土地建立了深厚的感情，践行了集团对内地市场的长期承诺。

回望十余年的开发与建设，集团及整个团队经历无数挑战，投入大量心血，一切历历在目，点滴在心头。

2003 年，非典来袭，人心惶惶，项目动迁工作一波三折。面对这样的危机，集团坚持"站得高一点、眼光远一点"，以耐心和细致应对。

2006 年，考虑到大中里地块对上海市整体发展的价值与长远的社会效益，查懋成先生主动提出将迅速回笼资金的住宅规划变更为纯商业用途，提振南京西路商圈的商业能级。此后，我们邀请有共同理念的太古地产加入，共同开发，共同运营，强强联合。作为项目的首任 CEO，个人肩负各方赋予的信任和期望，深感任重道远。

2008 年，全球金融海啸来袭，但这没有动摇我们的决心，集团全力以赴推进大中里项目的整体规划。

2010 年，项目内的百年建筑"民立中学 4 号楼"移位 57 米，启动大型修缮和保育工作，并命名为"查公馆"，借以传承集团创始人查济民博士的家国情怀，并使它在恢复昔日光彩的同时焕发新生。

2012 年，排除万难的动迁工作终告完成，项目开始施工。

至今仍让我深深怀念的是整个项目团队的合作精神。成员是来自五湖四海的精英，大家深知，由于房地产开发行业的性质，任务完成后便会各奔前程，但大家由始至终都是上下齐心，迎难而上，跨越一个又一个障碍，解决一个又一个看似无法解决的难题。

相遇是缘，相知是福。

从 2002 年拿下地块，到 2010 年破土动工，再到 2017 年 11 月正式开幕……谁都没想到，这个项目要千呼万唤十余载，我也从一个地地道道的香港人，变成了对上海充满感情的人。

过程中，各级领导对项目的支持和帮助令我铭记于心。每当我们向领导反映困难的时候，得到的回应常常是："我有什么可以帮到你们？"还记得有位领导曾对我说："你们公司对项目开发的用心令人动容，难怪各方领导都大力支持。"此外，我们广结良朋，许多专家、同行和朋友，都曾不遗余力地为项目出谋献策……每次回想起来，皆是好人好事，让我心怀感激。要感谢的人实在太多，难以一一书录，倘有挂一漏万，就借此后记正式鸣谢。

15 年磨一剑，项目跨越无数难关。2016 年 8 月 25 日，项目内的商场及 250 米高的办公大楼拿到了竣工验收备案，就此为项目树立了重要的里程碑。我曾写过这样几首诗，畅抒一路闯关的感受：

千帆尚在渡江中　　遇难逾上莫放松
养兵千日一朝用　　零六三零要竣工

2016 年 1 月

攻坚共渡六月关　　黄梅高温更添难
夜作日时未言累　　轻舟终过万重山

2016 年 8 月

每个时间节点既是压力，亦是动力。这种攻坚克难、止于至善的精神是刻在每个兴业人内心的信念，推动我们坚守愚公移山般的决心和拼劲，以匠人情怀精雕细琢项目的每个细节。集团全盘审视地区规划，荟萃新旧文化，尊重历史传承，注入创新活力，务求能持续释放项目的长远价值，最终让兴业太古汇彰显出与上海这座国际都市相匹配的非凡魅力。

"不为外撼，不以物移，而后可以任天下之大事。"现在，我们终于可以自豪地说，作为一个负责任的开发商，我们实现了对这片土地的承诺。兴业太古汇既是大上海的缩影，也可以看作是当代文化与商业结合的一种典范。

我们期待这座汇聚潮流时尚与品质生活的商业综合体，在未来的日子里，不断开创新篇，再创辉煌。

写于 2020 年盛夏

# Gratitude and Honour

**JACKIE TANG**

*Executive Director of HKR International Limited
and the first CEO of HKRI Taikoo Hui*

In the early 1980s I had a wonderful opportunity. I joined the company and participated in the Discovery Bay project on the northeastern side of Hong Kong's Lantau Island. At the time, this 650-hectare, environmentally-friendly town was only just beginning to take shape. As expected, it became the centre of decades of hard work for me. But, my connection to Discovery Bay actually began before I started at HKRI. After graduating from the University of Hong Kong's Faculty of Architecture, I took a position in an architectural design firm, and the first project I worked on was Discovery Bay.

After Discovery Bay became the benchmark for eco-friendly towns in Asia, HKRI began to look for property development opportunities in Shanghai. On New Year's Eve in 2002, Mr. Victor Cha signed a contract with Shanghai's Jing'an District Government on behalf of the company, and officially took over the development rights for the Dazhongli plot on West Nanjing Road. From that day forward, my work focus shifted from Hong Kong to Shanghai, marking the beginning of my connection to this wonderful city.

In the early 2000s, the rapid growth of business and the economy saw urban development accelerate as China began an unprecedented series of massive civil engineering and construction projects. When HKRI took over the 62,800-square-metre plot in Dazhongli, the company was not simply looking for a return on investment. We embraced Dazhongli with passion, and vowed to create a legendary project. Located in the heart of China's economic engine – Shanghai – it would be a project with as much impact as Discovery Bay.

What we did not expect was that the composite commercial and residential project, which we estimated would be completed within 3-5 years, would become a mixed-use commercial complex that took 15 years of continuous development. In the process, we established strong ties to the city and also fulfilled our company's long-term commitment to the local community.

Looking back at more than ten years of development and construction, the dedication of both the company and the entire team enabled us to overcome numerous challenges. We all remember everything like it was yesterday, and learned a great deal from this shared experience.

When SARS hit in 2003, people panicked and the project faced myriad difficulties. Despite the crisis, our company upheld its ideals of "standing taller and looking beyond the horizon," and responded with patience and dedication.

In 2006, Mr. Cha, who understood the potential and long-term value of Dazhongli to Shanghai's overall development, including the social benefits, proposed converting the plan. It would change from a quick-return residential housing model to pure commercial usage, with the goal of improving the commercial value and capacity of the West Nanjing Road Business District. We then invited Swire Properties Limited, a company that shared our vision and values, to become a joint venture partner. As the first CEO of the project, I shouldered the trust and expectations of both parties, and felt the responsibilities intensely.

The global financial crisis of 2008 did not shake our determination, and we worked hard to advance the development of the Dazhongli Project.

In 2010, the century-old Building No. 4 of Minli School was slid 57 metres to its present location. We began large-scale refurbishment and conservation work in order to restore the structure to its former glory. It was renamed "Cha House" as a tribute to the patriotism of our company's founder, Dr. Cha Chi-ming.

In 2012, we overcame a host of difficulties and completed the resettlement of residents to clear the site. Then construction began.

To this day, I still remember the spirit of teamwork that ran through the entire project. Team members included experts from a variety of different disciplines and professions. Due to the nature of the construction project, we knew we would all part ways after accomplishing the mission, but we always worked together to overcome problems, surmount obstacles, and resolve issues one after the other.

Fate brought us together and it was an honour.

No one would have thought that the project would take more than a decade – from when we took over the plot in 2002, the beginning of construction in 2010, to the official opening in November 2017. It has also transformed me from a down-to-earth Hongkonger into someone who is deeply passionate about Shanghai.

The support provided by government leaders at all levels in the process has left me with lasting memories. When we reported any difficulties, the most frequent response we would get was: "What can I do to help?" I remember that an official once told me: "Your company's dedication to the project is impressive. It is no wonder everyone here expresses such support." We met a lot of amazing people, and many experts, colleagues, and friends who dedicated themselves to providing advice and assistance to the project. Whenever I think back, I remember everything that these wonderful people did, and I am forever grateful. There are so many to thank, it would be difficult to mention all their names here. So, rather than risk omitting anyone, let this postscript serve as my official declaration of gratitude to everyone involved.

It took 15 years to, as we say in Chinese, "sharpen one sword." But, we came a long way and resolved countless difficulties. On 25 August 2016, the project reached an important milestone when we received the Certificate of Construction Completion and Acceptance for the shopping mall and the 250-metre-tall office tower. I wrote a few poems to express my feelings about overcoming the odds.

> **Across the sea a thousand sails head**
> **Challenges come, yet grips tighten**
> **Soldiers train a thousand days for one battle**
> **We build block by block for one final day**
>
> *January 2016*

> **Fight hard in June to complete**
> **Extreme weathers bring more difficulties**
> **Work day and night without tire**
> **Thousands of mountains passed by our skiff**
>
> *August 2016*

Every milestone provides both pressure and motivation. The spirit of surmounting obstacles in pursuit of perfection is the motto inscribed on the heart of every member of the HKRI family. Along with encouraging craftsmanship and meticulous attention to every detail, it powers our resolve and provides the courage to do the right thing. The group has carefully considered the unique location, interweaving new and old cultural elements to respect Dazhongli's heritage and inject a new, innovative spirit. We aim to continuously harness the long-term values of the project and allow HKRI Taikoo Hui to embody the unique charms that reflect the glamour of the international city of Shanghai.

There is an old Chinese saying that goes: "To achieve unprecedented goals, one's resolve should neither be shaken by external interference, nor beaten by unexpected hurdles." That is exactly what we did with this project. We can now finally and proudly say that, as a responsible developer, we have fulfilled our commitment to this piece of land. HKRI Taikoo Hui is the embodiment of Shanghai and a paradigm for the integration of contemporary culture and business.

We hope that, with its congregation of chic and tasteful living, this commercial complex will continue to shine and create many glorious new chapters.

Written in the summer of 2020

# 项 目 概 览 Fast Facts

| 项目名称<br>Project | 兴业太古汇 | HKRI Taikoo Hui |
|---|---|---|
| 地址<br>Address | 上海市静安区南京西路 789 号 | 789 West Nanjing Road, Jing'an District, Shanghai |
| 社会功能<br>Function | 商业综合体 | Mixed-use commercial complex |
| 地块<br>Land plot | 原大中里地块 | Formerly Dazhongli |
| 建筑群演变<br>Transformation | 由大中里石库门建筑群转型为城市更新范例 | From Shikumen residential estates to an urban renewal showcase |
| 创始开发商<br>Founding developer | 香港兴业国际集团有限公司 | HKR International Limited |
| 合资开发商<br>Joint developer | 太古地产有限公司 | Swire Properties Limited |
| 建设期投资<br>Construction investment | 170 亿人民币（截至 2017 年 11 月） | RMB 17 billion (as of Nov. 2017) |
| 盛大开业<br>Grand opening | 2017 年 11 月 3 日 | 3 November 2017 |
| 占地面积<br>Land area | 62,800 平方米 | 62,800 sqm |
| 总楼面面积<br>Total GFA | 322,000 平方米 | 322,000 sqm |
| 区位<br>Central location | 四至：南京西路、威海路、石门一路、青海路<br><br>内街：吴江路（部分）、愉景大道 | Surrounded by four main roads: West Nanjing Road, Weihai Road, Shimen Road No. 1, Qinghai Road<br><br>Inside the project: Wujiang Road (partial), Discovery Boulevard |
| 主干道路<br>Transportation hub | 邻近南北高架和延安高架 | Adjacent to the Yan'an Elevated Highway and the N-S Elevated Highway |
| 地铁交通<br>Metro network | 毗连地铁 2 号线、12 号线，无缝衔接 13 号线 | Access to Metro Line 2 and Line 12, with a seamless connection to Metro Line 13 |
| 总建筑师<br>Chief architect | 王欧阳（香港）有限公司 | Wong & Ouyang (HK) Limited |

| 设 计 概 念 Master design | 结合中西古今元素，面向未来 | Future-proof design with a balance of Chinese, international, traditional and modern elements |
|---|---|---|
| | 中国江南庭院 "一轴三节"，北旺南静 | A replication of classic Shanghainese mansions with a "one-axis, three-node" layout featuring a lively North Piazza and a serene South Garden |
| | 从南到北全长逾 450 米，重塑 "逛马路" | A central axis stretching 450 metres from north to south creates the feel of a pleasant stroll |
| 布 局 Structures | 一座大型购物中心（100,000 平方米） | Mega-size shopping mall (100,000 sqm) |
| | 两栋超高层甲级写字楼（170,000 平方米）香港兴业中心一座（51 层）香港兴业中心二座（35 层） | Two premium Grade-A office towers (170,000 sqm) HKRI Centre One (51 floors) HKRI Centre Two (35 floors) |
| | 两间酒店及一间公寓式酒店（逾 50,000 平方米，超过 400 间客房）上海素凯泰酒店 镛舍 镛舍公寓式酒店 | Two hotels and a serviced apartment tower: (50,000 sqm, 400+ rooms) The Sukhothai Shanghai The Middle House The Middle House Residences |
| | 多栋二至三层商业建筑沿街林立，包括星巴克臻选®上海烘焙工坊（2,700 平方米） | Multiple 2-3-storey buildings for retail business, including the Starbucks Reserve® Shanghai Roastery (2,700 sqm) |
| | 地铁廊购物空间连接 2 号及 13 号线 | MetroLink underground shopping space connected to Metro Line 2 and Line 13 |
| 社 区 Community | 静安区 20 万白领 | 200,000+ white-collar workers in Jing'an |
| | 超过 10 个户内外活动场地 | Over 10 indoor and outdoor event spaces |
| | 年终无休举办活动和表演 | Year-round events and activities |
| 保 育 Conservation | 原地保留逾 100 年树龄的广玉兰古树 | Preserved a 100+ year-old magnolia grandiflora tree in its original location |
| 活 化 Restoration | 平移、抬升、修缮百年上海优秀历史建筑 "民立中学 4 号楼"，并重新命名为 "查公馆" | Relocated and restored the century-old Building No. 4 of Minli School, and renamed it Cha House |
| 绿 化 Green ratio | 约 20% | ~20% |
| 环 保 认 证 Environmental certifications | 项目内新建单体建筑获美国绿色建筑协会 LEED®（能源与环境设计先锋）认证 | All the newly constructed buildings have been awarded LEED® (Leadership in Energy and Environmental Design) certifications |
| 购 物 中 心 品 牌 口 号 Shopping mall slogan | 爱混敢嗲 | Dare For More |

# 鸣 谢 Acknowledgements

谨代表 **香港兴业国际集团** 借本书对以下政府部门、机构、合资方、顾问单位、施工单位和个人在兴业太古汇建设过程中的支持、协作与贡献表示衷心感谢。

On behalf of **HKR International Limited**, we would like to acknowledge the collaboration of the following government departments, organisations, our joint venture partner, consultants, contractors, as well as individual team members who contributed to the development of HKRI Taikoo Hui.

### 合资方 | Joint Venture Partner

太古地产有限公司　Swire Properties Limited

### 建筑设计顾问 | Architectural Design

王欧阳（香港）有限公司　Wong & Ouyang (HK) Limited

上海建筑设计研究院有限公司　Institute of Shanghai Architectural Design & Research (Co., Ltd.)

上海现代建筑设计（集团）有限公司　Shanghai Xian Dai Architectural Design (Group) Co., Ltd.

### 结构设计顾问 | Structural Engineering

艾奕康咨询（深圳）有限公司　AECOM (Shenzhen) Co., Ltd.

奥雅纳工程顾问（上海）有限公司　Arup International Consultants

### 机电顾问 | Building Services Engineering

科进顾问（亚洲）有限公司　WSP (Asia) Limited

### 主要施工单位 | Building and Construction

上海建工集团股份有限公司　Shanghai Construction Group Co., Ltd.

上海市基础工程集团有限公司　Shanghai Foundation Engineering Group Co., Ltd.

### 其他主要顾问 | Other Main Consultants

上海申通地铁集团有限公司　Shanghai Shentong Metro Group Co., Ltd.

上海静安置业（集团）有限公司　Shanghai Jing'an Real Estate (Group) Co., Ltd.

**查公馆平移顾问单位** | Cha House Relocation Consultant

上海同华加固工程有限公司　Shanghai Tonghua Reinforcement Engineering Co., Ltd.

**查公馆保育顾问单位** | Cha House Restoration Consultant

上海章明建筑设计事务所　Shanghai Zhangming Architectural Design Firm

**上海素凯泰酒店室内设计** | The Sukhothai Shanghai – Interior Design

如恩设计研究室　Neri & Hu Design and Research Office

**镛舍及公寓式酒店室内设计** | The Middle House and the Serviced Apartment – Interior Design

Lissoni Architettura S.P.A.

**政府部门（上海市政府部门）** | Government（*Shanghai Municipal Government Organisations*）

上海市住房和城乡建设管理委员会
Shanghai Municipal Commission of Housing and Urban-Rural Development

上海市规划和自然资源局　Shanghai Municipal Planning and Natural Resources Bureau

上海市住房保障和房屋管理局　Shanghai Municipal Bureau of Housing Security and Management

上海市生态环境局　Shanghai Municipal Environmental Protection Bureau

上海市卫生健康委员会　Shanghai Municipal Health Commission

上海市商务委员会　Shanghai Municipal Commission of Commerce

上海市市场监督管理局　Shanghai Municipal Administration for Market Regulation

上海市绿化和市容管理局　Shanghai Landscaping & City Appearance Administrative Bureau

上海市应急管理局　Shanghai Emergency Management Bureau

上海市公安局交通警察总队　Shanghai Public Security Bureau Traffic Police Corps

上海市卫生局卫生监督所　Health Supervision Institute of the Shanghai Municipal Health Bureau

**政府部门（静安区政府部门）** | Government（*Jing'an District Government Organisations*）

静安区人民政府　People's Government of Jing'an District

静安区建设和管理委员会　Shanghai Jing'an District Construction and Administration Commission

静安区规划和自然资源局　Jing'an District Planning and Natural Resources Bureau

静安区住房保障和房屋管理局　Jing'an District Housing Security and Real Estate Management Bureau

静安区生态环境局　Jing'an District Environmental Protection Bureau

静安区卫生健康委员会　Jing'an District Health Commission

静安区商务委员会　Jing'an District Commerce Commission

静安区市场监督管理局　Jing'an District Market Supervision and Administration

国家税务总局上海市静安区税务局　Shanghai Municipal Bureau of Local Taxation Jing'an District Branch

静安区绿化和市容管理局　Jing'an District Greening and City Appearance Administration

静安区应急管理局　Jing'an District Emergency Management Bureau

上海市公安局静安分局　Shanghai Public Security Bureau Jing'an Branch

上海市公安局静安分局交通警察支队　Shanghai Public Security Bureau Traffic Police Detachment, Jing'an District

静安区人民政府南京西路街道办事处
West Nanjing Road Sub-district Office of the Jing'an District People's Government

静安区城市管理行政执法局执法大队　Urban Administrative and Law Enforcement Bureau, Jing'an District

静安区重大项目推进办公室　Jing'an District Major Project Promotion Office

其他顾问单位（按中文拼音排序）　| Other Consultants

---

艾奕康环境规划设计（上海）有限公司　AECOM Environmental Planning and Design (Shanghai) Co., Ltd.

锐贤酒店设施设计咨询（上海）有限公司　Angles and Curves Design and Consulting (Shanghai) Co., Ltd.

保力灯光设计有限公司　Pro-Lit Co Limited

贝尔高林国际（香港）有限公司　Belt Collins International Limited

Concept Saphyr

Design Realization Asia Ltd.

深圳革思亚设计有限公司　Graphia International Limited

广州市丽芙德酒店管理咨询有限公司　Guangzhou Lifude Hotel Management Consulting Co., Ltd.

Isometrix Lighting Design Limited

捷得国际建筑师事务所　The Jerde Partnership

金宝声学环保顾问有限公司　Campbell Shillinglaw Lau Limited

君合律师事务所　Jun He LLP

凯谛思工程咨询（上海）有限公司　Langdon & Seah Consultancy (Shanghai) Co., Ltd.

Lighting Planners Associates Inc.

罗氏职业安全顾问有限公司　Loss Control Engineering Limited

Orangerie International Limited

全景艺术有限公司　Panorama Art Limited

许李严建筑师有限公司　Rocco Design Architect Limited

上海浩淼科技有限公司　Shanghai Haomiao Technology Co., Ltd.

上海建瓴工程咨询有限公司　Shanghai Jianling Designing and Drawing Examining Co., Ltd.

上海利文交通科技有限公司　Shanghai Liwen Transportation Technology Co., Ltd.

上海三维工程建设咨询有限公司　Shanghai Three-dimensional Engineering Construction Consulting Co., Ltd.

上海市测绘院　Shanghai Surveying and Mapping Institute

上海视档建筑声像服务有限公司　Shanghai Shidang Construction Shengxiang Service Co., Ltd.

上海新华建筑设计有限公司　Shanghai Xinhua Construction Designing Co., Ltd.

上海新拓城资产管理有限公司　Shanghai Xintuocheng Asset Management Co., Ltd.

上海增德防火技术咨询服务有限公司　Shanghai Zengde Fanghuo Technology Consulting Service Co., Ltd.

上海震银城市规划咨询有限公司　Shanghai Zhenyin Urban Planning Consulting Co., Ltd.

深圳市梁黄顾艺恒建筑设计有限公司　LWK & Partners (Shenzhen) Ltd.

沈麦韦（上海）商务咨询有限公司　Shenmaiwei (Shanghai) Business Consulting Co., Ltd.

宋腾添玛沙帝建筑工程设计咨询（上海）有限公司
Thornton Tomasetti Construction Engineering Design Consulting (Shanghai) Co., Ltd.

Tassos Bizakis (Athens) Foss Lighting Design Foss SA

同济大学建筑设计研究院（集团）有限公司　Tongji Architectural Design (Group) Co., Ltd.

威煌安全顾问有限公司　Y.Y. Wong Safety Consultants Limited

武汉威邦安全顾问有限公司　Wuhan Weibang Safety Consulting Co., Ltd.

### 其他施工单位（按中文拼音排序） | Other Contractors

保得国际贸易（上海）有限公司　Polytek International Trading (Shanghai) Co., Ltd.

北京承达创建装饰工程有限公司　Sundart Engineering & Contracting (Beijing) Limited

北京鸿合电子工程技术有限公司　Beijing Hitevision Intelligent Solutions Co., Ltd.

北京慧诚沃特喷泉科技有限公司　Beijing Huicheng Wote Fountain Technology Co., Ltd.

北京江森自控有限公司　Beijing Johnson Controls Co., Ltd.

福建新文行灯饰有限公司　Wenton Lights Decoration Co., Ltd.

广州市博艺广告制作有限公司　Guangzhou Boyi Advertising Making Co., Ltd.

广州珠江装修工程有限公司　Guangzhou Pearl River Decoration Engineering Co., Ltd.

江门建声声学材料有限公司　Architectural Acoustics (Jiangmen) Co., Ltd.

三力网络有限公司　3D Networks Co., Ltd.

上海昂盛智能工程股份有限公司　Shanghai Blooming Grace Intelligence Engineering Inc.

上海大华装饰工程有限公司　Shanghai Dahua Decoration Engineering Co., Ltd.

上海富建士装饰工程有限公司　Shanghai Fujianshi Decoration Engineering Co., Ltd.

上海海华建筑装饰工程有限公司　Shanghai Haihua Furniture Decoration Engineering Co., Ltd.

上海辉固岩土工程技术有限公司　Shanghai Fugro Geotechnique Co., Ltd.

上海锦奥环境工程有限公司　Shanghai Jinao Environmental Engineering Co., Ltd.

上海康乾泳池技术有限公司　Shanghai Kangqian Swimming Pool Technology Co., Ltd.

上海康业建筑装饰工程有限公司　Shanghai Kangye Construction & Decoration Engineering Co., Ltd.

上海联悦机电安装工程有限公司　Shanghai Lianyue Electromechanical Installation Engineering Co., Ltd.

上海绿材园林材料有限公司　Shanghai Lvcai Gardens Materials Co., Ltd.

上海普英泰工程设备安装有限公司　Shanghai Puyingtai Equipment Engineering Installation Co., Ltd.

上海市安装工程集团有限公司　Shanghai Installation Engineering Co., Ltd.

上海市建筑科学研究院〔集团〕有限公司　Shanghai Research Institute of Building Sciences (Group) Co., Ltd.

上海市建筑装饰工程有限公司　Shanghai Building Decoration Engineering Group Co., Ltd.

上海腾隆〔集团〕有限公司　Shanghai Tenglong (Group) Co., Ltd.

上海威煌消防工程设备有限公司　Shanghai Weihuang Fire Engineering Equipment Co., Ltd.

上海园林〔集团〕有限公司　Shanghai Gardens (Group) Co., Ltd.

上海至亨招牌设计制作有限公司　Shanghai Zhiheng Placards Design Production Co., Ltd.

上海住总集团建设发展有限公司　Shanghai Zhuzong Group Construction Development Co., Ltd.

深圳长城家俱装饰工程有限公司　Great Wall Decoration Co., Ltd.

沈阳远大铝业工程有限公司　Shenyang Yuanda Aluminium Industry Engineering Co., Ltd.

通力电梯有限公司　Kone Elevator Limited

浙江精工钢结构有限公司　Zhejiang Jinggong Steel Structure Group Co., Ltd.

如有任何信息不准确或遗漏，请接受我们的诚挚歉意

Please accept our sincere apology for any errors or omissions.

# 附　录　Appendix

第三章

图书在版编目（CIP）数据

未艾·方兴：从大中里到兴业太古汇：汉英对照／
上海第一财经传媒集团有限公司编著 .－ 北京：中国建筑
工业出版社，2019.12
ISBN 978-7-112-24532-1

Ⅰ. ①未… Ⅱ. ①上… Ⅲ. ①城市道路－介绍－静安区
Ⅳ. ① K925.13

中国版本图书馆 CIP 数据核字 (2019) 第 277081 号

责任编辑：徐晓飞　张　明
责任校对：王　烨

书籍设计：北京吴勇设计事务所

未艾·方兴：从大中里到兴业太古汇
上海第一财经传媒集团有限公司　编著
*
中国建筑工业出版社出版、发行（北京海淀三里河路 9 号）
各地新华书店、建筑书店经销
北京雅昌艺术印刷有限公司制版
北京雅昌艺术印刷有限公司印刷
*
开本：889 毫米 ×1194 毫米　1/16　印张：16¾　字数：366 千字
2020 年 10 月第一版　2020 年 10 月第一次印刷
定价：168.00 元
ISBN 978-7-112-24532-1
　　　(35186)